The Empire City

The Empire City

NEW YORK AND ITS PEOPLE, 1624–1996

Selma Berrol

Westport, Connecticut
London

Library of Congress Cataloging-in-Publication Data

Berrol, Selma Cantor.
    The empire city : New York and its people, 1624–1996 / Selma
Berrol.
      p. cm.
    Includes bibliographical references and index.
    ISBN 0–275–95795–0 (alk. paper)—ISBN 0–275–96935–5 (pbk.)
    1. New York (N.Y.)—Emigration and immigration—History. 2. New
York (N.Y.)—History. 3. Immigrants—New York (State)—New York—
History. 4. Minorities—New York (State)—New York—History.
5. Pluralism (Social sciences)—New York (State)—New York. 6. New
York (N.Y.)—Social life and customs. I. Title.
F128.9.A1B42   1997
974.7′1—dc20   96–27455

British Library Cataloguing in Publication Data is available.

Library of Congress Catalog Card Number: 96–27455
ISBN: 0–275–96935–5 (pbk.)

First published in 1997

Praeger Publishers, 88 Post Road West, Westport, CT 06881
An imprint of Greenwood Publishing Group, Inc.
www.praeger.com

Printed in the United States of America

The paper used in this book complies with the
Permanent Paper Standard issued by the National
Information Standards Organization (Z39.48–1984).

10 9 8 7 6 5 4 3 2 1

This book is dedicated to the people of New York City, past and present.

Contents

Preface   ix

1. From Trading Post to Commercial City, 1624–1824   1

2. Growth and Change in the Commercial City, 1824–1870   39

3. A New Metropolis: New York and Its People, 1870–1920   75

4. Boom Times, Bad Times: New York and Its People, 1920–1945   103

5. Postwar New York: Bright City, Dark City, 1945–1970   125

6. Roller Coaster Years: New York and Its People, 1970–1996   149

Bibliographical Essay   177

Index   181

Preface

New York City has been viewed from many different perspectives by many different historians, but few, including this author, have undertaken the daunting task of writing a full-length synthesis. Indeed, only a book of encyclopedic proportions can encompass the 400-year history of this great city. The method that most historians have chosen in order to cope with the wealth of available material is to find a unifying theme that can be expanded into a book of manageable size. The theme that I have chosen to study in this book is the symbiosis that has marked New York City's history from its earliest days.

For almost four centuries, New York City, in all its incarnations, has been a promising destination for people seeking a better life. Aided and abetted by its marvelous location and a commercially minded leadership, the tiny settlement at the mouth of the Hudson River developed into a multiethnic giant because the people who came to New York and the city they settled into needed each other. Without the strength and ambition that the newcomers brought, New York could not have become the Empire City. Without the opportunities available in an open city, those who left their native land could not have improved their lives.

This book is divided into six chapters, arranged in chronological sequence. Chapter 1 illustrates the theme by pointing out the opportunities offered to the adventurers and refugees who settled at the port of New Amsterdam. At the same time, Chapter 1 shows how the unfree blacks and somewhat freer farmers, fur traders, sailors, and laborers enabled the settlement to survive and prosper. Chapter 2 extends the symbiosis theme by demonstrating how the growth and physical improvement of the city was stimulated by the needs and strength of newcomers from various parts of the British Isles and the Continent. The Croton water system, for example, was built with the labor of Irish immigrants, who thus reduced the danger of epidemics (especially cholera) to themselves as well as to the rest of the city while at the same time earning wages denied to them in their poverty-stricken homeland.

Chapter 3, which discusses Italian laborers, connects their arrival with the building of subways, which enabled the crowded city to expand in many directions. This chapter also describes the changes in the public schools, which were charged with Americanizing the children of the Russian Jews and others from middle and southern Europe. To accomplish this, the Board of Education began a massive building program and changed the curriculum. At the same time, the parents of the "little aliens" were enriching the city's manufacturers by their labor while improving their own standard of living.

Chapter 4 describes the city in the prosperous 1920s and depressed 1930s. During these two decades of economic ups and downs, symbiosis continued. Southern blacks migrated to New York to escape racism and poverty and benefited the city by taking the place of white immigrant workers, who were prevented from coming by restrictive immigration laws. Although black workers were poorly paid, they were spared the worst aspects of white racism, such as lynchings. Also in the 1930s, refugees from fascism in Europe enlarged the city's intellectual and scientific community while achieving a safe harbor for themselves.

In Chapter 5, for the first time, symbiosis is less apparent. More southern blacks and a new group of Hispanics, Puerto Ricans, found it much harder to find routes to upward mobility in a city that was losing a large portion of its white middle class to the suburbs and, more important, losing industries that had previously needed unskilled labor. These developments continued into the period discussed in Chapter 6, which nonetheless describes a partial renewal of symbiosis. An infusion of new workers from Asia and the Caribbean, pushed out by great poverty to come to a city that offered some opportunities, led to a revival of an old New York industry (garment making) and supplied declining neighborhoods with new stores as well as ethnic restaurants. At its conclusion, the book presents opposing viewpoints regarding the future of the city.

1

From Trading Post to Commercial City, 1624–1824

Although the Dutch can rightfully claim to be the first settlers in what was to become the city of New York, in 1524 Giovanni da Verrazano's ship, the *Dauphine*, was the first European vessel to enter the harbor. Apparently unmoved by the discovery, the French-sponsored expedition left soon after arrival. Except for a visit by Estaban Gomez and his crew two years later and an occasional fur trader, the island of Manhattan and its environs were left to nature and the native population for the next century.[1] The second visitor was Henry Hudson, one of many "explorers for hire," who had been engaged by the Dutch East India Company to do what Christopher Columbus had failed to do more than a hundred years earlier—find a route to China that did not necessitate going around Africa. Instead, on September 2, 1609, the master of the *Halve Moen* found an island and a river that permitted "navigation far into the unknown interior" as well as a population of Indians called Manates.[2]

Hudson did not remain in the harbor for very long because the natives were "warlike and threatening" but instead went upriver to find other Indians who were willing to trade their valuable furs for trinkets. It was this information, in addition to the desire to have a base for privateering during the seventeenth-century wars between Protestant Holland and Catholic Spain, that motivated the directors of the Dutch West India Company to send a shipload of men and women to the island that Hudson had discovered. In 1624, therefore, another Dutch ship, the *Nieuw Nederlandt*, dropped anchor in the bay and 110 men, women, and children debarked to start a settlement that would provide a base for privateering and fur trading.[3]

For these thirty French-speaking Protestant families, known as Walloons, the transoceanic move was but another step in a migration which had begun in the previous century. Their ancestors had been residents of the modern Département du Nord who had become Protestants in the middle of the sixteenth century and, as a result, were driven out of France. Searching for a haven, they moved further north to the more tolerant Netherlands and became part of a refugee community in Leyden, Holland.[4]

Among their fellow displaced persons were a band of dissenters, known to history as the Pilgrims, who had arranged with the English Virginia Company for the right to establish a settlement in North America. The Walloons, although they had found work as wool carders, weavers, clothiers, and dyers in Leyden, were interested in a further move and decided to do as the Pilgrims had done. They came under the auspices of the newly formed Dutch West India Company, whose leaders directed them to disembark at Manhattan Island because "the many waterways which came together there" made for a safe harbor and easy launching of ships.[5]

More settlers came during the next two years, and in 1626 there were 270 people living in thirty houses along the East River, most of which were made of bark. Indicating the importance of money and furs in the new settlement, only the Company's counting house, used to store money and furs, was made of stone and had a thatched roof. According to resident Nicholas Van Wassenaer, who kept a "Historical Account" of events in the young settlement, the men worked "as in Holland; one trades upwards, southwards and northwards, another builds houses, the third farms." Conditions, however, remained quite difficult. In 1628, the Reverend Jonas Michaelius, New Netherland's first ordained minister, said that there were "no horses, or cows and laborers' rations were mostly stale bread."[6]

Some of the original settlers had moved up the Hudson Valley as far as present-day Albany, but 173 newcomers arrived between 1630 and 1644 to more than make up for the loss. Overall, however, the little settlement grew very slowly, although the Dutch West India Company provided a free trip and was ready to give away parcels of land according to the size of the immigrant's family. The Company also supplied credit without charging interest for the purchase of livestock. In 1629 the Directors of the Company tried an additional ploy, offering "large estates to investors who would bring fifty colonists in four years," but the shortage of labor persisted. Recognizing that their colony would remain small and vulnerable without additional workers, the Company sent a group of black slaves to New Amsterdam.[7]

In part due to the slaves' labor, by the middle 1630s New Amsterdam boasted a "flour mill, two saw mills, a shed for shipbuilding, goat pens, and a church as well as a bakery and a midwife." Another kind of structure was also erected at the same time: a wooden palisade to keep out hostile Indians. At first the natives had been friendly and curious visitors to the colony, but their attitude toward the white settlers had soured by 1640. Good relations had been fostered by the whites to get valuable furs for little money, but when the Indians "learned to bargain shrewdly," there was considerable friction. The hostility was exacerbated by William Kieft, the Director General sent by the Company to manage the town, who tried to tax the Indians. Another reason for the conflict may have been the illegal activities of some of the residents, who violated company rules and sold alcohol, muskets, and ammunition to the natives. The result was sporadic violence, which discouraged less venturesome Europeans from coming to New Amsterdam.[8]

Kieft was followed by Peter Stuyvesant, who found the town to be a "slovenly, drunken [one-fourth of the buildings housed taverns], dishonest community." One of the few bright spots, however, was the trade the colony carried on with various English colonies. Tobacco was imported from Virginia, fish from New England, dyes and salt from Barbados while grain, timber, potash, and furs were shipped out. Within a decade of its first settlement, New Amsterdam had become an entrepôt, establishing a pattern that was to continue for the next two centuries.[9]

During the succeeding years, the town attracted a sizable number of English "immigrants," who came from Massachusetts, Connecticut, and eastern Long Island. Even more important, in an early example of the symbiosis that has characterized New York history, Dutch toleration of religious dissent attracted religious refugees from all over Europe. New Amsterdam provided them with a much needed haven, and their arrival enabled the colony to grow.

As Joyce Goodfriend says in *Before the Melting Pot*, the people who came to New Amsterdam and later New York "did so not because of any consistent immigration policy implemented by either the Dutch West India Company or the British [but rather] as a result of a complex of factors relating both to dislocating forces in their prior homes and the contour of society in seventeenth century New York." The "dislocating forces" included wars, often over religion; economic changes, which eliminated certain occupations; and increases in the population due to better sanitation and greater medical knowledge without equivalent expansion of land ownership and occupations. Those were the "push" factors. The "pull" was the "lure of economic . . . opportunity associated with the developing commercial life of the port reinforced by letters which spoke favorably of the colony."[10]

Other reasons for coming to New Amsterdam included specific links, such as the fact that Holland had a lively trade with Poland and, as a result, seventeenth-century Amsterdam had a Polish colony, some of whose members came to New Amsterdam. Some came as soldiers in the Dutch army, just as Scandinavians came as sailors in the Dutch navy, but once in North America, they worked at a variety of nonmilitary trades. As early as 1643, barely two decades after its founding, in addition to the groups already mentioned, there were Bohemians, Scotch, Waldensians, Portuguese, and Italians in New Amsterdam. No wonder that a visiting priest reported that eighteen different languages were spoken there. Almost as many religious faiths were represented. The Dutch Reformed Church was the established church of the colony, but Anglicans and other groups were free to worship as they wished. Only the Catholics, few in number, were forbidden to have a church of their own. Since the Dutch did not want to emigrate, the colony would have been unprofitable to the West India Company unless they allowed other ethnic groups to enter. As a result the cosmopolitan quality that has always characterized New York was apparent early on.[11]

Those who came began their money-making activities almost upon arrival. By the latter part of 1626, the settlement had taken shape and the inhabitants were able to send thousands of beaver, otter, mink, and wildcat skins back to Holland. The fur trade, as we have seen, was one of the great economic attractions of New Amsterdam; the other was its advantageous location. Just as the West India Company had hoped, the sheltered harbor, easy to enter and leave, was a haven for Dutch privateers, who made hit-and-run attacks on Spain's colonies in the Caribbean and on the slow-moving, gold-heavy Spanish galleons as they made their way back to Europe.

The settlement spread out somewhat during the 1630s, and a fort at the southernmost tip of the island was completed by 1635:

The building was approximately 300 feet long and 250 feet broad. The sides were, for the most part, earthen; the four corners, which formed arrowhead projections, were stone. Guns and mortars were emplaced along the parapets and a variety of buildings were housed inside the walls. The Director General's . . . home lay along the east wall, the quarters of the garrison's officers along the north and the soldier's barracks along the west.

Nearby was a large stone church, erected seven years after the fort, and on its northern side was Bowling Green, used as a parade ground, a playground, and, at specified times, a market.[12]

To the north of the Green, after 1653, was a great wall, which was called the "Singel" and was intended to protect New Amsterdam from the English, "whose colonies in New England and settlements on eastern Long Island were dangerously near," and from the Indians, who became increasingly restive as the Dutch settlement expanded.[13] The wall was more a symbol than a means of protection. Although it was built of "rounded timbers 12 feet high and pointed at the top" and extended from the East to the Hudson River, it was shoddy when first built, and lack of maintenance weakened it further. Floyd Shumway, in his book *The Seaport City*, sums it up: "The wall never stood off anything more dangerously aggressive than wandering cows." When it came down in 1699, the "Singel" became Wall Street, the city's first east-west axis.[14]

There was also an imposing Stadt Huys (City Hall) on what is today Pearl Street. It was fifty feet square and had stone walls three stories high, dwarfing its neighbors. By 1660 a number of streets had been laid out, including Broadway, which ran from Bowling Green to the Wall. A cemetery had been established on the west side of Broadway, with a separate one for the tiny colony of Jews placed outside the Wall. Another separate burial ground, for black slaves, was located apart from the other two.[15]

As Oliver Rink describes in his article on the Company and the Dutch Reformed Church, spiritual life in New York suffered from the conflict between those whose interests were in profits and those concerned with souls. One issue was economic. The headquarters of the Church in Amsterdam sent a minister, but the Company was expected to support him, his family, the church, and a school. Another issue was power—that is, "the role of the clergy in colonial government." In this regard, the Company thought that there was no role for a "predikant" (minister), but the ministers believed otherwise and much conflict ensued.[16]

The limited objectives of the West India Company—that is, the fur trade and piracy—coupled with Indian raids, many restrictive regulations, and general mismanagement kept New Amsterdam from growing as fast as it might otherwise have done. For most of the first two decades of its existence, this did not greatly concern the Directors in Holland because they were making substantial sums from the fur trade and profiteering. Their success led them to establish outposts in South America, but it proved costly to retain these settlements. By 1654, the West India Company was bankrupt and conditions on Manhattan Island left much to be desired. There were only fifty farms, the population had been decimated in wars with the Indians, and "disorder and discontent prevailed."[17]

At this point, the Directors reversed their earlier economic guidelines and asked Director General Peter Stuyvesant to abandon the multitude of regulations that had inhibited trade and made the colony unattractive to settlers. Since the Company could no longer support New Amsterdam, the Directors believed that the only hope for its future was to encourage individual investment. Capital, however, would be attracted to the colony only if restrictions that "unduly hampered the individual in his pursuit of profits" were lifted.[18]

For this reason, the Directors urged Stuyvesant to lower the fees for burgher rights (required to do any business in the town) and end the practice of granting monopolies. Capitalistic competition was to be the rule; individual initiative was to be encouraged. Earlier regulations prescribing the size, weight, ingredients, and price of bread, for example, were to be greatly modified; the bakers of New Amsterdam would attract customers by the quality of their bread. The prices would not be artificially set but would be allowed to rise and fall in accord with marketplace conditions.[19]

Neither Stuyvesant nor the burghers of New Amsterdam liked the new policy. In their opinion, it was the shortage of common laborers, not men with capital, that was slowing the colony's development. If the Company could find a way to bring more workers to New Amsterdam, the settlement, they said, would flourish. The Directors were aware of the labor shortage and, as we have seen, had tried to meet the need by importing black male slaves as early as the second year of the colony's existence. Later, they brought in several black women. The labor shortage continued, however, and as a result, in 1648, the Dutch government "authorized the people of New Netherlands to send grain and cattle . . . to Dutch settlers in Brazil in return for blacks." Four years later, the settlers were encouraged to import slaves directly from Angola, another Dutch colony. However, because slave owners preferred "seasoned" workers, after 1654, Curacao, a Dutch colony in the Caribbean, became the major supplier of slaves for New Amsterdam.[20]

The Dutch allowed slaves to farm land, keep the profits, and use their earnings to buy their freedom or the freedom of a wife. However, because they wanted to have a source of unfree labor available to the colony in the future, a child's freedom could not be purchased. Just before the British takeover in 1664, when blacks constituted 20 percent of the population, a dozen black slaves petitioned the Company for their freedom and got it. Their names would seem to indicate that they were from Angola, but at least one name (John Fort Orange) showed Dutch influence. With freedom came land, a practice that was customary throughout the Dutch period. This apparent generosity reflected practical, not idealistic, motives. White settlers were more interested in trading than farming and, as a result, the colony was sometimes short of food. Furthermore, outside the town, Indians were "burning houses, cattle, barns and crops and killing white farmers and their families." Understandably, considering the dangers outside the city and the opportunities within it, it was an unusual settler who chose to take up farming.[21]

As a result of white disaffection with agriculture, blacks owned and farmed land in what is now Greenwich Village along Spring, Broome, Houston, and Bleecker Streets. They were, however, seen all over the town, especially during a holiday called "Pinkster" (derived from the Dutch celebration of Pentecost in late spring). During Pinkster, a leading male member of the black community was crowned as king for a week and his "subjects," dressed flamboyantly, consumed "quantities of food and drink, played improvised music and danced." Clearly little work was done during this period, but according to an expert on Afro-American culture, white owners or employers encouraged the "celebratory activities" because they saw the blacks as children who could be "immensely entertaining," especially if the occasion occurred only once a year.[22]

Because Holland was far away and Stuyvesant was determined, many of the liberalizing directives drafted in Amsterdam were never implemented, and New Amsterdam's economic growth continued to be slow. It was, however, steady. The Directors in Holland, hoping for a quick return on their investment, underestimated the strength of the existing economy. From the earliest days of New Amsterdam's history, the people who settled there earned their living in diverse ways, as tanners, butchers, shipbuilders, brewers, coopers, armorers, tailors, cartmen, and shopkeepers. Also, as we have seen, New Amsterdam had begun to assume its future role as an entrepôt shortly after its founding.

By 1635, New Amsterdam's merchants participated in an intercolonial trade with the English colonies to the northeast and south and with other Dutch settlements in the Hudson Valley and on Long Island. Coastal vessels based in New Amsterdam, for example, carried tobacco and salt from Virginia to Boston. In 1652, the tobacco trade, in particular, became even more lucrative when the Company removed the export tax. Nine years later, an English visitor, possibly sent to assess the value of the colony in preparation for the takeover that came a few years later, reported that "because the town is planted commodiously for trade, that is their chief employment. They plant and sow little."[23]

A closer look at the flourishing intercolonial trade that existed in 1661 explains why, as the English observer had noted, there were a surprisingly small number of farms in New Amsterdam. From Long Island came beef, pork, wheat, butter, and tobacco. From New England came more of the same plus "flower [flour] and biskit," malt, fish, apples, iron, and tar. Virginia sent tobacco, oxhides, beef, pork, and fruit. In return for these items, New Amsterdam merchants sold linens from Holland, canvas, tape, thread, cordage, brass, stockings, spices, and "all useful manufactures" to the hinterlands while sending many raw materials, such as furs and tobacco, to Holland.[24]

It was this economic activity, as well as the need for a haven, that attracted the first Jewish settlers to New Amsterdam in 1654, when Asser Levy led forty-three men, women, and children into the colony to join the existing population of 1,000. Manhattan represented the end of a long journey for them. In the last decade of the sixteenth century, Marannos (Spanish Jews who had ostensibly converted to Catholicism during the Inquisition of the previous century) moved to Holland to practice their true religion. In 1633 some moved to Pernambuco in Dutch-owned Brazil, but when Catholic Portugal took over that colony, they were forced to flee again. They chose the settlement on Manhattan Island because they had not been persecuted in Holland and expected tolerance in New Amsterdam as well. They were not welcomed by Director General Stuyvesant, but the Company, in deference to its Jewish stockholders, insisted that they be allowed to stay. Stuyvesant had little to fear; the Jewish colony grew to only fifty people before the British takeover in 1664.[25]

Merchants and skilled workers, the Jewish newcomers saw the young colony as a place of opportunity. Eager to capitalize on the trading possibilities, "they struggled harder for the right to trade than for the right to have a burial ground or a synagogue." In their first years they celebrated their holy days in secret, but in a short time they were permitted to have their own cemetery. They did well because they or members of their family had lived in a number of different places; they had understood and could speak several languages; and, because they had kinfolk all over the world, they were able to maintain a network of trading relationships using the port of New Amsterdam as a base.[26]

By 1664, in spite of neglect, exploitation, and policies that might have destroyed a less advantageously situated settlement, New Amsterdam—although it reached only to present-day Wall Street—was a bustling, somewhat rowdy, cosmopolitan seaport town which continued to grow at a rapid rate. Many of the people who had come there to improve their fortunes had succeeded in doing so. As was to be true again and again, the settlement offered a real chance to those who, like the Walloons, Jews, Germans, Poles, and Dutch, came equipped with capital, experience, or skills. Even the erratic policies of the Dutch West India Company could not destroy the opportunities that existed on the island of Manhattan. By the same token, without the arrival of such entrepreneurs, New Amsterdam might have remained a small outpost in the Dutch Empire.

The increasing success of New Amsterdam as an entrepôt was, at least in part, responsible for the end of Dutch control. The London government had never agreed to the legal right of the Dutch to be in North America, but during the years in which England and Holland had been allies against Spain, little had been done to oust them. As the mercantile and naval rivalry between the two trading nations sharpened, however, the developing commerce of New Amsterdam came under increased English scrutiny and, in the Navigation Act of 1651, England tried to stifle it.

According to the Navigation Act, all trade with England or its colonies was to be limited to English ships with English captains and a crew that was at least three-fourths English.[27] The merchants of New Amsterdam violated this law as much as they possibly could, and after midcentury, English rulers, both Cromwellian and Stuart, realized that the possession of New Netherlands by the Dutch was a major obstacle to the enforcement of their mercantilist policy in North America. As a result, they were determined to bring the colony under their control. English men and women had already settled in several places on Long Island, and when Charles II became king in 1660, he decided to make the entire area the property of the English Crown—specifically, his brother James, the Duke of York.[28]

The first move came on Monday, August 25, 1664. An English ship, the *Guinea*, approached Long Island and the alarmed residents of New Amsterdam made preparation for the expected attack by organizing a guard composed of every able-bodied man and providing each one with "one pound of powder and one and one half pounds of lead." At great sacrifice (considering the Dutch affection for beer), "brewers were ordered not to malt any grain for eight days and only to brew low grade beer" in order to save grain if the town was cut off from outlying districts.[29]

Other ships joined the *Guinea*, and on August 27 the English took possession of the ferry that connected the small Dutch settlement called Breuklyn with New Amsterdam and prepared to invade. Governor Stuyvesant asked Dutch settlers from outside New Amsterdam to help defend the colony from the 400 advancing English troops, but he got no response. For the next few days, the British ships maneuvered around the island, using both the Hudson and the East River. After several tense days, the burghers urged Stuyvesant to give up because the defenders of New Amsterdam were clearly out manned and underequipped. On September 6, therefore, negotiators worked out a treaty that gave all of New Netherlands to the English. Two days later Stuyvesant reluctantly signed it. Forty years of Dutch ownership ended without a shot being fired.[30]

That, however, was not the end of the story. Although the Articles of Capitulation signed by Stuyvesant guaranteed the current inhabitants of New Amsterdam the "uninterrupted possession of their houses, goods and inheritances" and allowed them to continue worshipping in the Calvinist Dutch Reformed Church, there was a lingering resentment against the new rulers. When England and Holland went to war in 1672, therefore, Dutch soldiers from areas north of the town came down the Hudson and, abetted by some New Amsterdam residents, recaptured the settlement and renamed it Fort Orange. In 1674, however, it was once again New York because the Dutch did not want to keep it when they signed a peace treaty with England.[31]

The 1,500 people who lived in New York at that point—three-fourths of them Dutch—were involved, as always, with economic concerns. They looked forward to improving their fortunes under the new regime and, to a great extent, that is what happened. The newcomers were able to build on the healthy number of occupations already existing in the former Dutch colony because merchants and traders, now able to ship their goods under the Union Jack, had access to all the ports in the British Empire. For this and other reasons, in the first three decades of British rule, the population grew to well over 5,000 people and the wealth of the community similarly increased. There were also other improvements: The English Governors tore down the shabby, useless Wall and filled in the smelly Broad Street canal.[32]

Population growth was in large part the result of continuing migration and immigration. British, French Huguenots, additional Jews, Dutch, and Germans joined groups of their brethren who had arrived earlier. Although some of the newcomers (such as the Palatine Germans) who wanted to be farmers were more attracted to Long Island or Westchester, those whose interests lay in trade stayed in New York City. As had been true since its foundation, the fundamental economic activity of the settlement continued to be "the movement, for profit, of goods by water."[33]

In 1687, Governor Thomas Dongan reported that "New York . . . lives wholly upon trade with the Indians, England and the West Indies." A decade later, another Governor, the Earl of Belloment, said that "there is not a richer populace anywhere in the King's dominions than there is in this town."[34] A bustling city it was, but not an altogether friendly one. At the end of the seventeenth century, the English were very much a minority and many of the Dutch were hostile to them which, in turn, made the English demand oaths of allegiance and obedience to the Duke of York's wishes. There was, however, little violence because English government policy was basically accomodationist, leading to a relatively easy transition. Land ownership arrangements made in the pre-conquest period, for example, were quickly confirmed. At bottom, both the English and the Dutch were too intent on making money to waste time and strength on interethnic battling. They chose, rather, to separate themselves and lived in different wards, clustered with their own kind. In the eighteenth century there was more intermingling, and by 1776 only Jews and blacks were segregated.[35]

In the first years after the English takeover, Dutch customs (such as the Christmas Eve visits of Santa Claus) prevailed, as did their sports (bowling, skating, sleighing) and some of their vocabulary. "Boss, cookie, cruller, stoop" became part of the English language. In general, however, New York became more English with every passing month. Street names, for example, were Anglicized and the titles *schout, burgomaster,* and *schepen* were replaced by *mayor, alderman,* and *sheriff.* Dutch residents were sometimes part of the government, but more likely the officeholders would be English. The British desire to Anglicize the colony was illustrated by their suppression of the Dutch parochial schools and insistence on an English language calendar and English names for weights and measures. By the end of the century the Dutch were a numerical minority, outnumbered by the English and the many French Huguenots.[36]

Although they were not allowed to be part of the power structure, the Dutch accepted English rule without protest until the London government, in 1688, joined New York and New Jersey to their New England colonies. In the Dominion of New England, as it was named, the Dutch would be an almost invisible minority and therefore vulnerable to decisions that might injure their prosperity and security. For this reason, when the Glorious Revolution occurred in England a year later, there was considerable jubilation in New York. News of the deposition of Stuart King James II and the accession to the throne of his daughter Mary and her husband, the Dutch prince William of Orange, was welcomed by those New Yorkers who had been excluded from power. One such citizen was Jacob Leisler, a wealthy merchant who took advantage of the vacuum created by the change of regime in London and organized a successful rebellion. He and his supporters held power until 1691, when a new governor arrived from London. At that point, Leisler and his son-in-law, accused of treason, were executed.[37]

Immigration continued to swell the population. Between 1703 and 1712, the white population grew by 3.3 percent, and by 1731, 7,045 people of European descent lived in New York. The number would have been larger had not hundreds perished in epidemics of yellow fever and smallpox in 1702. Many of the newcomers came as indentured servants from Scotland, Ulster, and Ireland; others were established merchants, ambitious to increase their wealth. Most were from the British Isles, none were destitute; indeed, many brought capital and others brought skills. As a result, all were a great asset to the city.[38]

The failure of Leisler's revolt settled the question of governance. Freed from such worries, the inhabitants of New York turned their attention back to what was really important—trade. The variety of goods that entered and left the harbor was astounding. Exports continued to include furs, timber, whale oil, and tobacco to England; flour, bread, peas, pork, and horses to the West Indies. The king had granted New York a monopoly for "sifting and packing of flour and biscuit for export" in 1679, which further enlarged the scope of the city's trade. The seaport continued to be an entrepôt; much of what was exported and imported neither originated nor remained in New York but was merely jobbed there by paying commissions and fees to the factors who made the arrangements and extended credit.[39]

This lucrative trade was fostered by municipal officials and the royal governors in many different ways. Since 1683, the city had been governed under the Dongan Charter, a document which had confirmed much of the structure established under the Dutch. The Charter affirmed the existence of the new Corporation of New York, a body with considerable economic and judicial power. Although the Royal Governor appointed the mayor, sheriff, and recorder (counsel), the freemen of each of the six wards, into which the city was divided, elected one alderman and one assistant alderman, who, together with the mayor and recorder, constituted the Common Council.[40]

All of these officials had to meet property requirements to run for office, assuring that the city would be in the hands of the well-to-do. As a result, the aldermen were usually established merchants; the assistant aldermen most often were independent artisans. With only minor changes, mostly in the Montgomerie Charter of 1731, this structure was to remain the government of New York until after the Revolution. Like so much else in the city, these arrangements enhanced its attractiveness to men of trade. The franchise, and with it the power to influence the development of the city, belonged to those who did business there (freemen) or occupied, through ownership or rental, substantial property (burghers). Artisans, defined as "owners of professional skills and tools," were members of both groups.[41]

There was a clear-cut class structure in pre-Revolutionary New York, illustrated, among other things, by dress and housing. The upper 10 percent, involved with government, large-scale trade, land ownership, and the professions, held 45 percent of the wealth. Merchants wore waistcoats, long hair, buckled breeches, and ruffled shirts, while artisans dressed in simple breeches covered by leather aprons and wore caps. The wealthy lived in two- and three-story townhouses along Park Row and Broadway and had slaves and servants, while artisans lived in back of their shops and workrooms. Even less fortunate were the journeymen, who lived in the underdeveloped Out Wards (open land that was not technically part of the city), and the unmarried men, who slept in boarding houses near the waterfront.[42]

The population and physical size of the city grew a great deal in the decades that preceded independence. In 1760, the number of houses had doubled from the 1,300 that stood in 1745, and the population had reached 18,000. By 1771, almost 22,000 people lived in New York, and the boundaries of the city had been pushed beyond Bayard Street. Following the drainage of the swamps that lay west of Broadway, that part of the island was also beginning to fill. This development, which led to new housing, was welcomed, although the absence of public transportation meant that crowding at the city core would continue. The expansion and the high rents that were a consequence of the crowding made real estate investment and speculation very profitable.[43]

Even more profitable was the volume of commerce, domestic and foreign, that continued to expand during the eighteenth century. A variety of goods from all over the world were on display in the shops that lined Broadway, especially in the area of Hanover Square. Merchants, seamen, and ship captains, all of whom were associated with trade, formed the largest occupational group in the city. According to a historian of eighteenth-century New York life, "the . . . port was a great mart and clearing house. . . . Ships arrived daily from Europe and the West Indies, seven hundred a year, by mid-century. There was no drop later in the century; between 1747 and 1772, port records show a 600% increase in shipping traffic."[44] An observer reported that the people of New York seemed to be "infatuated with trade," and his statement reinforced another comment that said the location of the city and the "genius" of its people for trade had so inclined them to commerce that they "sought no other education for their children other than writing and arithmetick."[45] This good news, however, should not obscure the bad. In 1702, for example, a yellow fever epidemic killed 10 percent of the population; twenty-one years later, smallpox killed almost as many.[46]

Anything having to do with the trading life of the city was a top-priority item to the government and the merchant elite. In the early 1750s, for example, the Corporation had constructed the Great Dock at the foot of Broad Street, the Albany Dock adjacent to it, and the Corporation Dock on the Hudson. There were also many other improvements, some, such as paved streets, desperately needed. By 1775, cobblestones covered most streets, and there were even some sidewalks, all of which must have been a boon to pedestrians.[47]

Along the same lines, there were changes made in waste removal, which until 1731 was simply dumped in the open gutters that ran down the streets. At that point, a new law required every household to sweep its garbage into the street and pay an authorized cartman to remove it. Even earlier, sewers began to be built, and by 1769 New York was a much cleaner city. Street lighting, again partly paid for by homeowners, was another change for the better, as was the employment of paid firemen and the purchase of modern fire-fighting equipment. Prior to 1737, local volunteer fire wardens and buckets, purchased in varying numbers by every household, had been the only protection against fire. The number of buckets required depended on the number of hearths in the home and the occupations of the owner. Brewers, for example, had to keep six buckets, and bakers had to keep three.[48]

Decent water was something else New York did not have. It came from wells and "it was so foul and brackish that horses refused to drink it." Those who could afford to do so purchased their water from cartmen, who sold clean drinking and cooking water door to door. Good water or bad, there was never enough of it, which greatly increased the difficulty of extinguishing the frequent fires. An elaborate plan to build a waterworks plant, using a steam-powered pump, was arranged in 1774, but the Revolution prevented its completion.[49] The bad water may have been one reason for the multiplicity of taverns, but it is clear that they served other purposes as well. In 1770, there were 400 taverns in New York (one for every twelve adult males), which were used as places to transact business. "Mail was picked up, goods were auctioned, insurance coverage secured and sailors were found to man outgoing vessels."[50]

The proliferation of taverns also led to heavy drinking, which sometimes required the intervention of policemen, who were volunteers until 1762, after which the Corporation decided to spend some money on professionals. A jail had been built earlier on the Commons, an open area where Broadway was divided to form the Bowery Road. The Commons was also home to the city's social welfare institutions: the Almshouse and the Bridewell, the latter a holding area for "debtors and light offenders." Prior to the erection of the jail, malefactors sentenced to incarceration had been confined in the basement of City Hall. The new jail was surrounded by a whipping post, stocks, a cage, a pillory, and gallows, all of which were used. Two larcenous ladies, for example, were given thirty-nine lashes at the whipping post, followed by a week in jail and expulsion from the city. Interestingly, although prostitution was an occupation for as many as 500 women, who practiced their profession on the "Holy Ground" near St. Paul's Chapel on Broadway and the Commons, they were not usually arrested.[51]

Improvements in the health, safety, and convenience of New York, however, did not entirely account for the growth and prosperity of the city in the eighteenth century. During the wars that marked that century, the city's merchants learned to be flexible and unspecialized. They dealt with anything saleable and sold goods at auction or on consignment. They also were not inhibited by regulations made in London, and they made money by smuggling, privateering, and supplying the enemy— French, Spanish, or Indians. Even the narrowness of the city was an asset because goods, once unloaded from wharves on the east side or west side, never had to be carted over long distances; thus both labor and time were saved. Five flourishing markets, conducted under municipal supervision, facilitated the distribution of produce from outside the city. There were also several ferries, and mail service was excellent.[52]

The improvements and activities of the growing city, just as had been true in the seventeenth century, attracted newcomers to New York. They came to make money and did so. Although there were some depressed periods, there were more prosperous ones. Overall, the wealth of the city grew and, with it, its foreign-born population. Indeed, many of the new arrivals played a role in stimulating foreign trade. This was particularly true for the English and Huguenot merchants, who had agency relationships and sources of credit with their relatives in London and the West Indies.[53]

It was also applicable to the small Jewish community of New York, whose members were constantly reinforced by kinfolk from other places. Their number grew from 150 in 1700 to 225 in 1730, but even at the later date they constituted only a small part of the population. However, from 1701 to 1730, Jewish merchants sometimes conducted as much as 12 percent of the total import trade of the city, in addition to holding a sizable share of the insurance, credit, and banking business. Their prosperity enabled them to erect their first synagogue in 1730. This edifice, on Mill Street, was the first of several temples known as Shearith Israel and permitted the congregation to end the practice of worshipping in each others' homes. Men and women prayed separately (the former wearing hats, the latter wearing white scarves). All religious activity took place at the Bima, a platform in the center of the room. Economic success also prompted at least one well-to-do Jew to move into a previously all-Gentile neighborhood. This produced a letter "to the Israelite of the Tribe of Judah, lately removed near Fudge's Corner," attacking him for using his "enormous" wealth to outbid the Christian competition on the rent.[54]

Jews, Sephardic and Ashkenazic (the latter from one of the many parts of the Austro-Hungarian Empire), were only one of several religious groupings in the eighteenth-century city. Anglicans, Scotch Presbyterians, Reformed Dutch Calvinists, Quakers, Lutherans, French Huguenots, Moravians, Methodists, and Roman Catholics were all part of the city's religious fabric. All but the Roman Catholics had a building in which to worship. Until the community grew larger and could afford to contribute to the building of a church, New York Catholics worshipped in each others' homes with the aid of a priest, who came up from Maryland at regular intervals. A shift in the relative size and importance of the three major denominations—Anglican, Presbyterian, and Reformed Dutch—took place just before the Revolution, when the Dutch church slipped to third place. One reason for the change was the decision of younger Dutch families to join the groups that included more of the elite of the city, Anglicans and Presbyterians.[55]

But not only men with money and connections saw the young city as a place to improve their fortunes. Because small-scale manufacturing also grew in the decades immediately preceding the Revolution, foreign artisans as well as men without specific skills but possessed of a strong back emigrated to the city. Coopers (who made the essential barrels used in the seaport city), sailmakers, ship carpenters, millers, linen weavers, whalebone processors, sugar refiners, nailmakers, leather workers, goldsmiths, and iron foundry workers all found employment in eighteenth-century New York.[56]

These craftsmen were mostly from England, but there were also Huguenot silversmiths, German metal workers and printers, Irish clockmakers and silk dyers, as well as coachmakers from various parts of the British Isles. Wig makers, barbers, and hairdressers came from Italy; their services were much in demand by the merchant elite.[57] Most of the newcomers came as free labor, but there was also a sizable number of indentured servants, many of whom came from the British Isles, and a significant number of Germans. Some of the free workers were more successful than others; skilled Irish workers from Ulster, for example, did well; others, such as Catholics from southern Ireland, settled for poorly paid and insecure work as common laborers and cartmen. Yorkshire weavers, who came around 1730, did not prosper because New Yorkers, constrained by the British from exporting textiles, produced only a little cloth for the home market. Most working-class families, however, apparently supported themselves, and the poor list throughout this period was small.[58]

Although there were substantial differences in the life style of rich and poor New Yorkers, there was also "a potential for personal and intergenerational mobility." Twenty percent of the leading property holders in the early eighteenth century, for example, had fathers who had been seamen, day laborers, or cartmen. Opportunities for upward mobility seemed to have declined somewhat later in the century. The leading shipowners in 1764, for example, "were the children of the topmost élite of the generation of the 1720's and '30's."[59] Class, of course, also affected the political life of the city. As the century moved on, the members of the Common Council were more likely to be wealthy or the sons of previous members.[60]

There is much evidence that labor continued to be in great demand throughout most of the eighteenth century. Although the Corporation insisted that only freemen could do business, work, or vote in the city, by midcentury it was easy to obtain that rank. Anyone born in New York was a freeman by virtue of birth and needed only to register. Those who came from elsewhere were required to pay a sliding fee (3 pounds for merchants or shopkeepers, 20 shillings for manual workers). Skilled workers were more welcome than unskilled; according to the Naturalization Act of 1713, an immigrant without a trade had to give two years' security to show that he would not be a burden to the Corporation. In contrast, a newcomer with a skill was welcome free of charge. Furthermore, both "help" and "situation wanted" notices demonstrated that there was a reasonably good match between the skills the immigrants brought and the opportunities the city offered.[61]

On the eve of the Revolution, the people of the city were assembled in a hierarchical but flexible structure, with large merchants, crown officers, landowners, lawyers, shopkeepers, and artisans in the first group; poorer freeholders (with property worth less than 40 pounds or mortgaged) in the second; and clerks, laborers, and journeymen (often grouped as mechanics) at the bottom.[62] In some respects, however, the bottom was not so far from the top. Although the most wealthy had elegant city homes as well as country estates in Brooklyn, Whitestone, Flushing, Hoboken, Staten Island, and across the Harlem River in Kingsbridge, due to the absence of adequate transportation everyone lived for most of the year in proximity to the commercial district, which centered on the East River docks. It was generally agreed that the East River, rather than the Hudson, was the best for shipping because it had a slow current and offered easy access to Long Island Sound and hence to the Atlantic Ocean.[63]

Many of the wealthy merchants had stores and counting houses adjoining or within their homes. While the portion of Broadway that ran from the Battery to Trinity Church, called the Mall, was home to the well-to-do, as it had been for most of the century, just in back of it or a few blocks away lived the mechanics, who, in the absence of house numbers, located themselves by the signs of their trade.[64] The wealthiest families of New York were rich indeed, often as a result of a combination of professions: landowners, merchants, and law. The largest single group of merchants were English, many of whom had come to the city as youngsters and had bypassed formal education to become apprentices in established businesses.[65]

Putting class above ethnicity, the upper class married without concern for the country of origin of their chosen partners. The Beekmans from Germany married Bayards and Jays from France, and Livingstons from England married the Anglo-Dutch Roosevelts. Most of them lived in Georgian-style houses, "square, painted brick buildings five windows wide with centered entrances and balconies." Inside, the furnishings, such as English china and silver and Oriental porcelain and fabrics, reflected both the owner's wealth and the far-flung trade of the city. The residents of these homes displayed their status by their clothing as well as their homes, dressing in a fussy style imported from London and referred to as "the Macaroni." Their outfits included "short waistcoats, enormous wigs and small cocked hats." They also bought coaches imported from England, disdaining those made in New York.[66]

Middle-class housing was quite different. These families lived in two- or three-story Dutch-style houses with gabled roofs and half doors. The kitchen was usually in the cellar, and the other rooms were often above a shop or office. The poorest New Yorkers lived west of Broadway in the least-developed part of the city, the area north of Warren Street on the West Side. Their homes were "crude shanties with dirt floors and unplastered walls." The area had been considered an unsuitable place to live because it was swampy and mosquitoes, the source of yellow fever, swarmed there. After 1760, however, when efforts to drain the swamps succeeded, houses were built and people began to move into the area. In spite of this improvement, there was never enough housing for the growing population. It was, of course, possible for people to "commute," especially from Brooklyn, because three different ferry services were in operation, but for most workers, paying the ferry fare was an unwanted added expense. Since the service was also uncertain, the ferries were not much used for daily travel.[67]

Regardless of where they lived, most of the citizens profited, directly or indirectly, from the lucrative shipping trade presided over by the merchants of the city. It would not be correct to see eighteenth-century New York as a one-industry city, but there can be no doubt that overseas trade was central to its economic prosperity. The trade served another purpose as well: Every voyage made from New York advertised the city's existence and prosperity and thus helped to attract additional population and capital. A large proportion of New Yorkers labored at the port, and many others worked in offices, managing the finances of the trade. Still more were employed in the shops that sold the imported goods. Also contributing to the bustling economy in the pre-Revolutionary years were the city's craftsmen, most of them from England.[68]

The city's newspapers, the *New York Journal, Gazetteer,* and *Gazette,* advertised the availability of goods imported or made locally, such as London-tailored clothing, imported wines, sailcloth, and delicacies such as "pickled oysters." Most of these items were available in small retail shops, but basic food and drink was sold in the city's six markets—four on the populous East Side, two on the less inhabited West Side. Milk was delivered directly to homes.[69]

Class and family income played an important role in schooling. The children of the wealthiest families were educated by tutors in their homes. Middle-class youngsters were most likely to attend denominational schools. The poorest children might attend a charity school, but more likely they went to work at an early age. None of the available schools were highly valued; indeed, one contemporary said that "our schools are of the lowest order . . . the instructors want instruction." Overall, mid-eighteenth-century New Yorkers were not much interested in intellectual pursuits. They did not read much beyond the newspapers. There was one subscription library but no place to hear secular music or see art.[70]

Taken as a whole, New York, in the years just before the Revolution, had a heterogeneous, cosmopolitan, and growing population which had been attracted to the city by its economic opportunities. By their presence these people were adding to the city's attractiveness. There were 26,000 New Yorkers in 1775, and just before the outbreak of hostilities they lived in over 3,200 houses stretching up to Reade Street on the west side and Bayard Street on the east.[71]

The expansion and prosperity of the city during the 1750s and 1760s was due in large part to the American portion of the Seven Years' War, known on this side of the Atlantic as the French and Indian War, which began in 1754. For one thing, British preoccupation with a long war being fought on several continents made it easier for the American colonists to evade laws designed to protect British ports. Even more important, however, New York was the headquarters of the British armed forces, who needed food, housing, and equipment. The city's merchants got lucrative supply contracts, manufacturers hired more workers, and the city prospered. Some entrepreneurs made fortunes from stealing French ships, and others found profit from "clandestine trade with the enemy."[72]

All things considered, New Yorkers did not rejoice when the North American phase of the war ended in a British victory and Canada became part of the British Empire. Four more years of opportunity lay ahead, however, since the final ending of the Seven Years' War did not come until the Peace of Paris was signed in 1763. At that point, a depression struck the city, exacerbated by new British policies which seemed likely to limit New York's economic prospects. The government at Whitehall was anxious to punish those Americans who allegedly had prolonged the French and Indian portion of the war by supplying the French with food and trading with the French West Indies.[73]

Parliamentary actions, such as the passage of the Sugar Act of 1764 and the Stamp Act a year later, produced much opposition in New York because both acts levied taxes that cut into the profits made from trade. In the case of the first Act, it made sugar more expensive and therefore there were fewer customers able and willing to buy it. The second Act, which required that stamps be affixed to all documents, newspapers, and other printed material (including marriage licenses), was a burden to the business community but also to consumers because the cost of procuring the stamps was passed on to them.[74]

When the first stamps reached New York on October 23, 1765, the American ships in the harbor "lowered their colors as a declaration of grief," and threats were pasted on the doors of public offices saying that "the first man that . . . distributes or makes use of the Stamp paper, let him take care of his house, person and effects." A few days later, on November 1, there was a riot during which a sizable mob paraded in the streets and burned an effigy of the Lieutenant Governor, Cadwallader Colden. Because of actions like these, even more violent in Boston, the Stamp Act was repealed in 1766.[75]

There was reasonable unity in the protests against the new taxes, but as the Revolutionary crisis deepened and independence, followed by war, seemed a strong possibility, a large part of the city's mercantile community drew back. Their concern was that war, even more than taxes, could destroy trade. As a result of such conservative attitudes (which contrasted dramatically with the much more radical opinions that were also present), New York, just before the Revolution, was a divided city. An example of the bitterness appeared in a definition printed in the *New York Journal* which supported a boycott of trade with England: "A Tory is a thing whose head is in England and its body in America and whose neck ought to be stretched."[76]

The British government had a number of grievances against the colonists: their flagrant privateering, trading with the enemy, violations of the Navigation Acts, which prohibited such trade, and the refusal of New York's provincial government to vote the sums of money needed to feed and house the soldiers or buy guns. To make matters worse, all this was occurring while Britain was paying in lives and money to keep the French away. The cost had been high. Great Britain had huge debts, and the colonists were expected to help pay the bills. Actually, the Stamp and Sugar Acts were only the beginning of the campaign.

Lord Grenville and his associates in London had additional plans: making the colonists pay for feeding and housing British troops stationed in the various colonies (the Quartering Act), enforcing the Navigation Acts and thus preventing trade with English ports, limiting the amount of specie and forbidding the use of paper money (the Currency Act), and impressing young male colonists into the British navy. Some of the new taxes, such as the one on sugar, were merely a newer version of the Molasses Act, which was passed thirty years earlier (although not enforced), but the Stamp Act and Tea Act were innovations. Furthermore, the latter Act, by giving the British-owned East India Company a monopoly, undermined the New York smugglers, who had been importing tea and avoiding taxes.[77]

Americans had a number of grievances of their own. First, the British currency they were forced to use was unstable; second, there was never enough specie with which to carry out normal business. The Sugar Act, which (in addition to levying a tax on sugar from the British West Indies) placed new duties on imports from the other islands, created much anger. This was exacerbated by London's announced intention to use the money so collected for an increasing military presence in New York and Britain's other North American colonies.[78]

His Majesty's government then added further fuel to the fire by plac-ing a new set of import duties on glass, lead, paint, paper, and tea in 1767, collectively known as the Townshend Acts. The new tax on tea, a widely used product not possible to grow domestically, assumed a cen-tral position in the escalating quarrel. Boston's reaction is better known, but New York also had a tea party. When a ship called the *Nancy*, known to be carrying tea, appeared in New York Bay, "the firing of the cannons and a massive protest rally convinced its captain to depart without unloading." Worse was yet to come. On April 22, 1774, the cargo of another tea ship, the *London*, was dumped into New York Bay.[79]

These rebellious actions were in part the work of the Sons of Liberty, who made their first appearance during the Stamp Act crisis. The mem-bers were "middling merchants, former sea captains and mechanics whose goal was to win concessions from the British but who also wanted to prevent the mobocracy" from ruining the city. When the first stamps arrived on a British merchant ship, three of the Sons—Isaac Sears, John Lamb, and Alexander McDougall—organized a protest, forc-ing the British to move the stamps to an armed warship and then to the Fort for safety. The Sons gained further prominence in January 1770, when British soldiers nailed up "broadsides attacking them for erecting a Liberty Bell on the Commons near City Hall" and causing the Battle of Golden Hill. More riot than battle, the fracas began when two of the Sons seized some British soldiers. Efforts to free them led to hand-to-hand fighting between the British and hundreds of civilians recruited by Sears and Lamb. Only a few people were wounded, but the incident allowed the Sons of Liberty to become the spokesmen for those New Yorkers who opposed accomodation with Great Britain.[80]

Partly as a result of the Sons' agitation, New York joined the other colonies at the First Continental Congress in 1774. Within the city, a Committee of Sixty was elected to move New York closer to rebellion. Matters came to a head when news of first blood was shed outside of Boston. The radicals in the Sons of Liberty took control and, with a Committee of One Hundred, seized muskets and organized a militia. In August, blood was also shed in New York. British troops had evacuated the Fort and were now on ships in the harbor, whence one of them, the *Asia*, "loosed a barrage against the city." At summer's end Royal Gover-nor Tryon was no longer able to control the city.[81]

These events did not signify that all New Yorkers were ready to fight. The division in public opinion was not along ethnic lines. It is more likely that class, occupation, and fear were the factors that influenced people's opinions regarding rebellion. Those who remained loyal to Brit-ain said the Fort could not protect them, that they were vulnerable to attack from the islands that surrounded Manhattan, and that their "crowded, heavily built up city, containing houses with wood shingle roofs" could be easily destroyed by fires resulting from bombardment by the British ships in the harbor.

Such fears could apply to all citizens, but men who had attained prosperity because of their connection to Great Britain and its Empire were unwilling to disrupt a relationship that had been useful to them. Those most opposed to rebellion included large property owners, government employees, merchants, and the Anglican clergy. The various concerns led the New York delegation to the First Continental Congress to abstain from the vote on the Declaration of Independence and made many eligible young men unwilling "to sign up for the common defense." Those most opposed left the city entirely and moved to Canada.[82]

In the first phase of the war, General Washington and his army forced the British to evacuate Boston and then marched triumphantly to New York City, arriving in April 1776. His triumph, however, was short lived because he was followed four months later by Lord William Howe and "the largest expeditionary force ever raised by England," which encamped on the south shore of Brooklyn. By August, 7,000 American militiamen faced 20,000 British regulars.

The battle raged for eight days, but, as would be expected, the disparity in strength led to a disaster for the Americans. Washington's staff urged him to prevent the British from using the city by burning it to the ground and advised him to leave the area and fight from a stronger position elsewhere. One of his lieutenants, Nathanial Greene, told his chief that "two-thirds of the property in the city of New York belonged to Tories and that therefore we have no very great reason to run any risk for its defense." The Continental Congress, however, would agree only to an evacuation, and Washington himself opposed the plan to destroy the city, partly because he was afraid that doing so would make the very discouraged survivors of the Battle of Brooklyn desert in even larger numbers than they had been doing. He therefore chose to leave the city intact and face the British again in Westchester, where he hoped to win a battle and thus convince his soldiers that the British were something less than invincible.[83]

Had Howe been quick to pursue, the entire rebellion might have ended right there. Fortunately for Washington and his army, the General was slow to move and Washington was able to extricate his remaining 5,000 troops. In September the battle resumed at Kips Bay on the eastern side of Manhattan, where Howe's forces bombarded the shore for two hours and then landed. The American militia stationed at Kips Bay could do no more than briefly slow the British advance and were therefore evacuated.[84]

A farm owned by a family named Murray was located at the spot where the British disembarked. Mrs. Murray has been considered a patriotic heroine who gave the redcoats food and drink and thus delayed their pursuit of the American forces. In reality, she and her husband were wealthy Tory landowners, and while she did give General Howe and his officers cakes and wine, the brief interlude did little to delay their pursuit of Washington's forces, who were making their way north to Harlem.[85] In the battle of Harlem Heights, the British were temporarily repulsed. They soon, however, resumed the chase and Washington was forced to continue to retreat up the Hudson Valley, fighting and losing a big battle at White Plains and smaller ones elsewhere. By November 1775, New York was firmly in British hands and remained so until 1783.[86]

The city that Washington and his army had left behind was a Tory haven for the duration of the war, but with victory it became the temporary capital of the new nation. With each of these changes, thousands of people departed and others arrived, so that between 1776 and 1783, the population dropped to 5,000, rose to 33,000, and fell again to 12,000— the point it was at when the war ended. Overall, the city lost about one-third of its prewar population, many of whom left when Washington's army did, leaving their landholdings behind.[87]

Although most of the inhabitants, some of whom were Tory refugees from rebel-controlled areas, suffered a good deal during the war, a portion of the population grew richer than ever because commercial activity did not cease. British soldiers needed goods and services, and enterprising merchants profited by supplying the British military establishment and carrying on trade with unoccupied portions of British North America. The major impediments to business were shortages of all kinds—especially housing, due to two disastrous fires in 1776 and 1778, which destroyed almost a third of the city west of Broadway and north of Broad Street. There were still other hardships during the occupation. Cut off from from its normal suppliers on Long Island and Staten Island, both of which were in rebel hands, New Yorkers cut down shade trees for fuel, houses decayed, and farms were left in disarray.[88]

Because of the continuation of trade, military and otherwise, during the Revolution, at war's end the wharves, warehouses, and other accoutrements of commerce, most of which were on the east side of the city, were intact and in good repair. This had much to do with the fact (remarked upon by contemporary observers and historians alike) that New York recovered very quickly from the effects of war, fire, and occupation and by 1788 had rebuilt its burned-out area, added considerable population, and was once again the profitable commercial center it had been prior to hostilities.

A parade held in that same year was organized by occupations, thus revealing the varied opportunities available to workers in New York. In addition to the more familiar artisans, there were foresters, grain measurers, peruke makers, ivory turners, nailers, and pump makers, all of whom advertised their specialties.[89] Every year saw an increase in the number of ships that arrived in New York harbor, and the port's exports rose from 2,505,465 tons in 1790 to 19,851,136 in 1800. This was in contrast to Newport, Rhode Island and Boston, which never recovered from the effects of the war and never regained their pre-revolutionary economic stature.[90]

The war produced significant changes in the social and political structure of New York. For one thing, it "brought to a halt . . . the gradual flow of political and economic power to a small multi-generational elite." Confiscations of Tory property during and immediately after the war, combined with changes in the trading network, "opened a large number of positions in the upper ranks." These opportunities were taken by "new men," some moving up from the lower classes, others moving into the city from France, Ireland, and New England. The newcomers did not change the ethnic balance of the city but rather reinforced the prewar mixture. What also remained from the colonial era was religious tolerance. Understandably, the position of the Anglican Church was somewhat weaker, but the pattern of coexistence among the various religious groups remained intact.[91]

So did some of the discrimination. The New York State Constitution of 1777 contained no restrictions on voting or officeholding for Jews or Catholics but did require a naturalization oath, which included a renunciation of "all allegiances and subjegation to every foreign king, prince, potentate or state, in matters ecclesiastical as well as civil"—a provision that effectively barred Catholics from citizenship, the ballot, or public office. The Jewish community was not affected by this clause but had some difficulty reorganizing its religious life after wartime disruptions because the majority of the prewar congregation of Shearith Israel had chosen to go to Philadelphia to wait out the war.[92]

Postrevolutionary changes included some very important modifications in race relations. As previously noted, blacks had been living on Manhattan Island since 1626. They lived in shabby quarters attached to the homes of their owners or, if they were free, they occupied houses set apart from whites. In either case, they were seen as inferior. Accurate statistics are hard to come by, but reliable estimates indicate that there were 300 blacks in New York City when the British took over. The new ruler of the colony, the Duke of York, had a monetary interest in the Royal African Company, whose business was the slave trade, and therefore he approved of the establishment of a thriving slave market at the foot of Wall Street. Many of the newcomers came from Africa, particularly Angola, but even more came from the West Indies. As a result, New York's black population constituted a "strikingly heterogeneous community consisting of native born New Yorkers," "seasoned slaves from the West Indies and the southern colonies, as well as more recently captured men and women from West Africa and Madagascar." Thanks to the Dutch, who, as stated earlier, freed some of the slaves and gave some of them land, about 2 percent were free and had settled on land on the outskirts of the city.[93]

Unlike plantation owners in the South, New Yorkers did as the Dutch had done and used the blacks mostly as artisans and house servants. Under the British, more white indentures arrived to do this kind of work. As a result, fewer blacks were imported. This, however, did not lead to a decrease in the total black population of the city, which numbered 2,400 in 1746 and 3,000 when the Revolution began. Their proportion in the population, however, moved steadily downward; by 1799, they comprised only 10 percent of the population, and most were free.[94] The first legal steps toward the goal of ending slavery in New York City were taken in 1781, when the New York State Legislature voted to free blacks who had fought on the American side during the Revolution. Four years later, the importation of slaves was prohibited; in 1786, slaves from the forfeited Tory estates were freed. A gradual emancipation law was passed in 1799 which provided that the children of slaves born after that date would be free at age eighteen (males) and age twenty-five (females). This was broadened by another law passed in 1817, which stated that all slaves born before 1799 were to be freed by 1827. In 1841, slavery in all of New York State was finally ended.[95]

Many individual owners had freed their slaves before the state laws were passed because in "the burgeoning post-Revolutionary city they were not useful." Master "craftsmen tended to dispense with skilled slave assistants in favor of using cheap or indentured white immigrant labor." Most blacks, therefore, became house servants. Those who did not live in a white household resided in "half underground cellars that seemed to symbolize their status as being only half free." Those who worked on the outside were most likely to be part of the crew on one of the ferryboats that crossed the Hudson and East Rivers or drivers of carts and haulers of drinking water.[96]

The post-Revolution legal changes in the condition of black New Yorkers were not driven by economic reasons alone, and lawmakers were not much influenced by liberal ideas generated by the American Revolution. It was fear, more than any other emotion, that led to the gradual end of slavery in New York. To begin with, it was very difficult to control the slaves in the expanding cosmopolitan city. Many ran away, taking some of their master's property with them; others "engaged in riotous behavior."

In 1712, for example, a group of slaves set fire to some buildings and killed five of the whites who came to put out the flames. As punishment, the right of blacks to own land, as the Dutch had permitted, was revoked. As a result of another uprising, in 1716, thirteen of the rioters were burned to death, eighteen hanged, and seventy transported to the West Indies. In 1741, news of a "Great Slave Plot to burn down the city" brought panic to the white population.[97] At the same time that a portion of the black community was expressing its anger by violence, many others were more interested in building a community. In the 1790s blacks organized their own churches, thus showing by constructive means, their anger at being forced to sit in the back of white churches. In 1787, blacks organized an African Free School, which grew to hold 110 students in 1800.[98]

Although New York's business life returned to its healthy pre-Revolution state, the trade that had been sufficient for a colonial city in the 1770s was not enough for the American city ten years later. In the immediate postwar years, however, New York was not able to expand the volume of its commerce very much. The troubles and uncertainties of the Confederation period were only part of the reason for this. In addition, the loss of Tory merchants and their capital was a real blow, as was the invasion of the "Hessian Fly," which reduced the supply of flour available for export. Also problematic were new British trading restrictions that came with independence. Although they were often violated, new Orders-in-Council, promulgated in 1783, barred American shippers from trading with their prewar partners, the British West Indies. This led to more trade with the French, Spanish, Dutch, and Danish Caribbean islands. There was no decrease in overall trading volume, but an increase was difficult to achieve.[99]

Trade with the British Isles, Holland, Spain, Portugal, or Madeira generally continued, although restrictions stating that raw materials in American bottoms had to come directly from the United States in order to enter British waters prevented American ships from following previous practices, such as picking up grain, sugar, and other products produced in South America and the Caribbean and delivering them to England. Overall, the new procedures hampered New York commerce a good deal.[100]

It helped a bit that New York was the terminus of the monthly mail ships from Britain and the government packets from France. New initiatives, however, were needed for growth, so the New York merchants looked into other trading patterns. The first was brand new and quite successful. In 1784, the *Empress of China* departed from New York bound for Canton, China with a cargo of fur, wine, and lumber and brought back various exotic items from Asia. Only sixteen years later, there was a great demand for tea, silk, and spices in New York; 147 ships in the Far East trade docked in the harbor and the reach of New York's businessmen had been expanded to Calcutta and Batavia.[101]

A second thrust was to the South. The New York mercantile community made a great effort to improve on their already lucrative prewar coastal trade with the cotton-producing states. This was the so-called cotton triangle, the three-cornered trade that brought Charleston and Savannah cotton to New York, where it was unloaded and then reloaded on ocean-going ships bound for England's textile factories. As a result of this trade, New York's contacts with Liverpool were greater than with any other port in the world.[102]

Because of its far-flung trading patterns and its developing hinterland (New York State had opened its western lands for settlement in 1784), postrevolutionary New York regained and then expanded its historic role as an entrepôt. In 1790, for example, it exported wine, spirits, tea, coffee, molasses, cocoa, chocolate, sugar, nuts, spices, indigo, and, of course, cotton, none of which was produced anywhere near the city. It also exported its own staple, flour, subject to State inspection for the worrisome Hessian fly. In that same year, one-fourth of the nation's imports went through the New York Customs House.[103]

There was also an increase in manufacturing activity in the last decade of the eighteenth century, continuing into the nineteenth century. Some of this represented greater production of familiar items connected with shipbuilding, but, in addition, ready-made clothing, boots, shoes, and printing became more important to the city's economy. For most of the period, manufacturing was still done by craftsmen, but by the 1820s, small factories began to replace home workshops.[104]

Processing raw materials continued to be central to the city's economic life. The refining of West Indian sugar, a field in which German immigrant William Havemeyer earned a great fortune, was one example of this. Flour milling also continued to be important, as was liquor distilling, beer brewing, and the processing of leather and tobacco. Havemeyer's success was exceeded by that of another German immigrant of the period, John Jacob Astor, whose wealth came from a variety of activities, including real estate speculation. The growing city, which had reached Houston Street by 1800, was a fertile field for those with access to the capital needed to buy property.[105]

Partly to supply capital and manage investments, several banks were organized. A branch of the Bank of North America, whose headquarters were in Philadelphia, opened a New York office in 1784. In the same year, the Bank of New York and a branch of the Bank of the United States established themselves in the city. The Bank of Manhattan was organized three years later, followed by the Merchants Bank in 1801.[106] At the same time, the municipality ended its "corporate paternalism" and established a more open atmosphere for business development. The apprentice system was abandoned, along with complicated freemanship procedures, price fixing, and monopolies. In its role as supporter of economic development, rather than regulator, the city undertook an extensive and successful renovation of the waterfront, which was completed in 1801.[107]

As a result of all these initiatives and in spite of six yellow fever epidemics between 1798 and 1822, New York grew by two to three thousand people a year from the 1790s through the first quarter of the nineteenth century. Even the devastating fire of 1818, which wiped out a million dollars' worth of shops and merchandise, did not result in permanent damage to the economy.[108] Possibly because of the city's healthy growth, the loss of both the state and national capital was hardly noticed. After a brief two-year stay in New York, in 1790 the federal capital moved to Philadelphia for ten years, while a permanent capital was being built in the District of Columbia. The move was engineered by Alexander Hamilton in return for the federal government's assumption of debts that the state had accumulated during the Revolution. The loss of the state capital to Albany was the result of political considerations: The pre-Revolutionary struggle between upstaters and the city over taxation and other issues was reawakened in the 1790s and culminated in the move of the Legislature to Albany in 1797.[109]

The growth of population between 1790 and 1800—from 33,131 to 60,515, an 80 percent increase—was remarkable. The reason was primarily immigration, although internal migration also played a part. According to the principal historian of this period of New York's history, Sidney Pomerantz, 3,000 people a year arrived at the Port of New York from Europe between 1789 and 1793 and another 6,000 between the latter date and the end of century. Furthermore, most of them stayed in New York. As the city continued to gain an increasingly larger share of foreign and coastal trade, it became a "magnet for drawing people and holding them." [110]

The newcomers were a diverse lot. Between 1790 and 1800, Irish, Germans (especially Hessians), and French refugees from both Haiti and revolutionary France were attracted to New York. Many were skilled workers, but more were needy. By the late 1790s, in contrast to earlier years, the large volume of immigration began to be seen as a problem. It was said that the newcomers were a burden on the rudimentary poor relief facilities and were carriers of the dread yellow fever bacteria. Furthermore, the new arrivals needed protection and direction. "Sharpers and unscrupulous ship captains exploited them, and this led to the establishment, in 1794, of the Society for the Information and Assistance of Persons Emigrating from Foreign Countries." In spite of their efforts, the newcomers continued to be a burden on the municipal treasury. After considerable pressure, in 1797 New York State gave the city $2,500 for the refugees from Haiti. The federal government sent a smaller sum.[111]

The Irish and French, who came as refugees from revolution, were a varied lot. The Irish were the instigators of a failed revolt against England, and the French from Haiti were victims of an uprising that succeeded. Most of the newcomers, however, were not refugees but rather artisans from England, where their earning power was being undermined by industrialization. Unwilling to become factory laborers, they chose to work in the preindustrial New York economy, where their skills were still in great demand. As a result of this late-eighteenth-century immigration, in a clear-cut example of the match that has been so important to New York history, new artisans were added to the city's economy, such as cutlers, musical and mathematical instrument makers, lace and fringe weavers, coach and harness makers, and pewterers, to name only a few.[112]

In some respects, the late-eighteenth-century arrivals resembled those who had come earlier, but there was a difference in status. The availability of workers who did not need to be supported led to a decline in the number of indentured servants employed in New York. As a result, this particular form of labor organization disappeared. Another difference was the result of New York State policy. After the opening of state-owned western lands in 1784, many of the new arrivals, especially the Germans, only passed through the city on their way west.[113]

The growth and prosperity of New York in the 1790s might have been even greater had it not been for the wars that resulted from the French Revolution. Beginning in 1793, the battles between France and England caused considerable difficulties for the United States and its premier trading city. In an attempt by both the Americans and British to continue business as usual, John Jay negotiated a treaty with Great Britain which modified previous restrictions on American trade with the West Indies, tacitly put the United States on the side of its former mother country, and seemed to assure peace.[114]

The treaty, however, was extremely unpopular with those New Yorkers who sided with France, and the conflict led to a deepening of political divisions that had originated in earlier developments related to the organization of the national government. The Federalists, led by Alexander Hamilton, were pro-British and favored a strong central government. The Jeffersonian Republicans, on the other hand, wanted more power to go the states and attached themselves to the cause of France's revolutionary government. These divisions also affected national immigration and naturalization policies, which were very liberal and required only that free whites reside in the United States for three years in order to become citizens. Fearing that most of the new arrivals would support the Republicans, however, the Federalist-controlled Congress raised the residency requirement to five years in 1795 and, three years later, to fourteen years. When the Republicans came to power in 1801, however, they moved the requirement back to five years.[115]

In any case, the Jay Treaty did not preserve the peace for long. By 1806, impressment of Americans by the British became a burning issue once again, and the city's merchants became alarmed at the prospect of a British blockade of the harbor. To prevent this, defensive works were started at the tip of Manhattan (these were later known as Castle Clinton and were used for other purposes). As the quarrel with Great Britain escalated, Congress passed an Embargo Act in December 1807, which prevented all trade with Europe and precipitated a panic in New York. There were many evasions, but on the whole the embargo was a distinct hardship for New York, whose economy was so closely tied to the sea trade. Three years later, the embargo was somewhat loosened by the passage of the Non-Intercourse Act, and graduallly the port became busy again—only to come to a halt once more in 1812 with the start of the war with Great Britain. The argument continued to be over impressment, a nonissue as far as the New York mercantile community was concerned. Blocked from normal trade, the merchants resorted to an old way to make money during war time—privateering. The signing of the Treaty of Ghent in 1815 brought a welcome end to the war, and piracy fell into disuse.[116]

As soon as trade could resume, the city's businesses benefited enormously from the decision of British manufacturers to "dump" their accumulated surpluses in New York rather than in Philadelphia or Boston. "Behind the ship that brought the news of peace came a fleet of British ships which for three months dumped enormous quantities of goods into a ravenous market." After "dumping" ended, coastal trade continued to make New York the major economic center of the United States. Ships brought raw cotton from the South, leading to the creation of a textile industry in the city, while other New York ships, filled with cotton, sailed directly to Europe from the South and returned to their home port laden with textiles, manufactured goods, and immigrants from the British Isles and Germany.[117]

Economic and demographic growth was reflected in other areas as well. By the second decade of the nineteenth century, there were fourteen banks in New York, which greatly increased available credit. There was also a spurt in the number of auction sales because the system was very attractive to British exporters, who preferred to consign their goods to an American auctioneer, thus retaining title to them until they were sold. Auctions could be advertised and business stimulated even before the goods arrived because after 1818 there was regular packet service from New York to Liverpool. The ships of the Black Ball line made the trip whether there was cargo or not, and this reliability made their business grow.[118]

The packets, the auctions, and the multiplying insurance companies (four by 1798), because they lessened commercial uncertainties, increased New York City's attractiveness. In addition, in certain areas, such as commercial banking, New York outran all its rivals because its pioneering bankers organized a commercial paper market before any other American city did so, were the only ones to develop a call-money market (an option procedure which allows a buyer to put a "hold" on a specific stock or commodity purchase at an agreed upon price and pay up within a stated time period), and were very aggressive in seeking depositors. By 1817, there were enough securities brokers to form a Board of Brokers and, due to a law passed by the State Legislature six years earlier, enough corporations to keep them busy.[119]

While giving full credit to the entrepreneurial talents of New York's businessmen and bankers, economic historians have also emphasized the importance of its hinterland. Here too, however, humankind deserves credit along with nature. Between 1799 and 1819, the city strengthened its ties to the countryside by the construction of turnpikes and bridges. By 1808, New Yorkers had invested more money in turnpike stock than had the residents of any other state. Even before the completion of the Erie Canal in 1825, therefore, enterprising New Yorkers were able to see that their economic growth depended on their surroundings and see that no city, like no person, could really be an island.[120]

The Canal, however, was of great importance because it enabled New York "to become the essential middlemen between the farmers and trappers of America's West, the east coast and even Europe." De Witt Clinton, as mayor and governor, provided the impetus for building the Canal and also received much of the criticism, as demonstrated by the witticism "Clinton, the federal son of a bitch, taxes our dollars to build him a ditch." When he poured Lake Erie water into the Atlantic Ocean on November 4, 1825, his action symbolized the belief that New York would become a world city. The governor prophesized that the urban center on the Hudson "would become the emporium of commerce, the seat of manufactures and that whole island of Manhattan . . . , replenished with dense population, would constitute one vast city."[121]

The combination of private initiative, governmental leadership, and immigration produced a dynamic and prosperous city by the second decade of the nineteenth century. President Timothy Dwight of Yale University, on a visit to New York, spoke of the "bustle in the streets, the perpetual activity of the carts, the noise and hurry at the docks . . . the sound of saws, axes and hammers at the shipyards, the continually repeated views of numerous buildings . . . the vast number of vessels, continually plying on the bay and rivers."[122]

Dwight's report and Clinton's oratory presented New York, present and future, in a very bright light. Were there no dark spots? Was the prosperity widespread? To a great extent, yes. There were certainly poor people in New York, and in times of depression, public assistance had to be provided. The almshouse was never empty, and the entire problem of poverty was a concern of the city's humanitarians. Their interest, however, did not mean that the poor in New York were so numerous but rather that they stood out so clearly in the otherwise booming city.

Who were the poor? They were the disabled, the infirm, dependent children, the sick, the aged, the blind, the mentally defective, women widowed by death or desertion, and the families of seamen who had left them without funds. These were the unfortunates who could be found in any city at any time in history. They were in dire straits in early nineteenth-century New York because they could not work. Had they been able to do so, they could have supported themselves. The other groups who sometimes needed help were the working poor—apprentices, domestics, scavengers, chimney sweeps, ditchdiggers, all of whose work was irregular and whose earnings very small. A third group of poor were destitute immigrants, predominantly Irish. In the middle of the 1790s, almost half the people in the almshouse were new arrivals from the Emerald Isle. Every ethnic group, however, was represented. In 1796, for example, the records show that an aged Jew named Jacob Abrahams lived in the almshouse and requested kosher food.[123]

The financial burden of poor relief was much resented by municipal officials, especially when, as in 1815, it was the largest single item in the city budget. As that decade went on, however, more and more private charitable agencies were formed (they numbered 100 by 1825). The recipients of the private funds were varied, but the recently arrived poor, especially the Irish, were always in the majority. Help was not graciously given to the Irish. Their poverty, assumed criminality, propensity to riot, heavy drinking, and Catholicism exacerbated nativism. In a classic case of blaming the poor for their poverty, the nearly destitute Irish were held responsible for creating the inadequate housing in which they lived. Their homes were mostly in the northern wards—Five, Six, Seven, and Ten—and their housing was in crowded slums, two to three people in a room in tenements, cellars, and rundown boarding houses. Corlear's Hook in the Seventh Ward was one of the worst sections. Another area considered undesirable was Bancker Street in the Fourth Ward, part of a large black ghetto spreading east from City Hall. By 1820, the outskirts of the city had become squatter camps for Irish and German poor.[124]

This is a grim picture, but it should not be allowed to dominate the total portrait of early nineteenth-century New York. In reasonably good times (which was most of the time) and with good health, the dynamic economic structure of New York made the city one of promise for the unskilled almost as much as for the craftsman or the man with capital to invest. As long as the match between the city's needs and the talents and strengths of the population was maintained, New York would remain a mecca for immigrants. For this reason, when population pressures and the dislocations accompanying industrial and agricultural changes "pushed" so many millions out of nineteenth-century Europe, more were "pulled" to New York than to any other American city.[125]

NOTES

1. Eugenie Birch, "Prelude to World City: New York City From Dutch Colony to Economic Capital, 1625–1860," ed. David R. Hill, *Working Paper Series, 1990*, Society for American City Regional Planning History, 1.

2. Eric Homberger, *The Historical Atlas of New York City* (New York: Henry Holt & Co., 1994), 12.

3. Ibid., 20.

4. Charles W. Baird, *History of the Huguenot Emigration to America* (New York: Doubleday & Co., 1922), Vol. I, 149, 153, 158.

5. Thomas Janvier, *The Dutch Founding of New York* (New York: Harper & Brothers, 1903), 57, 87.

6. J. Franklin Jameson, ed., *Narratives of New Netherland, 1609–1664* (New York: Barnes and Noble, 1959), 424; Oliver A. Rink, "Private Interest and Godly Gain: The West India Company and the Dutch Reformed Church in New Netherland, 1624–1664," *New York History* (July 1994), 247.

7. Homberger, *Atlas,* 20, 26.

8. Thomas Archdeacon, "Anglo-Dutch New York, 1676" in Milton M. Klein, ed., *New York: The Centennial Years, 1676–1976* (Port Washington, N.Y.: Kennikat Press, 1976), 26, 27; Homberger, *Atlas,* 30.

9. Homberger, *Atlas,* 24.

10. Joyce Goodfriend, *Before the Melting Pot: Society and Culture in Colonial New York, 1664–1730* (Princeton: Princeton University Press, 1992), 40–41.

11. Nan A. Rothschild, *New York City Neighborhoods: The 18th Century* (New York: Academic Press, 1990), 81; Miecislaus Haiman, *Poles in New York in the 17th and 18th Centuries* (Chicago: Polish Roman Catholic Union of America, 1938), 27, 29; Floyd Shumway, *Seaport City* (New York: South Street Seaport Museum, 1975), 9; Marianna Van Rensselaer, *History of the City of New York in the 17th Century* (New York: New York University Press, 1956), 209.

12. Archdeacon, "Anglo-Dutch," 14.

13. Ibid., 17–18.

14. Shumway, *Seaport,* 18.

15. Homberger, *Atlas,* map, 31.

16. Rink, "Private Interest," 246–247.

17. Jameson, *Narratives,* 103.

18. Harold C. Syrett, "Private Enterprise in New Amsterdam," *William and Mary Quarterly* (October 1954), 543.

19. Archdeacon, "Anglo-Dutch," 24.

20. Ibid., 27–28.

21. Shumway, *Seaport*, 42–43; Ira Rosenwaike, *Population History of New York* (Syracuse: Syracuse University Press, 1972), 11.

22. Kenneth Scott, "Ethnics in New Amsterdam," paper delivered at Kingsboro Community College, CUNY Conference, May 16, 1977; David Narrett, "Ethnicity and Race in Early New York"; Review Essay of Shane White, *Somewhat More Independent: End of Slavery in New York, 1770–1810* (Athens: University of Georgia Press, 1991) in *Journal of American Ethnic Studies* (Summer 1993), 29–31.

23. Bayard Still, *Mirror for Gotham* (New York: New York University Press, 1956), 9.

24. Ibid.

25. Archdeacon, "Anglo-Dutch," 29; Leo Hershkowitz, "Some Aspects of the New York Jewish Merchant Community, 1654–1820," *American Jewish Historical Quarterly* (September 1976), 11.

26. Shumway, *Seaport*, 39.

27. Oscar T. Barck, Jr., *New York City during the War for Independence* (New York: Columbia University Press, 1931), 19.

28. Archdeacon, "Anglo-Dutch," 30.

29. George Lankevich with Howard Furer, *A Brief History of New York City* (Port Washington, N.Y.: Associated Universities Press, 1984), 24–25; Herman and Barbara Van Der Zee, *A Sweet and Alien Land, Story of Dutch New York* (New York: Viking Press, 1978), 10.

30. Van Der Zee, *Sweet Land*, 11.

31. Archdeacon, "Anglo-Dutch," 30.

32. Rothschild, *Neighborhoods*, 16.

33. Shumway, *Seaport*, 9; Joyce Goodfriend, *Before the Melting Pot* (Princeton: Princeton University Press, 1992), 40.

34. Archdeacon, "Anglo-Dutch," 21.

35. Rothschild, *Neighborhoods*, 89; Goodfriend, *Melting Pot*, 110.

36. Rothschild, *Neighborhoods*, 100; Goodfriend, *Melting Pot*, 187, 190.

37. Archdeacon, "Anglo-Dutch," 34–35.

38. Douglas Nash and Robert Thomas, *Growth of the American Economy to 1820* (Columbia: University of South Carolina Press, 1968), 71.

39. Still, *Mirror*, 18; Homberger, *Atlas*, 36.

40. Paul A. Gilje, *Road to Mobocracy* (Chapel Hill: University of North Carolina Press, 1987), 1; Archdeacon, "Anglo-Dutch," 33; Bruce Wilkenfeld, "Revolutionary New York, 1776" in Milton Klein, ed., *New York, The Centennial Years* (Port Washington, N.Y.: Kennikat Press, 1976), 48–49.

41. Goodfriend, *Melting Pot*, 167.

42. Howard B. Rock, "The American Revolution and the Mechanics of New York City: One Generation Later," *New York History* (July 1976), 368–369.

43. Shumway, *Seaport*, 21.

44. Wilkenfeld, "Revolutionary," 49; Archdeacon, "Anglo-Dutch," 84.

45. Wilkenfeld, "Revolutionary," 54, 55; Esther Singleton, *Social New York under the Georges* (New York: Benjamin Blom, 1902), 3, 19.

46. Goodfriend, *Melting Pot*, 53, 113.

47. Carl Bridenbaugh, *Cities in Revolt* (New York: Capricorn Books, 1955), 271;

Charles Glaab and A. Theodore Brown, *History of Urban America* (New York: Macmillan, 1967), 20–21.

48. Wilkenfeld, "Revolutionary," 50.

49. Archdeacon, "Anglo-Dutch," 20; Shumway, *Seaport*, 54.

50. Shumway, *Seaport*, 55; Wilkenfeld, "Revolutionary," 51.

51. Wilkenfeld, "Revolutionary," 52.

52. Ibid., 51; Shumway, *Seaport*, 55–56; Singleton, *Social New York*, 56.

53. Shumway, *Seaport*, 32; Singleton, *Social New York*, 56.

54. Hyman Grinstein, *The Rise of the Jewish Community of New York* (Philadelphia: Jewish Publication Society, 1945), 39; Hershkowitz, "Jewish Community," 11; Still, *Mirror*, 24; Singleton, *Social New York*, 35.

55. Wilkenfeld, "Revolutionary," 63.

56. Ibid., 55–56.

57. Shumway, *Seaport*, 33; Howard Marraro, "Italo-Americans in Late 18th Century New York City," *New York History* (July 1940), 322; Samuel McKee, "Labor in Colonial New York, 1664–1776," Ph.D. dissertation, Columbia University, 1935, 30.

58. Bridenbaugh, *Cities*, 201.

59. Ibid., 420; Bruce Wilkenfeld, "Social and Economic Structure of the City of New York, 1695–1796," Columbia University dissertation, 1973, 82; Gilje, *Mobocracy*, 127.

60. Wilkenfeld, "Revolutionary," 60–61.

61. Arthur Peterson and George Edwards, *New York as an 18th Century Municipality* (Port Washington, N.Y.: Ira J. Friedman, 1967), 53–54, 85; McKee, "Colonial Labor," 37.

62. Peterson and Edwards, *New York Municipality*, 53–54.

63. Wilkenfeld, "Revolutionary," 47.

64. Wilkenfeld, "New York Neighborhoods, 1730," *New York History* (April 1976), 11, 171.

65. Harrington, *Social New York*, 34–35.

66. Shumway, *Seaport*, 52; Wilkenfeld, *"Revolutionary,"* 48, 50, 56.

67. Shumway, *Seaport*, 32–33.

68. Ibid., 35.

69. Ibid., 45.

70. Ibid., 27.

71. Rothschild, *Neighborhoods*, 33–40.

72. Arthur Schlesinger, *Colonial Merchants and the American Revolution, 1763–1776* (New York: Facsimile Library, 1939), 17, 45; Alan Rogers, *Empire and Liberty: American Resistance to British Authority, 1755–1763* (Berkley: University of California Press, 1947), 37.

73. Rogers, *Empire*, 42; Schlesinger, *Merchants*, 17.

74. Shumway, *Seaport*, 59.

75. Ibid., 60.

76. Virginia Harrington, *New York Merchants on the Eve of the Revolution* (New York: Columbia University Press, 1935), 326.

77. Oscar Barck, *New York City during the War for Independence* (New York: Columbia University Press, 1931), 19.

78. Lankevich, *Brief History*, 46.

79. Harrington, *Merchants,* 319, 321, 342–343.

80. Lankevich, *Brief History,* 50.

81. Gilje, *Mobocracy,* 57.

82. Lankevich, *Brief History,* 50–57.

83. Barck, *War for Independence,* 31; Wilkenfeld, "Revolutionary," 65–66; Bruce Bliven, *Battle for Manhattan* (Baltimore: Penguin Books, 1956), 10.

84. Lankevich, *Brief History,* 53; Barck, *War for Independence,* 12.

85. Bliven, *Battle,* 15, 17.

86. Ibid., 59.

87. Rosenwaike, *Population,* 15.

88. Lankevich, *Brief History,* 54.

89. Wilson Smith, *Cities of Our Past* (New York: John Wiley, 1964), 81.

90. Sidney Pomerantz, *New York, American City* (Port Washington: Kennicar Press, 1952), 158–159.

91. Wilkenfeld, "Revolutionary," 67; Barck, *War for Independence,* 79–83.

92. Pomerantz, *American City,* 373, 385.

93. Goodfriend, *Melting Pot,* 111–112; Pomerantz, *American City,* 221.

94. McKee, "Colonial Labor," 116, 124–125.

95. Archdeacon, "Anglo-Dutch," 28; Wilkenfeld, "Revolutionary," 44; Narrett, Review of *Somewhat More Independent,* 28–30.

96. Gilje, *Mobocracy,* 153–154, 156–157; Pomerantz, *American City,* 221–224; McKee, "Colonial Labor," 166.

97. McKee, "Colonial Labor," 133, 159–165; Homberger, *Atlas,* 44.

98. McKee, "Colonial Labor," 167; Gilje, *Mobocracy,* 156–157.

99. Robert Albion, "New York Port in the New Republic," *New York History* (October 1940), 388, 390, 392.

100. Ibid., 397.

101. Pomerantz, *American City,* 152; Myron Luke, "Port of New York, 1800–1810," New York University dissertation, 1950, 21.

102. Albion, "Port," 398.

103. Pomerantz, *American City,* 158, 165.

104. Raymond Mohl, *Poverty in New York, 1783–1825* (New York: Oxford University Press, 1971), 6.

105. Pomerantz, *American City,* 178, 196.

106. Ibid., 185.

107. Ibid., 218–219; Luke, "Port of New York," 12.

108. Lankevich, *Brief History,* 103; map of New York City at the end of the eighteenth century in Pomerantz, *American City,* 258–259.

109. Pomerantz, *American City,* 200.

110. Ibid., 203.

111. Mohl, *Poverty,* 173; Rosenwaike, *Population,* 17; Pomerantz, *American City,* 204.

112. Pomerantz, *American City,* 201, 220; William Alexander Duer, "Reminiscences of an Old New Yorker," in Wilson Smith, ed., *Cities of Our Past and Present* (New York: John Wiley, 1964), 29–30.

113. Pomerantz, *American City,* 201.

114. Gilje, *Mobocracy,* 100–101; Lankevich, *Brief History,* 69.

115. Lankevich, *Brief History,* 74.

116. Ibid., 76, 77.

117. Glaab and Brown, *Urban America,* 37.

118. David Gilchrist, ed., *Growth of Seaport Cities, 1790–1825* (Charlottesville: University of North Carolina Press, 1967), 70, 71; Glaab and Brown, *Urban America,* 39.

119. Glaab and Brown, *Urban America,* 37; Lankevich, *Brief History,* 76, 77; Albion, "Port," 398; Gilchrist, *Seaport Cities,* 70.

120. Gilchrist, *Seaport Cities,* 110, 114–115.

121. Ibid., 75.

122. Lankevich, *Brief History,* 83–84.

123. Mohl, *Poverty,* 7; Glaab and Brown, *Urban America,* 72.

124. Mohl, *Poverty,* 17, 23, 25, 28–29.

125. Ibid., 21; Pomerantz, *American City,* 333.

2

Growth and Change in the Commercial City, 1824–1870

The factors, geographical and otherwise, that had caused New York to grow into a flourishing commercial city by the third decade of the nineteenth century continued to account for its expansion into what was sometimes called the "Great Metropolis" fifty years later. The population grew rapidly between 1830 and 1870, and twelve new wards were created during the same period. Growth slowed somewhat during the Civil War years but picked up again when hostilities ended.[1]

In spite of the physical expansion northward, the population density of the older downtown wards increased from 94.5 percent to 163.5 percent per acre between 1820 and 1850. By the latter date there was an enormous contrast between the uptown residential wards and those further downtown. In the Fifteenth Ward, centered on elegant Washington Square, "a population . . . as large as that of the Sixth Ward lived on three times as much area" and had the lowest death rate in the city. In the latter ward "each person had one third the space enjoyed by the fortunate . . . and one in every twenty-eight people died each year."[2]

Between 1845 and 1880, the population north of Fourteenth Street increased by 290,000 people, which was "almost as many [people] as the entire city [had] contained in 1840."[3] Anticipating further growth, the grid plan was extended to streets north of 155th Street. New York City grew faster than New York State or the entire nation in the two decades prior to the Civil War, and by 1860 it contained more than 50 percent of the 1.5 million people living in the ten counties that surrounded it. The population statistics might have been even higher if the census takers could have counted the transient sailors and elusive "ne'er do wells" who also lived in the city.[4]

A total of 726,386 people inhabited Manhattan Island in 1865, living in twenty-two wards that stretched from the tip of the island to above Eighty-sixth Street, river to river. By 1880, 1,206,000 people lived in a city that had become, at least in size, a metropolis.[5] It could also have been called a world city because steady immigration during the first half of the nineteenth century, had, by 1855, led to a foreign-born majority in nine of the city's wards and was approaching that point in five others. In the Fourth and Sixth Wards, which constituted the lower east side, 70 percent of the population jammed into an area one-quarter of a square mile in size were foreign born. These two wards were the ones most densely populated by immigrants, but the First and Second Wards at the very tip of Manhattan Island were not far behind (this was also true for the Eleventh, Fourteenth, and Nineteenth Wards north and west of the Lower East Side).[6]

The large population in all these districts was the result of a 140 percent increase in the number of foreign-born New Yorkers between 1845 and 1855, twice as great as the percentage increase in the same period for the entire population of the city.[7] Thousands of people from the British Isles—English, Scotch, Welsh, and, most of all, Irish—had chosen to make New York their home.[8] They were joined by a large number of emigrants from Germany and a somewhat smaller number from France and Poland. There were also a smattering of people from Belgium, Holland, Prussia (then a separate state in what was to become the German Empire in 1871), Austria, Switzerland, Italy, Spain, Portugal, Sweden, Denmark, and China. In addition, Canada and its neighboring provinces of New Brunswick and Nova Scotia were well represented, as were migrants from New England, New Jersey, Long Island, and Pennsylvania. In 1855, 60 percent of the population had been born elsewhere.[9]

Although in several wards a single ethnic group might be in the majority, in the antebellum period, New York had no ghettoes for the foreign born. There was instead a mixture of people, ethnically and in terms of social class, in every ward. As one commentator remarked, "The inhabitants of New York, because they come from all over, exhibit a sort of patchwork quilt in which the materials have been brought together from all quarters."[10] Furthermore, all of the residents moved frequently, for better housing if their income grew larger or for a cheaper place to live if their luck was bad. The population of any given area, therefore, was always in flux. Enough German immigrants, for example, lived in the Tenth, Eleventh, and Thirteenth Wards to give the area the name *Kleindeutschland* (little Germany), but they moved frequently and by 1872 had broken the Fourteenth Street "boundary," leaving the Lower East Side to the eastern European Jews.[11]

Visitors commented on the mix of peoples to be found in all parts of the city: "Natives of almost any country in the world may be found in the streets and counting houses," said one tourist; and another, Anthony Trollope, remarked that "in no other city in the world is there a population so mixed and cosmopolitan in their modes of life." He also foresaw that this would continue and prophesized that in a few years New York would have filled the streets north of the 154th Street boundary, which appeared on the maps available when he was visiting in 1861.[12] Trollope was absolutely correct because the reasons that had impelled several million people to emigrate from to the United States and settle in New York remained and grew more significant in the years after the Civil War.

Everywhere in Europe, better hygiene and greater medical knowledge, "from starting points that cannot be measured with precision," had lowered infant mortality and increased longevity, leading to great increases in the population. The specifics might vary from country to country, but overall, in most of the nations of Europe, a greatly increased number of people were unable to earn a decent living. The "increase could sometimes be met by putting more land under cultivation, by changing the use of what was already being cultivated, by developing alternative occupations or by moving out to search for more lucrative work." Such movement might mean only going from a farm to a nearby city, but it could also result in going much further, to another country or another continent.[13]

The demographic factor was the basic reason for immigration to the United States as well as to other parts of the world. Modernization, which included industrialization and the consequent displacement of artisans, provided another reason. The creation of "speedier and more convenient ways to emigrate" in combination with these other factors stimulated a historic movement out of Europe. In the absence of any legal barriers, the immigrant flow that had begun in the nineteenth century continued and grew stronger.[14]

Between 1820 and 1830, 92,844 immigrants from the British Isles arrived in New York. The largest number were Irish, but over 20,000 were from Scotland, Wales, and England. The New York State census of 1855 showed that there were 32,135 Britishers in New York, third in number to the Irish and Germans but larger than any other group. Many had been farmers who lost their land when Parliament enacted enclosure acts, which broke up the open fields previously used for communal farming. Those without legal title to their land "sought employment in the towns and some scraped together enough to pay their passage across the sea."[15]

Other changes that affected artisans also led to emigration from Britain. In the 1820s and 1830s, statutes making it unlawful for skilled workmen to leave Britain were repealed and thousands of workers, displaced by the increasing number of factories, followed a pattern established earlier in the nineteenth century and moved to the United States, bringing their talents with them. The index to Robert Ernst's *Immigrant Life in New York* shows ten skilled trades under the heading "English immigrants," and his table, based on the 1855 census, shows that their presence in the clothing, shoemaking, furniture, metallurgy, and shipbuilding trades was considerable.

Because the skills they had learned in their native land had become obsolete as a result of industrialization but were welcome in New York, English artisans made the Atlantic crossing. Charlotte Erickson, who calls the arrivals from Britain "Invisible Immigrants," offers another reason for their move. Those who came may not have had the qualifications needed to get the best-paying jobs in Britain but were skillful enough to be fully employed and well paid in New York City.[16]

The largest group of immigrants to settle in New York were the Irish. There were 175,735 individuals who had been born in Ireland living in New York in 1855, a number that would grow to 198,595 by 1880.[17] As we have seen, emigrants from Ireland were not new in New York; they had been settling in the city since colonial times. Until the middle of the nineteenth century, however, most of the Irish newcomers were Protestant Scotch-Irish, descendents of people who had been settled in Ireland centuries before in order to restrain rebellious Catholic Irish in the southern part of the country. The descendents of those Catholic Irish were the ones now arriving in New York City. Immigrants from Ulster, as the northern portion of Ireland was known, continued to come but were soon outnumbered by their Catholic countrymen.[18]

As a result of prosperity during the last decades of the eighteenth century and the first years of the nineteenth, the population of Ireland had increased from 5 million to 8 million souls. Britain, involved in the wars of the French Revolution and Napoleonic Era, encouraged the farmers of Ireland, always their bread basket, to grow more grain and raise more cattle. Higher income led to earlier marriages (age sixteen for girls, eighteen for boys) and more births as well as higher land prices.[19] "As population grew and competition for land became more intense . . . subletting and subdivision reduced the size of farms" and led to the development of the conacre system, under which laborers were able to occupy tiny parcels of land and grow enough potatoes to feed a family of five for ten months.[20]

After the Napoleonic wars, in 1815, grain prices fell and even the larger Irish tenant farmers were hard pressed to meet the rent on land they had leased when prospects were bright. As a result, estate owners, seeing greater profits from using the land for pasture, evicted their tenants and raised cattle and sheep instead.[21] "Because there was simply no other way to feed one's family in rural Ireland . . . land on which to grow potatoes was an absolute necessity." For this reason, small land-owners, following the conacre pattern with their own kin, divided their property into tiny parcels so that their sons could marry and raise enough potatoes for survival. Land was therefore subdivided until "three, six or even ten families were settled on a piece of land that could have provided for only one." [22]

Matters grew even worse when, in 1846, Britain repealed the Corn Laws (tariffs on imported grain), which had given Ireland a protected market. At this exact moment, a fungal infection, *Phytoptora infestus,* struck and for the next five years, on and off, the potatoes on which so many were dependent rotted in the fields. "The leaves of the potato plant turned black, crumbling into ashes when touched and the very air was laden with the sickly odor of decay." [23] Some of the destitute peasants were admitted to workhouses, where they might get the bitter and limited food of charity; voluntary relief committees fed 40 percent of the population in the terrible winters of 1846 and 1847. In spite of such efforts, thousands, weakened by malnutrition, died of typhus. A priest, Father John O'Sullivan, told of bodies lying unburied for days, of a child half eaten by the starving family cat, and ended his report by saying, "Flesh and blood cannot bear up against" the horrors he had seen. In the worst years, such as 1847, the roads to the Irish port towns were jammed with refugees, who fought with each other to get on a ship. [24]

Several million people emigrated, most to the United States and smaller numbers to Canada. Many of those going to Canada paid ten shillings, less than those who came to New York, but they traveled on open-deck ships making a return journey after delivering timber to the British Isles. Britain encouraged the Irish to go abroad, especially to Canada, for two reasons: They feared an exodus to England, Scotland, or Wales, and they wanted to build a large English-speaking population in the colony that had once belonged to France. [25]

Because Ireland purchased cotton, wheat, flax, tobacco, and other products from American producers, returning ships brought the refugees to New York, Philadelphia, Baltimore, Charleston, and New Orleans. Also, many of the refugees who landed in Quebec made their way to New England, especially to Boston, as well as to smaller cities in Rhode Island and Connecticut. The largest number, however, came to New York. [26]

Since most of the ships carrying Irish men, women, and children to the New World departed from Liverpool, many of the emigrants began their journey by crossing the Irish Sea to England, a trip that took one full day. [27] Forty days later, if they came on a sailing ship (as most did before 1869), they would land in New York or another East Coast city. Most had paid four pounds, or about twenty dollars, for the journey. [28]

Some were able to pay this sum thanks to relatives in America; others were financed by poor-house officials unable to support them in Ireland; and still others followed a method used by Ulstermen earlier: They made the trip without paying for a ticket, and when the ship landed, the captain arranged for them to be indentured to an employer, who then paid for the cost of their passage. The immigrant then worked off the debt as he labored without pay for the man who had "redeemed" him.[29]

The most desperate emigrants tried to travel as stowaways, which led ship captains to search their vessels before lifting anchor. Children under eight had to pay half of what adults did; to avoid paying even a small amount, mothers pretended to suckle a child if he or she was small enough to mislead the ticket sellers.[30]

Conditions aboard ship were dreadful. In the era of sailing ships, 30 percent of the passengers bound for Canada and 9 percent of those coming to New York died en route from hunger and disease, leading the emigrant vessels to be called "coffin ships" or "swimming coffins." On the steerage deck, which was usually four feet high, there were two tiers of bunks. Conditions were even worse on the "orlop" deck below steerage, which was little more than a hole with no ventilation. Passengers paid almost nothing for this space but had to provide their own food.[31] Worst of all was the crossing for the unfortunates who made the trip on the open decks. In spite of improved conditions on steamships after 1830, of 440 passengers on the *Lark* in 1847, 150 died while at sea and 186 were sick enough to be taken to the Marine Hospital when they arrived in New York.[32]

In the same year that the *Lark* landed, New York City had followed the example set earlier by the private Society for the Information and Assistance of Persons Emigrating from Foreign Countries and established a Board of Commissioners of Emigration, who gave advice and aid to the survivors of the transatlantic journey. Following the pattern of many ethnic groups, the Irish who had come earlier—fearing the economic burden represented by their destitute brethren but, even more, fearing an increase in the already widespread bigotry from which they suffered—urged the newcomers to leave the city. When recruited by labor contractors, some did.[33]

In response to the arrival of 651,931 Irish immigrants—55 percent of the total number of immigrants arriving in the United States between 1846 and 1851—New York City established Castle Garden, an immigrant receiving center at the tip of Manhattan Island which had been Fort Amsterdam when the Dutch were in power and then became Fort George after the British took over.[34] In its third incarnation, there were interpreters, medical personnel, small banks which changed money, and advisors who urged the newcomers to leave New York as soon as possible. Before any of these services were performed, however, the new arrivals were bathed in two gender-separated wooden tubs that held twelve people apiece and were forced to stand up and scrub their bodies and especially their hair, which often contained lice, while the attendants watched. The same attendants would then provide them with towels and march them off for medical inspection. When they emerged from the Garden, the newcomers had to face another hazard: "sharpers," who took what little money they had on the pretext of finding them jobs and housing. Although preying on immigrants was never entirely eliminated, action by the Castle Garden authorities diminished its importance.[35]

The services offered to the Irish were also available to the other immigrant groups who arrived in the middle of the nineteenth century and thereafter. Germans, including Jews, were the most numerous of the non-Irish arrivals, but there were also a sizable number of people coming from elsewhere in Europe. Some did not remain in New York. Many Scandinavians dispersed to the Middle West, as did a large number of Germans. Others moved to the South, but more remained and became part of New York's multicultural society.

As early as 1855, the New York State census indicated that 95,952 individuals born in the various German states—Bavaria (which sent the largest single group), Baden, Wurttemburg, and Hesse—lived in New York City. In general, they had been peasants who had been unable to sustain themselves due to changes in agriculture and the loss of secondary employment as artisans. Some had been "dwarf" farmers with tiny plots, but there were also many craftsmen (particularly weavers) displaced, as the nineteenth century moved on, by growing industrialization. Even if these skilled workers had been able to find jobs, their income would be smaller than what it had been and their standard of living lower.[36]

Once again, the bottom line was demographic. Population pressure had "caused subdivision of land beyond anything that could provide a tolerable living." Small holdings and heavy taxes forced many farmers to work for a large landholder as laborers and survive, but because they were unable or unwilling to subdivide their property further and even laboring jobs were scarce, their children had no way of making a living and emigrated. As a result of a complex of factors, including poor harvests and a one-year visitation of the potato blight, emigration seemed desirable.[37]

Another group of Germans, from the Kingdom of Prussia, also emigrated. Most of the farmland in the eastern portion of what was to become the German Empire was composed of great estates, worked by landless laborers whose ancestors had been serfs. Here, as in other parts of Europe, population increases led to new problems. Unwilling to provide poor relief to a burgeoning population that could not be self-supporting, estate owners limited housebuilding on their lands, hoping thereby to discourage marriages and reduce the birth rate. At the same time, however, they took advantage of the oversupply of laborers and cut costs by paying the lowest possible wages. As a result, farm workers and their families were "unable to maintain a decent standard of living" and joined the exodus to the New World.[38]

Robert Ernst, when he discovered that the 1855 census did not list Jews as a separate group, computed the approximate number living in New York City at that time by separating Jewish-sounding names from the mass of German and Polish ones. This led him to estimate that 10,798 Jews lived in New York in the middle of the nineteenth century. Some of them were Sephardic Jews, descendents of the ones who had settled, as we have seen, in seventeenth-century New Amsterdam. Others were Ashkenazi Jews from eastern and central Europe.[39] For all Jews, New York was likely to be their second residence after leaving the place where they had been born. Many members of the earliest Sephardic Jewish community, for example, had moved to London from Amsterdam and thence to New Amsterdam. In the nineteenth century, they continued to follow the same route. Their moves were motivated by both economic and religious factors, and the combination made them the largest number of Dutch citizens to emigrate to either London or New York.

They began to leave when Napoleon's forces occupied the Netherlands because "their long standing trading ties to England suffered severely from disruptions in international trade due to blockades and embargoes." By 1802, 82 percent of Amsterdam's Jews were on the public dole. The wealthier ones found it very expensive to support them and urged them to look for greener pastures.[40] There were also some religious reasons for leaving. The Dutch monarchy had granted Jews civil rights in 1776, but after 1819, when the Catholic French government headed by Napoleon's brother, Louis Bonaparte, began to rule the Netherlands, their freedom to worship seemed less secure and provided another reason, beyond economics, for going to England or America. Most went to Baltimore on ships returning to the United States after delivering tobacco to Holland, the next largest number to Philadelphia, and only 10 percent to New York, where they joined the existing Jewish community.[41]

Jews from the various German states and some portions of the Austro-Hungarian Empire had somewhat different reasons for emigrating. Unlike the Dutch Sephardim, who anticipated antisemitic regulation, they were already prevented from earning a decent living by restrictions and discrimination. In Bohemia, which later became part of Czechoslovakia, they were vulnerable to changes in the Hapsburg monarch's policies for their Jewish subjects; in Bavaria they were restrained by a government-imposed quota on innkeeping licenses; in Württemberg their efforts to buy land were limited; and, in general, opportunities for advancement grew smaller every year.[42]

As a result, the Jewish population of West Prussia dropped by almost 14,000 between 1824 and 1871. The figures for Posen were even more dramatic: Between 1816 and 1871, the province lost more than 35,000 Jews. This was to be expected; Posen was the most restrictive of the German provinces. Jews were not allowed to be citizens and were barred from most artisanal trades.[43]

Like the Sephardim, they too went first to London and established a settlement in the district known as the East End or Whitechapel. Many stayed and became loyal British subjects and prosperous merchants. Although never completely accepted by the Jews who had come earlier nor the larger English society, they were free to worship and to reach a higher standard of living than they could have done on the Continent. For those for whom this was not enough, however, America beckoned and they came to the United States, usually landing first in New York.[44]

By 1860, there were 35,000 Jews from various backgrounds living in New York, enough to establish twenty-three synagogues (some poor and tiny) and forty-four charitable societies. Many of the German Jewish immigrants were not members of any of these institutions but had rather chosen a different path and "sought to assimilate into the larger German immigrant society of the city," something that it was not difficult to do in a metropolis like New York. It is possible that this behavior was the result of the cool reception they had received from the established Sephardic Jews, who by the middle of the nineteenth century had been able to leave *Kleindeutschland* and move north and west to the Chelsea area around Seventeenth Street and Nineteenth Street.[45]

They moved because they were able to afford better housing and wanted to disassociate themselves from the new arrivals from Central Europe, but they could not escape the burden of helping those who arrived with empty pockets. The burden, however, was lifted from their shoulders in a relatively short time. Some of the newcomers brought capital and experience in banking and, as a result, the Seligmans, Kuhns, Loebs, Schiffs, Warburgs, and Lehmans were able to reconstitute banking firms originally established in Germany.[46]

Most of the German Jewish arrivals, while not reaching such heights, established small clothing manufacturing shops or became peddlers and traders. The old clothes shops near the port, for example, became a German Jewish monopoly. In addition, according to a historian who has closely studied this group, "their skills were just at that time in demand by an emerging and rapidly expanding industry": the production of cheap, ready-to-wear men's clothing. Unquestionably, there were failures in the German Jewish community, but on the whole, they appear to have made an almost ideal adjustment to life in New York City. For some, their residence in low-rent *Kleindeutschland* was relatively brief and by the late 1850s they were able to join the Sephardim in high-rent Chelsea.[47]

European immigrants, first from northern and western Europe and later from southern and eastern portions, dominated the foreign-born population of New York all through the nineteenth and well into the twentieth centuries, but there were also newcomers from Asia. "Meaningful Chinese immigration to the United States began roughly with the California gold rush in 1849." Young men came to what they called the "gold mountain" as sojurners, expecting to return to China and buy land. Between 1848 and 1882, when the Chinese Exclusion Act became law, about 300,000 Chinese entered the United States. The Chinese had a long migratory tradition, but their earlier destinations had usually been in Southeast Asia. In the nineteenth century, however, they came to the Caribbean and Latin America as indentures, who, as Roger Daniels says, were "surrogates for African slaves" imported earlier. Very few came to New York. Robert Ernst, describing the city in 1855, said "a tiny body of Chinese" were settling in lower Manhattan, in an area that became almost all Chinese by the end of the century.[48]

A combination of events outside of New York was the reason why the "tiny body" slowly grew as the century wore on. First, the "mountain of gold" proved to be inaccessible to the Chinese laborers who came to the California gold mines. By legislation and force, they were barred from being miners. When they left the goldfields and tried to live in the California cities, especially San Francisco, they experienced enormous hostility. In spite of this, because it proved difficult to find white workers to take on the brutal work of building the transcontinental railroads, the Chinese were hired to do it.

Some did not survive, but many of those who did migrated to the East Coast, hoping for better treatment and more opportunity. Furthermore, the passage of the Chinese Exclusion Act in 1882, together with a previous one enacted in 1880, made it impossible for all Chinese except teachers, students, merchants, and tourists to enter the United States. These laws provided another reason to leave the West Coast. Since it was no longer possible to leave the United States and come back, as many had been doing, they might as well move to the less threatening New York area. They worked as laundrymen, opened small restaurants to feed their own people, and, because of the absence of women, remained a small community. As late as 1890, only 14,000 Chinese, representing 13 percent of the total number of Chinese in the United States, lived in New York.[49]

On the West Coast they were victims of various degrees of racism, ranging from bloody riots, especially during depressions, to pigtail cutting and occupational discrimination. In New York, they drew little attention until Jacob Riis included them in *How the Other Half Lives*. Riis, a liberal by late-nineteenth-century standards, said the Chinese were stealthy and secretive, gambled, sold and used opium, participated in the white slave trade, and were frequent customers of prostitutes. The only kind words he could say for them is that they were clean and minded their own business.[50]

For most of the period under discussion, New York City was also home to another, considerably larger, racial minority—blacks, who differed from the Chinese as well as from newly arrived European immigrants because they had been born in the United States. As noted in the previous chapter, black New Yorkers were free long before the ratification of the Thirteenth Amendment to the Constitution. As early as 1820, there were only 518 slaves in New York compared to 10,368 free blacks. Together, they constituted 9.4 percent of the population.[51]

They were, however, an oppressed minority, whose institutions, such as churches and mutual benefit societies, were subject to attacks by bigoted whites. They also lacked political clout because in order to vote they had to meet a high property qualification, a barrier which remained for them long after 1826, when it ended for whites. In spite of their difficulties, the free black community had established a newspaper, *Freedom's Journal*, by 1817 (two others were to follow later) as well as a theater called the African Globe, located between Bleecker and Mercer Streets in Greenwich Village, the area in which most blacks lived.[52]

Although they were free men and women as opposed to their brethren in the South, at no time in the period from 1827 to 1861, discussed by Rhoda Freeman in her article on the leadership of the black community, did the number of blacks exceed 17,000 persons; the number decreased as the century went on. When the Civil War began, there were only slightly more than 12,000. Some had left the United States entirely and moved to Africa or the Caribbean, but more had moved to New England. As Ms. Freeman says, "New York City was neither a heaven nor a haven for the free black community." There was, rather, segregation and discrimination.[53]

In spite of this, after the ratification of the Thirteenth Amendment, when blacks were legally free to leave the South, enough came to New York to create a community of 15,000. Because so many European immigrants were coming to New York at the same time, however, in 1870 blacks constituted only 1.4 percent of the population. Most were doing domestic or menial labor, but there was also a small leadership class "who earned their living either in a business or profession."[54] Members of this class were not altogether passive. At the corner of Charles and Pearl Streets in July 1854, Elizabeth Jennings, a twenty-four-year-old African-American school teacher, attempted to board a Third Avenue Railway Company car but, because there was a sign stating "NO COLORED PEOPLE ALLOWED IN THIS CAR," she was forcibly removed. Ms. Jennings sued the Railway Company and won, although, unlike the results of a similar episode in Montgomery, Alabama, a century later, no Civil Rights revolution followed.[55]

Early in the nineteenth century, an observer of New York said that "the commercial character of the city is such that natives of almost country in the world may be found in the streets and counting houses."[56] Historian Robert Albion, writing a century later, endorsed this idea and gave a reason: "New York became the nation's richest city [by 1860] by managing to disperse most of its commercial imports throughout the country [and] increase its importance as the nation's biggest city by keeping a much larger share of its human imports within its own environs."[57] Both of these commentators expressed the idea that is basic to the history of the Empire City: the symbiotic relationship between the arrival of vast numbers of people, who provided the workers and consumers that enabled New York to grow and prosper, and the growth and prosperity itself, which attracted still more men and women (who were oppressed and depressed in their native lands) to come to the city that seemed to offer them survival and advancement. Even the Civil War did not slow immigration; 75,000 new arrivals came in 1862, 150,000 in the next year, 15,000 during the following twelve months, and 200,000 in 1864.[58]

The previous pages have described the "push and pull" factors involved in going to America and particularly to New York. Immigrants chose the Empire City in preference to Boston, where people asked "How much does he know?", or class-conscious Philadelphia, where the question was "Who were his parents?". In New York, the only criterion was "How much is he worth?". The city they came to, however, offered many of them only a poor welcome, and for some, emigration was a bitter disappointment. Why did most of them stay? Why did more of them come? The answer is that New York continued to offer more opportunities than back home or elsewhere in America and, in spite of corruption and inefficiency, depressions and war, changed and improved in a multitude of ways between 1825 and 1870. By the end of the period, New York was a larger and more livable city than it had been earlier.

Edward Spann begins his book entitled *A New Metropolis: New York City, 1840–1857* with a description of the commercial city in 1840. "South Street on the East River was the primary center of America's foreign trade, a street of merchants' stores and warehouses screened by a forest of masts and sails from many nations." On the Hudson River side of Manhattan Island, one could see the smokestacks of many steamships.

In 1828, enough duties were collected at the New York Customs House to pay all of the running expenses of the national government, exclusive of the payments on the national debt. By 1849, 3,000 ships entered New York harbor from 150 foreign ports, and the city handled over half the imports and a third of the exports of the United States.[59]

More duties went to the customs inspectors stationed in New York than in any other port city, which is not surprising since the city had a foreign commerce worth $323 million per year. In 1860, 1,678 tons were exported and over $2 million worth of goods were imported and distributed all over the United States. There were a variety of approaches and, of course, departures: for example, the Gedney Channel between Sandy Hook and Manhattan Island, which led to the Main Ship Channel, through the Narrows, into the Upper Bay, and to a dock at the Battery. For domestic shippers, the East River led into Long Island Sound and thence to New England, and the Hudson River provided a path to the Erie Canal and points west. There was also another path out of the harbor, past New Jersey, leading to the South and its cotton and tobacco.[60]

With the growth of railroads (the New York and Erie Railroad opened in 1851), some paralleling the waterways, New York was ideally suited to continue to be an entrepôt. Thus, manufacturing was a secondary part of the economy, trade came first, and lower Broadway was its center. By 1836, the affluent New Yorkers who had previously lived in the lower city moved north to Washington Square and Houston Street, and the City Hall district became the place for hotels, entertainments, theaters, and shops. All in all, New York did not lack for places of amusement. Day or night "Broadway was increasingly glutted with coaches, carriages, wagons and horse drawn omnibuses." Wall Street continued to be the focus of finance; after 1841 a new Merchant's Exchange nearby provided "a meeting place for the fast expanding business community."[61]

This community consisted of shipbuilders and owners, brokers and agents, as well as importers, commission merchants, auctioneers, and jobbers, all clustered around South Street, Wall Street, and Pearl Street. "The yards along the East River launched whalers, clippers and packets made of white oak . . . locust, yellow pine and white pine."[62] In a continuation of earlier developments, by 1855 there were fifty banks in New York with a combined capital of more than $60 million, "one fifth of the banking resources of the whole nation." There were also many insurance companies grouped in the area, all involved with trade. "The dock, the wharf, the countinghouse and the warehouse were the principal foci of the urban economy and the merchant middleman and the agent middleman [brokers, auctioneers, commission merchants, and factors] were the city's primary capital accumulators."[63]

Using *Doggett's New York Business Directory*, Robert Albion compiled a chart of the commercial functions carried on in New York in 1846 and 1847. The relative size of the categories presents a clear picture of the city's economic life. There were 228 "general" merchants connected with the mechanics and financing of shipping and a much larger number (over 900) importers, dealing in an amazing variety of products, from artificial flowers to woolens. Dry goods and cutlery seemed to be most in demand; tea and coffee were close seconds. Because the port was an entrepôt, there were 66 auctioneers, 502 commission merchants, 875 jobbers, and 228 agents. Under the heading "Other Functions," Albion listed every occupation connected with the port and its business life. This column ran from "Accountants to Weighers," the latter group being one of the largest but outnumbered by "Sailor's Boarding Houses." [64]

Business was good in New York, and to celebrate that fact, the commercial leaders of the city emulated London and erected a magnificent iron and glass exhibit pavilion, the Crystal Palace, which was opened in 1853 at Forty-second Street between Fifth and Sixth Avenues. Like its London namesake, the Palace was intended to be a showplace of inventions, products, and art that would bring visitors from all over the United States and the world, thus enhancing New York's prestige. [65]

As had been true in the eighteenth and early nineteenth centuries, the wealthiest New Yorkers were merchants, who numbered 6,001 in the 1855 census. They were not members of the original Dutch merchant families, who were content to sit back and see the value of their real estate holdings appreciate as "Manhattan swept northward," but rather more recent arrivals from Great Britain and New England. Men bearing names that were to become famous, such as John Jacob Astor, Archibald Gracie, and Robert Lenox, came from Europe; many lesser known but very successful businessmen came from Connecticut, Rhode Island, and southern Massachusetts. "Some were expanding their shipping enterprises . . . others were sea captains who decided to go into business in the big city or adventurous youths who had reached New York and worked their way to prominence." According to an observer who wrote in 1827, between 1820 and 1860, New Englanders dominated New York's mercantile life. [66]

Many of the adventurous youths began their careers as clerks, positions they usually obtained through family connections. At first, they did all sorts of odd jobs but then worked their way up to become copyists (no duplicating machines were to be found in the nineteenth century) and bookkeepers. By saving their money and doing good work, they were able to buy into a prosperous firm and become a partner. This process was essentially an apprenticeship system for middle-class youth. [67]

Another student of New York between 1820 and 1870 said that it was a "city of storekeepers, small sweatshops, factories . . . of a scattering of shops and workrooms" as well as being a seaport city. He might have added that it was also a processing city, a place where raw sugar was refined, leather tanned and processed, tobacco milled, and raw cotton turned into cheap clothes for sailors and servants. What it was not was a manufacturing city. Except for the production of construction materials and some consumer goods (furniture, clothing, carriages) and a thriving printing and publishing industry, New York remained a mercantile city.[68]

The relative absence of manufacturing was partly the choice of the moneyed classes, who preferred to invest in small-scale factories and real estate. Other factors included the costliness of a trained labor supply and the absence of nearby coal and water resources to provide the energy needed by heavy machinery. As a result, New York's largest manufacturing plants were the Allaire ironworks, which employed 200 laborers, and the Harper publishing company, with 140 printers and pressmen.[69] Not until the great migrations of the 1840s and thereafter, "bringing thousands of new workers willing to labor for low wages," was the city "able to develop a large manufacturing sector," which continued to grow in the later years of the nineteenth century, when the port was less active. In the 1880s, the high cost of land, "higher wages scales, growing material costs and a change to iron hulled vessels" combined to move shipbuilding out of Manhattan.[70]

Other economic pursuits more than made up for the decline of shipbuilding. Except for several depressions, the most severe in 1873, the city's economy continued to grow, as did the number of people living there. New York's population doubled from 500,000 to 1,200,000 between 1850 and 1880. If the not yet urbanized areas of Brooklyn, lower Westchester, Nassau, and Richmond were included, the total was even higher: 1,478,000.[71] The increase in numbers eventually forced settlement northward and outward. Before this happened, however, people and businesses were crammed into the area south of Fourteenth Street. Allan Pred describes the resulting chaos: "the odorous, overcrowded, wooden piers jammed with carts, drays and wheelbarrows, with sailors, merchants, laborers and carters—decaying and sagging buildings amidst the forest of masts; . . . the dirty squalid streets, trafficked by scavengering pigs and flanked by hastily erected . . . flimsy wooden structures of two to six stories."[72]

Within these chaotic districts, however, "the morphology [format and structure] of the mercantile city was discernible." Charts from Pred's article on manufacturing in New York City show that in 1840, individual craftsmen were localized. An area stretching from Corlear's Hook on the East River to Twelfth Street and inland up to Avenue C was known as the dry dock quarter, a conglomeration of shipyards, laborers, and artisans still concerned, at midcentury, with building and repairing ships. The printing and publishing trades were sandwiched between Wall Street and City Hall, although the high rents in that district forced the manufacturers of printing presses, such as the famous Hoe Company, to locate elsewhere.[73] Twenty years later, localization was less apparent. In the Fifteenth Ward, around Washington Square, there were forty-eight small factories, which turned out pianos, furniture, trunks, sewing machines, chocolates, and hoopskirts; an oderiferous slaughter house; saloons (234); and seventy-six brothels. There were also many householders because inadequate transportation made it essential for all but the wealthy to live as close as possible to their workplace.[74]

In 1840, twelve passenger horse-drawn omnibuses, which were slow and expensive (twelve and a half cents one way, very high for the dollar and seventy-five cents per diem wages of a shipwright, for example), were mostly used by merchants coming into the center from the suburbs north of Fourteenth Street. Relatively high cost was also true for the slightly more rapid but even more expensive horse-drawn street railroad, the New York and Harlem, which was first licensed by the City Council in 1831 and fitted with upholstered benches running the length of each car. As a result, continuing an earlier pattern, many of New York's workers tried to live where they worked. "Lowly paid tailors, journeymen, shoemakers, milliners and piecework dressmakers . . . slept and earned a living in the same quarters." Some employers, anxious to keep a well-trained worker, provided a room for him above or behind the workshop.[75]

More ferries from Brooklyn, Staten Island, and New Jersey, which carried 90,000 passengers annually and charged only two to four cents a trip, helped somewhat, as did the cable cars, which moved at thirty miles an hour. Unfortunately, they complicated street traffic more than the horse-drawn omnibuses had done. Until the introduction of the steam engine, getting to a job and back after a ten-hour day, six days a week, was a serious obstacle to lessening the congestion below Fourteenth Street.[76]

By the late 1850s, however, the Age of Steam had arrived and led to an expansion of transportation options. Steam-driven railroads, for example, could bring people into New York from nearby New Jersey, Queens, and Westchester. Rail travel was, of course, more expensive. It cost $37 a year, for example, to go from Wall Street to the village of Morrisania in what is now the Bronx. As a result, it was primarily the upper middle class who now saw that they could live outside the city but continue to do business there. The loss of the "best people" and the taxes they had paid was bemoaned by those left behind.[77]

Transportation improved in the 1850s and 1860s when franchises were issued to private companies to run steam-driven street railways on Second, Third, and Eighth Avenues. These street railways were seen as a great improvement over the clumsy, messy, noisy cable cars, which had carried 94 million passengers a year but had produced many accidents and ruined streets, which the city was slow to repair. The railroad, unfortunately, was also enough of a nuisance to allow wealthy department store owner A. T. Stewart to prevent the Broadway route from passing his store at Tenth Street. The issuing of franchises in perpetuity on any street was accompanied by corruption during the 1850s and throughout the Tweed era, but the fares were low (three to five cents) and there was some public regulation. In any case, street railways remained the only mass transportation in the city until the 1870s, which, as we shall see, brought elevated transit. As a result of better transport, by 1875 only 50 percent of the population remained below Fourteenth Street.[78]

As public transportation improved and new areas of the city became accessible, occupations, income, social class, and, indirectly, ethnicity determined a family's residence. The wealthiest lived in the westerly districts of the Eighteenth and Twenty-first Wards located between Fourteenth and Fortieth Streets, Sixth Avenue and the East River. In a fashion also typical of other areas in the city, however, not only the wealthy lived there. The census records for 1855 indicate that the most easterly areas of these wealthy wards were also home to craftsmen (the largest group), clerks, government employees, and salesmen, all of whom could be considered middle class. They were able to live "uptown," albeit in much more modest quarters than their wealthy neighbors, because twenty-four different manufacturing or processing plants were located somewhere in the district, mostly along the East River.[79]

"As wholesale activities concentrated in the warehouses in the most easily reached parts of the business district and as the growing spatial needs of finances and retailing increased land values, small scale manufacturing was forced to seek new facilities on the advancing edge of the business districts or in completely new locations."[80] For this reason, small factory owners were attracted to the Eighteenth and Twenty-first Wards. One part of the district, just south of Houston Street (today famous as SoHo), became a "warren of warehouses and small workshops" and was given the nickname "Hell's Hundred Acres" because of the many fires that occurred there.[81] When the fire-ravaged buildings were rebuilt, they were constructed of cast iron in the Palladian or Italianate style and remain in that form today.[82]

Greater choice of housing for New Yorkers as well as transportation advances were part of of a number of much-needed improvements made in the period from 1840 to 1870. Congestion in lower Manhattan, for example, had made crossing Broadway near City Hall life threatening. The sad condition of dwellings, the polluted water supply, public health crises, increasing crime, and inadequate schools were the most obvious of the matters that received attention and helped make New

York a more livable city and thus more attractive to the thousands who poured into the city in midcentury.[83]

Once again, this illustrates the symbiotic nature of the city's history. Some of the improvements, such as safe water, would have occurred without mass immigration; but others, such as truly public schools, might not have come until later. The increase in population and physical size of New York, the needs of the newcomers, and the problems they brought with them or created when they arrived forced the municipal authorities to take action. Those authorities, for much of the period, were very corrupt, and it may well be that their desire to stay in power helped bring about improvements. Because every change in the infrastructure required laborers, politicians saw an opportunity to employ the new arrivals (especially the Irish), pay them low wages, and win their votes once they were naturalized.

Since a roof over one's head is a basic need for most people, the inadequate housing conditions that existed in New York during the period under discussion were a major area in need of improvement. By 1825, the wealthiest merchants, who had lived in the mansions in the waterfront area since the late eighteenth century, had "transferred their residences to streets beyond the din; compensating for the remoteness from their counting houses by the advantage of quiet and luxury." The large homes they had occupied became boarding houses or were purchased by real estate investors, who divided them into two or more "commodious" apartments at rents that working-class people, employed at the port, could afford.[84]

As the city's economic activity increased, property values in Manhattan rose and so did rents. The craftsmen and small tradesmen who had occupied the subdivided mansions could not afford to live in lower Manhattan any longer and migrated to the upper wards. At that point, about 1833, investors bought the older buildings and changed them "into barracks, dividing their space into the smallest proportion capable of containing human life within four walls." Within a brief period, a Federal-era merchant's house could be turned into a slum property housing dozens of people. The results were the earliest tenement houses and were occupied by the poor, especially immigrants. "Ten or twelve families would crowd into what had once been a private dwelling, overburdening its primitive sanitary condition." After a heavy rain, due to the absence of sewers, the basements occupied by the most destitute were flooded, bringing in fecal matter and bacteria and resulting in devastating mortality rates. In 1840, for example, one out of forty whites and one out of thirty-four blacks died as a result of waterborne infections. Ten years later, the Chief of Police reported that 18,456 of the city's residents lived in low-ceilinged cellars where the dirt floor turned into germ-laden mud after a rainstorm.[85]

Newly built tenements were no better; indeed one, the infamous Gotham Court, was much worse. The tenements were five stories high, with 116 apartments reached by a narrow, winding staircase, and the small, two-room residences were assaulted by smells from the "communal doorless privies" and ventilated by small windows. The Court, which opened its doors in 1851, was soon occupied by "wretched Irish families and came to be a breeding place for disease and rats" because of its open drains. In spite of conditions that horrified the middle- and upper-class members of the Association for the Improvement of the Condition of the Poor (AICP), the desperately poor tenants remained at Gotham Court until they were evicted for nonpayment of rent. Their ability to live in the damp, smelly, and jammed rooms was explained away on the basis of the primitive housing they had lived with in Ireland; indeed, it was said that the Irish immigrants, who constituted most of the tenants, were to blame for the filth and degredation.[86]

The poor, both native born or recent arrivals, lived in slum housing, but Germans escaped the worst horrors, such as Gotham Court, and resided instead in two-story houses, now somewhat divided, that had been home to middle-class families on the lower east side. The district constituted a sizable portion of Manhattan. It was originally home to both of the major immigrant groups (including Sephardic and German Jews) who came to New York in the middle of the nineteenth century, but after 1860 the population was over 67 percent German and was known as *Kleindeutschland*.[87]

There were three areas of substandard mutiple dwellings in New York in the 1830s: Corlear's Hook, in the Seventh Ward, which continued to be one of the worst sections; the black ghetto around Bancker Street; and the Five Points, located at the intersection of Park and Worth Streets on the site of the former Fresh Water Pond. The Pond had not contained much fresh water since Dutch days, when it had been a favorite courting spot for young New Amsterdammers. In the eighteenth century it was known as the Collect Pond because everything, including dead horses, was dumped there. It was finally covered in 1808 and was better filled than empty, but it remained a swampy area unsuited for middle-class housing. The Points got its terrible reputation from the gangs, such as the "Plug Uglies" and "Dead Rabbits," that roamed its streets. It was nicknamed the "Den of Thieves" and was a place where a "Murder a Night" occurred. As a cautionary touch, the public gallows was moved there from City Hall Park and the Tombs prison was located nearby in 1838.[88]

The Points also contained numerous saloons and liquor stores and was the parade ground of many prostitutes. As a result, it had a sinister reputation in the outside world. If contemporary descriptions are to be believed, this is not surprising. "Barefoot, ragged children played in garbage strewn gutters or drank the last few drops from near empty whiskey bottles." The youngsters were on the street because their homes were packed full. In 1853, one newspaper reporter found five families, a total of twenty-two people, jammed into one twelve-foot-square room. There were also hundreds of homeless children and adults who slept in the alleys. Not surprisingly, the Five Points was a breeding ground for disease, and there were many early deaths.[89]

As immigration continued and the population grew, housing for the poor continued to be built and slums continued to spread. The movement was eastward, as the individual homes once owned by merchants and tradesmen were converted into tiny apartments. One method of getting more rental space on the very small lots was to build a rear house, blocked from the street and without much light or air. No space was overlooked. Old stables and warehouses were also converted into tiny apartments and were rented.[90]

Even with the conversions, however, there was never enough housing. By the 1840s, a new kind of tenement was being built in and around *Kleindeutschland*. These apartments consisted of combination of living room and kitchen facing the street or a narrow courtyard and one or two bedrooms without any windows at all. Some had running water (a great improvement) in the public hall sinks, but there were only two privies in a central courtyard. Most of the residents used chamber pots, which they emptied into the streets or the courtyard.[91]

There was no further change in the housing situation until 1867, when the city enacted a Tenement House Law. Airshafts were to be cut through a building to reach windowless rooms, and most cellar housing was closed down. Enforcement, however, was spotty and old-style tenements continued to be built. It was only at the end of the period under discussion in this chapter that an entirely new concept of apartment house building, the "dumbell" tenement, took hold. The nickname comes from the floor plan, which tapered in the middle, like the handle of a dumbell, and permitted two airshafts to bring light and air to the rooms in the middle of the floor. The airshaft often became clogged and acted as an echo chamber, but in other ways the new apartments were an improvement because there were two toilets serving four apartments on each floor and a combination laundry and bath tub in the kitchen.[92]

Indoor toilets and tubs became possible because of a historic change in the water supply system of the city. In 1842, after seven years of discussion and labor, the Croton Aqueduct in Westchester became the source of healthy water for the city. It was long overdue; arguments in favor of building the aqueduct had come from the brewery industry, whose product was affected by the bad-tasting water coming from the wells and springs; from temperance advocates, who hoped to decrease liquor consumption; from real estate owners, who wished to prevent fires, such as a dreadful one in 1835; and, most of all, from the medical profession, who, although "ignorant of the germ theory of disease, recognized that contaminated water caused disease and death."[93]

Preventing disease was much desired. A fearful cholera epidemic in 1832 had caused 3,500 deaths and cost the city more than $110,000 in lost business. The Five Points area felt the full brunt of the disaster "because of one much used pump whose water had been contaminated by nearby privies." Almost all who died were buried in Potter's Field because St. Patrick's cemetery, where most of the Irish residents of the Five Points would have preferred to be interred, could not handle the large number of destitute deceased Catholics.[94]

Cholera came again in 1833, 1834, and again in 1849; so did yellow fever in 1822 and, a bit later, typhus. It took no great intelligence to see why New York suffered as it did. The city was filthy—"the thousands of swine who roamed its streets were its only efficient scavengers." Citizens were required to sweep their rubbish into a pile in the gutter in front of their houses, to be picked up by city workers, but the "resulting corporation pie [New Yorkers referred to their government as the Corporation] was usually neglected and became a decomposing mass of filth." More cleansing might have been done if the city had an adequate supply of good water and sewers, and the results might have prevented epidemics.[95]

Although there were certainly other reasons for improving the sanitary conditions of the city, one motive for doing so was related to the arrival of thousands of sick immigrants from what were often called "plague" ships and to the diseases that were so prevalent in the districts in which they lived. In another example of the role of symbiosis in New York City history, heavy immigration led to greater interest in improved health and housing. As a result of the deterioration of health conditions between 1845 and 1865, a Metropolitan Health Act was passed in 1866 and, together with a good water supply, led to improved living conditions for all the residents of the city. Without question, New York was a safer place when it finally got 148 miles of sewers in midcentury.[96]

Another good result, the employment of 3,000 "mostly recent immigrants from Ireland," came from the construction of a new water system, which included miles of aqueducts and reservoirs. This was not treated as good news by those who hated the Irish. A prominent citizen, George Templeton Strong, said that the "aqueducts had been used as a necessary by all the Hiberian vagabonds who worked upon it." Perhaps so, but the Croton system was also necessary in a different sense because it provided desperately needed wages. After the construction of the water system in 1844, the weekly newspaper, the *Workingman's Advocate,* said that one out of every seven New Yorkers was a pauper. Earlier, especially during the frequent depressions that afflicted the city (such as the

long one that lasted from 1837 to 1839), as many as a third of the workforce was unemployed. In other bad years, such as 1832, 1854, 1855, and
1857, there was much suffering in New York. An etching entitled "The
Poor in Winter" showed a woman carrying a basket of twigs in her
arms and a bundle of rags on her back through a snowstorm while her
underdressed, barefoot, crying toddler clings to her skirt as they walk.[97]

Hard times in 1844–1845 attracted more journalistic attention than
usual. In addition to the *Workingman's Advocate*'s grim statistic, Horace
Greely, the editor of the *New York Tribune*, said that "there were fifty
thousand people in the city who had not the means for a week's subsis-
tence and knew not where to obtain it." Based on the huge number of
people (over 53,000) who applied for public aid in 1844, it would appear
that he was right.[98]

Depressions during the years under discussion were a fact of life in
New York. In 1834 the number receiving relief was high, and close to
3,000 people ended up in the poorhouse. The crisis years, however, were
not the only times that people, especially the Irish, were in need. Germans also experienced hardship, but the Irish poor "outnumbered all
others." In the 1860s, when the Irish constituted 30 percent of the population, they made up 64 percent of the almshouse population and 70
percent of the recipients of charity.[99]

It was estimated that half of the people helped by the Association for
the Improvement of the Condition of the Poor (AICP) in 1852 were Irish.
In spite of these statistics and the hostile generalizations of the WASP
(white Anglo-Saxon Protestant) majority, the Irish were not the only
needy people in New York City. As we have seen, organizations for the
relief of paupers antedated the arrival of mass immigration from the
Emerald Isle, and the "pitiable beggars" seen all over the downtown
districts were as likely to be native born as foreigners.

Why was there so much poverty in a city whose economy, in general,
was growing by leaps and bounds? The basic reason was that the population was expanding even more than the economy, creating a gap that
led to low wages and unemployment, especially during the winter,
"when the canals froze and commerce dwindled." After some months,
shortages caused food prices to rise, leading to an increase in the population of the almshouse, of "street arabs" (begging children), evicted
renters, and abandoned families.[100]

Those New Yorkers, immigrant or foreign born, who possessed skills
were more likely to manage even when times were hard. Germans, for
example, who comprised 15 percent of the population in 1855, "constituted more half of the city's bakers and confectioners, cabinet makers,
tobacconists, tailors and woodworkers." At the same time, when the
Irish constituted about 30 percent of the population, 60 percent of them
were working as servants, laborers, laundresses, carters, and coachmen,

earning little money and unable to accumulate a reserve for bad times. Furthermore, they competed with blacks for these jobs, which led to racial hatred and riots.[101]

It was widely believed that intemperance was the major cause of Irish poverty. The AICP report for 1857 said that in the whole of New York City there was but one tavern for every eighteen families, "but in the precincts of the lower classes, they were found in double and treble that ratio so that there was one grog shop for every five families." Modern students see the heavy drinking, frequent desertion, and high death rate among Irish males as being, at least in part, the result of their background in Ireland. As we have seen, rural Ireland presented few opportunities to learn skills that would be useful in New York.[102]

It would have been better to avoid the depressions, low wages, and seasonal unemployment that caused so much misery, but since that did not seem feasible, the role played by various organizations and the municipality did alleviate the suffering somewhat. A Society for the Prevention of Pauperism (SPP) had been organized in 1817, and an almshouse that had been part of the city since 1736 expanded, moved, and was renovated in the nineteenth century.[103] In addition to the AICP, which was founded in 1843 and was dedicated to "inculcating habits of frugality, temperance industry and self dependence," there was the New York Society for the Reformation of Juvenile Delinquents, which supervised the House of Refuge. Other charitable agencies included the Humane Society, "established originally to relieve the plight of the wives and children of imprisoned debtors," but by midcentury it was concerned with ameliorating the condition of the poor in general.

There were also a host of specialized institutions. They included the American Female Guardian Society (intended to protect female virtue by assisting indigent women and girls); the Society for the Relief of Poor Widows with Small Children; a House of Industry and a House for the Friendless, both intended to save destitute women and neglected children from the Five Points; a Christian Home for Female Servants; and a Society for the Employment and Relief of the Poor. During a crisis, people were fed (albeit pauper's meals), and attempts to reform the poor by temperance and thrift were constant.[104]

Special attention was given to the needs of pregnant women at the Lying In Hospital at Seventeenth Street and Second Avenue. The New York Juvenile Asylum was opened to limit the number of "street arabs." In the same decade, the 1850s, the Children's Aid Society began its work, which included efforts to convert their Catholic charges to Protestantism while feeding, clothing, and schooling them.[105]

Some reformers, anticipating twentieth-century attitudes, advocated schooling as a way to move the permanent poor, or more likely their children, out of poverty. Their efforts achieved some success. As de-

scribed in the previous chapter, the Free School Society had been organized in 1805 as a private antipoverty program and opened its first
school for poor boys a year later. In a short time, the well-connected
trustees were able to get funding from the city and state and began to
expand. By 1839, more than 20,000 children were enrolled in the Society's schools. The trustees were challenged at various times by other
groups, such as the Bethel Baptist Church, which had opened a school
for children of all faiths in 1820 and was awarded money from the same
source as the Free School Society, the State's Common School Fund.
Other churches opened free, nonsectarian schools using public money,
all of which alarmed the Free School Society trustees. Due to their pressure, in 1825 the Common Council denied such funding to any religious
society. Exhilarated by this victory, the Free School Society changed its
name to the Public School Society and became, in essence, the public
school system of the city.[106]

But this was not the end of the story. When Irish immigrants began
to arrive in large numbers, sending their children to school was not high
on their priority list. Their presence in the city, however, was important
to the Society's trustees, who, as early as 1831, recommended that a
separate school be opened in the Five Points district "for the large number of children destitute of literary and moral instruction . . . who have
so long been subjected to the worst examples, that it is not thought
proper to associate them with the respectable and orderly children who
attend the Public Schools." [107]

The overwhelming majority of the new Irish arrivals were Catholic,
and for this reason the Church represented another group interested in
educating young immigrants from the Emerald Isle. Since they were
barred from receiving tax dollars for their schools and, as we have seen,
most of their constituents were desperately poor and could not pay fees,
with a few exceptions, the children of the enlarged Catholic community
of New York would have to go the Public School Society's schools or no
school at all. The first option was as distasteful as the second because,
although the Public School Society maintained otherwise, its "version of
nonsectarian was really sectless Protestanism" and the textbooks used
in its schools contained many slurs against Catholicism.[108]

Beginning in 1839, the appointment of a new aggressive young
Bishop, John Hughes (himself an Irish immigrant), brought about what
Diane Ravitch has called the "First School War." It lasted until 1842 and
ended with the defeat of both the Church and the Public School Society.
Instead, all the children of New York could attend truly public schools
governed by elected local school boards. The freedom allowed these lo-
cal bodies was designed to satisfy Catholic demands. Since the New
York City schools were neighborhood schools, it was expected that the

trustees in a ward such as the Sixth would be Irish Catholics and choose books and a curriculum that would not offend their beliefs.[109]

One might call this a fair and democratic settlement, but that would be too optimistic. Just as nature abhors a vacuum, politicians know an opportunity when they see one, and the decentralized school system provided them with a chance to gain votes, power, and money. Beginning in 1853, when the Public School Society formally ended its work, the ward school boards accepted bribes from applicants for teaching jobs or offered appointments in exchange for votes, bought their books from publishers who paid them off, hired janitors who could be counted on to vote properly on election day, and, in general, were more interested in personal and party enrichment than education. The corruption did not go unnoticed. In 1864, another Education Act limited some of the worst abuses and, in comparison with politics in the rest of the city in the 1860s, "the ward system seemed honest and pure."[110]

The absence of a free secondary school in New York was not an issue in the first school war, but the need for free education beyond the eighth grade was a concern of many well-meaning individuals. As a result, following the settlement of the first war, a Free Academy was established that was designed to provide secondary education to boys willing and able to continue their education. By 1866, it had acquired sufficient educational éclat to offer a baccalaureate degree and was named the City College of New York, the nucleus of what became, a century later, the vast City University of New York.[111]

There does not seem to have been as much overt corruption associated with higher education, as was the case with the lower schools, but it is probable that, given the political structure of the city in this era, favoritism surely played a role. The municipal government structure in the 1840s seems to have been complex, chaotic and open to corruption. There was a figurehead mayor and a bicameral Council composed of a Board of Aldermen and Board of Assistant Aldermen, whose members were overworked, paid little or nothing, and were, partly for these reasons, openly venal. They were also very inefficient and, as a result, the city suffered from misgovernment in almost every area. As reform Mayor Robert Morris (who also failed to make any changes) said, the Council arranged for "pretended, unecessary and half performed services" and the members, Whigs or Democrats, reaped monetary and political rewards. Filthy streets were particularly troublesome, but since the street sweepers were appointed and retained on the basis of their political support, they were not expected to be efficient.[112]

The creation of a uniformed police force to supplant the amateur watch system was much needed but did not become reality until 1845. One sticking point was the uniform, which some saw as too authoritarian for a democratic city; others argued that it would make the police an easy target for armed criminals. On the other hand, there was no confidence in the watch system. Indeed, one jibe said, "While the city sleeps, the watch does too." Crimes became more frequent as the city grew, but the number of arrests declined. Each change in party meant a virtually complete restaffing of the watch and, since the men chosen depended on the good will of the politicians for their jobs, they made no attempt to prevent illegal acts by the politicians' supporters.[113]

None of this was a secret, but public opinion seemed willing to tolerate it rather than risk a strong police force that would threaten their civil liberties. Mayor Morris's efforts failed to get the approval of the Council on this and other issues, but when he lost his place to James Harper, the leader of the nativist American Republican Party (also known as the Native Americans or "Know Nothings" because they answered all queries about their organization by saying they didn't know anything), police reform made progress.[114]

A new law provided for a force of 800 men, divided among the city's wards, each with their own station house, captain, and other officers. There would also be a chief of police for the entire city, appointed, like the men in the force, by the mayor from nominees submitted by the aldermen and assistant aldermen in each ward. Because of objections raised by civil libertarians, the appointees could only serve for one year, although by 1853, a policeman with a clear record could serve longer. Clearly, the new police force, not yet uniformed but identified by a copper star badge (which led to the nickname "cop" or "copper") was still heavily political and only a slight improvement over previous arrangements. The men were compelled to contribute to political campaigns and were given furloughs on election day to keep known opponents of their ward leaders away from the polls. Although it was inadequate, in May 1845 the law went into effect and New York finally had a police force.[115]

Looking at the politics of the city in the following years, this hardly seemed to matter. In 1851, William Marcy Tweed (whose name has become a synonym for political corruption) was elected to the upper house of the Common Council, the Board of Aldermen, and learned his trade from the other members, who were known as the "Forty Thieves." At that point, Mayor Fernando Wood presided over flagrant corruption, thus providing Tweed with useful training. Wood was also strongly pro-South in the prewar years and proposed that New York secede from the Union rather than disrupt its lucrative trade with the cotton states. His idea was not accepted, and New York supported the Union effort with money and manpower when the war became reality.[116]

Tweed's best years were 1857 to 1870, when, as the most powerful politician in the city, he was able to control public improvements, taxation, and the finances of the various city departments. He also could name election inspectors, which made it possible for his supporters to "vote early and often." Additional patronage was available when he became Deputy Street Commissioner, and ultimately his power was formalized when he was made Grand Sachem of the Tammany Society in 1863. The Tammany Society was named after a Manate chief, but was actually the New York City Branch of the National Democratic Party.[117]

In another example of immigrant-city symbiosis, Tammany's success in mid-nineteenth-century New York was not due to Tweed alone but also to the huge number of immigrant voters, who were wooed with much-needed economic help (including jobs) and reciprocated by voting for the machine's candidates. In the absence of governmental assistance and without being lectured to or patronized, as the poor were by the "do-good" organizations, Tammany Hall was seen as the immigrant's friend. Tweed himself, as well as many of his henchmen, was not Irish, as is usually assumed. The Boss was a Scot and a nativist who did not like the Catholic Irish. Earlier in his career, however, before he became a powerful figure in local government, he was defeated by the candidate of the ferociously nativist Know Nothing Party when he ran for reelection to Congress. This enabled him to mask his own bigotry and allowed him to be seen as the Irishman's friend.[118]

His transformation duplicated the change that was taking place in his party. Tammany Hall, the headquarters of the New York City Democratic Party, had been 100 percent American until, in 1809, an Irishman was given a place on the Democratic ticket. Eight years later, it took a march by the Irish on Tammany Hall to force the nomination of Thomas Emmett, a prominent orator and Irish patriot, to a Congressional seat. Increasing Irish immigration, however, forced the Tammany sachems to renounce bigotry, arrange for token amounts of state aid to parochial schools and Catholic churches, and support universal manhood suffrage without encumbrances in order to gain their votes. And gain their votes they did. The Irish became a bulwark of strength for the Democratic Party in New York City.[119]

Seymour Mandelbaum says that in Boss Tweed's New York, "William Marcy Tweed, for all his bulk, is a man hidden in the shadows of Thomas Nast's leering cartoons in *Harper's Weekly,*" where he was portrayed as a "lecherous, corrupt and powerful Falstaff." Mandelbaum, however, sees him as more than a large-scale thief, although it was thievery that brought about his downfall in 1871. Instead, he credits the Boss with improving the structure and operation of a chaotic and inefficient city government, which included better enforcement of an earlier sanitation regulation and resulted in cleaner streets, more efficient sewers, purer water, much-needed bridges in upper Manhattan, and the completion of the "jewel" of the city, Central Park.[120]

Work on the park had begun in 1853, when the State Legislature approved its construction on an open pasture north of Fifty-ninth Street, which was then a collection of shanty towns "inhabited by rag pickers whose pigs and goats roamed freely." Somewhat later, Frederic Law Olmstead and Calvin Vaux won a contest designed to produce the best plan for the park. Work then progressed rapidly, except during the Civil War years, when labor was scarce.[121]

Tweed's tangible improvements were welcome, but in the process of making them, "he made the public treasury his own by forcing every city contractor to pay the amounts he set" and thus provided a "rake-off" for himself and his associates, Richard Connally, the Comptroller, and Peter Sweeny, the City Chamberlain. As these names show, politics provided more than enough reason for honest citizens to criticize the Irish, but the extensive bigotry directed at them in mid-nineteenth-century New York stemmed from other causes as well.[122]

They were seen as a burden on the public treasury, they were Catholics in a largely Protestant city, they were not passive (as illustrated by the First School War), they were viewed as criminals because of their overrepresentation in the city jails, and they were heavy drinkers. A quotation from a leading New York City newspaper, the *Evening Post*, in 1834 gives the prevailing view: "Everybody knows the peculiarities of the Irish character. Quick, irritable and gregarious . . . combined with impatience. No rational man would go to work . . . to light a fire among such combustible materials."[123]

Three decades later, during the Civil War, exactly such a fire was lit, and the results were as predicted. Early on the morning of July 13, 1863, crowds began to march north on Eighth and Ninth Avenues, growing larger as they went. They converged at Fifty-ninth Street, near the entrance to the newly completed Central Park, and then marched south on Fifth and Sixth Avenues, turning east on Fourty-sixth and Fourty-seventh Streets toward the United States Provost Marshal's office. Their object was to protest against the Act for Enrolling and Calling Out the National Forces, which had been passed by Congress the previous March in response to a downturn in volunteers, a high rate of desertion, and Confederate victories (which had driven Union troops north to Pennsylvania). New Yorkers were not alone in protesting the draft; in several western states, riots caused great danger to the lives of government officials trying to carry out the Act. Because New York was strongly Democratic and therefore hostile to the Republican government in Washington, the New York riot was the worst.[124]

Enlisting was an option and should have been popular because a volunteer could receive a bonus of $300 when he signed up. Blacks could also volunteer, and some did, but they received only $10. The Act required all men (including aliens) between the ages of twenty and forty-five and all unmarried men between the ages of thirty-five and forty-five to be enrolled in the army unless they paid $300 to hire a substitute. Manifestly unfair, it placed an undue burden on families dependent on the wages of a young conscript and was, therefore, a major cause of the week-long riot that followed the first call-up on July 13.[125] There were, however, several other reasons for the outbreak of violence.

President Lincoln's attempt to weaken the Confederacy by emancipating the slaves in rebel-held territory, thus encouraging them to flee, was not popular with many white, working-class New Yorkers, especially those (such as the Irish) who competed with blacks for unskilled and menial jobs. As early as the 1840s, Irish immigrants hunted "nigs" and beat them up when they caught them. This competition had been exacerbated by a depression that followed the start of the Civil War, when the city's creditor-debtor relationship with the South's cotton planters ended. Furthermore, although business had switched to war production and jobs were plentiful, inflation drove prices up by 43 percent while wages rose by only 12 percent. For prosperous New Yorkers, the Civil War brought great wealth; the value of property in New York County nearly doubled. As a result, rents soared and there were many strikes. One of them, mostly by Irish longshoremen working on the docks, was broken by hiring black workers.[126]

One of the first targets of the mob's anger were the industrial firms that had replaced unskilled white labor with blacks. Railroad tracks were torn up and factories with labor-saving machinery were burned. There was also great anger and some violence directed at the Metropolitan Police, the uniformed force established by the State Legislature in 1857 to supplant the corrupt "coppers" of earlier years, because it was these men who enforced temperence laws and thus affected the "most political of Irish institutions, the saloon."[127]

Ivor Bernstein, in a paper prepared for delivery at the New York Historical Society, saw two riots taking place during that hot and muggy week in June 1863. The first and earliest group of rioters was composed of workers employed in skilled and stable jobs and not predominantly Irish; the second, far more violent, represented common laborers, heavily Irish Catholics. There were only 800 troops in the city because New York State Governor Horatio Seymour had sent 2,000 men to help the besieged Union forces at Gettysburg.

The soldiers who were available were mostly wounded men recuperating from injuries suffered earlier in the war and were not able to stem the rampage that followed the marches. The draft, therefore, was temporarily suspended, but the violence continued. Telegraph wires were cut, the Armory at Twenty-first Street and Second Avenue was raided for arms, abolitionist editor Horace Greeley was endangered by the crowd that invaded the *Tribune* Building and shouted "Down with the old white coat who thinks the nigger is as good as the Irishman," streetcars stopped running, and business was at a standstill.[128]

Black New Yorkers had a very difficult time and were chased, beaten, maimed, shot, and hung. Black homes were destroyed, employers were warned to dismiss black workers and not hire others, and the Colored Orphan Asylum at Fourty-second Street and Fifth Avenue was looted and burned, causing all the children to flee and one to die. Fires raged all over the city, leading those who could leave to do so. "Trains and boats leaving New York were packed," and Philadelphia hotel owners profited. Most blacks, however, were not able to leave and continued to suffer, even after a heavy rainfall broke the heat wave and, following the Union victory at Gettysburg, more soldiers arrived. The violence against them subsided, but due to the fires the rioters had set, much of the housing in black neighborhoods had been destroyed. Even more serious, many employers refused to rehire black workers, and a new policy prevented them from riding on street cars.[129]

There was a relief committee to help them, but in spite of the committee's efforts, the city's black population was 10 percent smaller after the summer of 1863 because many of them left. They mostly went to other northern cities, but some emigrated to Africa and South America. During the worst of the violence, although they were a tiny minority in the city, a few Chinese peddlers were attacked and a "Mohawk Indian named Peter Heuston was taken for a Negro and beaten to death."[130]

The draft resumed on August 19, when a battalion of New York's own all-Irish 69th regiment came to New York from Gettysburg, Pennsylvania and were able to calm their fellow Hiberians. There was no further violence but there was an increase in anti-Irish feeling, manifested by further job discrimination ("No Irish Need Apply") and other forms of bigotry.[131] The riots, after all, had been the work of the Irish and resulting damages to property were considerable. In spite of this, and with the passage of time, the Irish community became absorbed into a city that continued to expand and, in most years, flourish. Bigotry never disappeared, but nativists were diverted by the coming of newer immigrants, almost as poor as the earlier Irish arrivals, certainly as different from the Protestant majority as the Irish were, but usually able, after much struggle, to find a place in the metropolis, as the following chapters will show.

They were able to do this because, at the end of the Civil War, despite the loss of the Southern trade, New York was ready for continued expansion of the economy. The National Banking Act, which was passed in 1863, enabled the city's banks to become the holders of the reserves of smaller banks all over the United States and become "the national Marketplace for banker's acceptances, all loans, commercial paper and government securities." The city also resumed its role as the "great workshop of the Western World, the busy hive of industry with its tens of thousands of artisans, mechanics and merchants," as the 1866 *Guide to New York* described it. The Census of 1870 showed that the population of New York had risen to 942,292 and that factories were producing goods valued at more than twice the level of 1869. Truly, New York could by seen by those looking for a better life as "A Promised City." [132]

NOTES

1. Simeon Crowther, "Urban Growth in the Mid-Atlantic States," *Journal of Economic History* (September 1976), 634; Alan Horlick, *Country Boys and Merchant Princes: The Social Control of Young Men in New York* (Lewisburg, Pa.: Bucknell University Press, 1975), 25, 34.

2. Edward Spann, *A New Metropolis: New York City, 1840–1857* (New York: Columbia University Press, 1981), 105.

3. Ibid., 101.

4. Ibid., and 183, 191, 315; Eric Homberger, *Historical Atlas of New York City* (New York: Henry Holt, 1994), 70.

5. Robert Ernst, *Immigrant Life in New York City, 1825–1863* (Port Washington, N.Y.: Ira J. Friedman, 1949), map, 93; table, 192.

6. Spann, *Metropolis*, 148, 336.

7. Ibid., 315.

8. Robert Albion, *Rise of the Port of New York, 1815–1860* (New York: Charles Scribner's Sons, 1939), 346.

9. Ernst, *Immigrant Life*, tables, 194–195.

10. Wilson Smith, *Cities of Our Past and Present* (New York: John Wiley, 1964), 83.

11. Arthur Pound, *Golden Earth* (New York: Macmillan, 1935), 202–203.

12. John Adams Dix, *Sketch of the Resources of the City of New York* (New York: G&C Carville, 1827), 38; Anthony Trollope, *North America* (Hammondswork, England: Penguin Press, 1968), 111, 125.

13. Philip Taylor, *Distant Magnet* (New York: Harper & Row, 1971), 21.

14. Roger Daniels, *Coming to America* (New York: Harper Perennial, 1990), 149.

15. Ernst, *Immigrant Life*, 3, 194.

16. Ibid., 82, charts, 76, 78, 85; Charlotte Erickson, *Invisible Immigrants* (Coral Gables, Fla.: University of Miami Press, 1972), 279.

17. Ira Rosenwaike, *Population History of New York* (Syracuse: Syracuse University Press, 1972), 67.

18. Doreen Magee, "Emigration from Irish Ports," *Journal of American Ethnic History* (Fall 1993), 7–8.

19. Thomas N. Brown, *Irish American Nationalism, 1870–1890* (New York: J. B. Lippincott, 1966), 2.

20. Cecil Woodham-Smith, *Great Hunger* (London: Hamish Hamilton, 1962), 34.

21. Ernst, *Immigrant Life*, 6.

22. Carol Groneman, "The Bloody Ould Sixth: A Social Analysis of a New York City Working Class," unpublished Ph.D. dissertation, University of Rochester, 1973, 3, 4; Woodham-Smith, *Hunger,* 32.

23. Ernst, *Immigrant Life,* 6; Kirby Miller, *Emigrants and Exiles* (New York: Oxford University Press, 1985), 281.

24. Barbara Kaye Greenleaf, *America Fever* (New York: New American Library, 1970), 37–38; Woodham-Smith, *Hunger,* 182.

25. Woodham-Smith, *Hunger,* 207.

26. Ray Billington, *Protestant Crusade, 1800–1860* (Chicago: Quadrangle Books, 1964), 33–34.

27. Walter Nugent, *Crossings* (Bloomington: Indiana University Press, 1942), 50.

28. Albion, *Port,* 340.

29. Edwin Guillet, *Great Migration* (Toronto: University of Toronto Press, 1937), 35.

30. Ibid., 64–65.

31. Ibid., 53, 72; Carl Wittke, *We Who Built America: The Saga of the Immigrant* (Cleveland: Press of Case Western Reserve University, 1939), 115.

32. Wittke, *Built America,* 127.

33. Ibid., 126.

34. Ibid., 133.

35. Ibid., 121.

36. Taylor, *Magnet,* 37–38; Homberger, *Atlas,* 99.

37. Ernst, *Immigrant Life,* 8; Taylor, *Magnet,* 38.

38. Taylor, *Magnet,* 40.

39. Ernst, *Immigrant Life,* 249, n. 28.

40. Robert Swierenga, *Dutch Jews in the North American Diaspora* (Detroit: Wayne State University Press, 1994), 4.

41. Ibid.

42. Avram Barkai, *Branching Out: German Jewish Immigrants in the United States* (New York: Holmes & Meier, 1994), 95.

43. *Jewish Lexicon,* Berlin, vol. 639; Barkai, *Branching,* 2.

44. Ernst, *Immigrant Life,* 40; Barkai, *Branching,* 179.

45. Barkai, *Branching,* 80, 86, 98.

46. Ibid., 81.

47. Ibid., 86; Ernst, *Immigrant Life,* 45.

48. Daniels, *Coming to America,* 239–240; Ernst, *Immigrant Life,* 45.

49. Wittke, *Built America,* 463; Ronald Takai, *Strangers from a Different Shore* (New York: Penguin Books, 1989), 84–85.

50. Jacob Riis, *How the Other Half Lives* (New York: Charles Scribner's Sons, 1890), 68–70; Takaki, *Strangers,* 92.

51. Rhoda Freeman, "The Leadership of the Black Community in New York City, 1827–1861," typescript, copyrighted 1972, 12.

52. Paul Gilje, *The Road to Mobocracy* (Chapel Hill: University of North Carolina Press, 1987), 156.

53. Freeman, "Black Community," 2.

54. Ibid.

55. Kathleen Benson, "A Civil Rights Victory in Old New York," Letter to the Editor, *New York Times,* September 7, 1994.

56. Dix, *Sketch*, 38.

57. Albion, *Port*, 336.

58. Smith, *Cities*, 114.

59. Spann, *Metropolis*, 2; Terry Coleman, *Going to America* (Garden City, N.Y.: Doubleday, 1973), 166; Albion, *Port*, 224.

60. Coleman, *America*, 167; Albion, *Port*, map, 18; table, 399.

61. Coleman, *America*, 166; Spann, *Metropolis*, 4; Homberger, *Atlas*, 87.

62. Amos Hawley, *Human Ecology* (New York: Ronald Press, 1950), 31; Coleman, *America*, 166; Allan Pred, *Spatial Dynamics of United States Industrial Growth* (Cambridge, Mass.: Harvard University Press, 1966), 309.

63. Henry Lanier, *A Century of Banking* (New York: Gillis Press, 1922), 31.

64. Albion, *Port*, 421–422.

65. Margot Gayle and Stephen Garney, "The New York Crystal Palace, 1853/1858," pamphlet (New York: Friends of Cast Iron Structures, 1974).

66. James Hardie, *Description of the City of New York* (New York: Samuel Marks, 1827), 72; Ernst, *Immigrant Life*, 15–16.

67. Horlick, *Country Boys*, 167.

68. Pred, *Spatial Dynamics*, 321, 324.

69. Ibid., 316.

70. Ibid., 314.

71. Ibid., 326–327; Sam Bass Warner, *Urban Wilderness* (New York: Harper & Row, 1972), 70; Albert Fein, "Centennial New York, 1876" in *New York: The Centennial Years, 1676–1976* (Port Washington, N.Y.: Kennikat Press, 1976), 75.

72. Pred, *Spatial Dynamics*, 325–326.

73. Ibid., 329–330.

74. Warner, *Wilderness*, 82.

75. Pred, *Spatial Dynamics*, 332; Homberger, *Atlas*, 76, 77; Fein, "Centennial New York," 83.

76. Spann, *Metropolis*, 188.

77. Ibid., 191.

78. Ibid., 301, 491; Fein, "Centennial New York," 75.

79. New York State, Secretary of State, *Census of the State of New York for 1855* (Albany: Van Benthuy, 1857), 117–118.

80. David Ward, *Cities and Immigrants* (New York: Oxford University Press, 1971), 105.

81. *New York Times*, December 18, 1994, 6.

82. Gayle and Garney, "Crystal Palace."

83. Anthony Jackson, *A Place Called Home* (Cambridge, Mass.: MIT Press, 1976), 1.

84. Jackson, *Home*, 2; Carroll Rosenberg, *Religion and the Rise of the City* (Ithaca, N.Y.: Cornell University Press, 1971), 33; Homberger, *Atlas*, 78.

85. Ernst, *Immigrant Life*, 54.

86. Jackson, *Home*, 10.

87. Pound, *Golden Earth*, 202–203; Homberger, *Atlas*, 99.

88. "Five Points Moral," *New York Times*, June 12, 1988, A:11.

89. Homberger, *Atlas*, 84.

90. Jackson, *Home*, 5; Rosenberg, *Religion*, 31–32.

91. Jackson, *Home*, 17.

92. Moses Rischin, *Promised City* (Cambridge, Mass.: Harvard University Press, 1948), 83.

93. Spann, *Metropolis*, 118; George Lankevich with Howard Furer, *A Brief History of New York City* (Port Washington, N.Y.: Associated Universities Press, 1984), 104; Rischin, *City*, 85.

94. Nelson Blake, *Water for the Cities* (Syracuse: Syracuse University Press, 1956), 132; Charles Rosenberg, *Cholera Years* (Chicago: University of Chicago Press, 1962), 38, 57.

95. Christine Stansell, "The Crisis of the Fifties," typescript, n.d, 10–11; Rosenberg, *Cholera*, 17; Homberger, *Atlas*, 82.

96. Ernst, *Immigrant Life*, 54; Blake, *Water*, 149, 169.

97. Norman Ware, *Industrial Worker, 1840–1860* (Chicago: Quadrangle Books, 1964), 26, 27; Homberger, *Atlas*, 81.

98. Ernst, *Immigrant Life*, 56; Spann, *Metropolis*, 71.

99. Jay Dolan, *Immigrant Church* (Baltimore: Johns Hopkins Press), 32, 33.

100. Spann, *Metropolis*, 72–73.

101. Ibid., 26–27.

102. David Rothman, *Discovery of Asylum* (Boston: Little, Brown & Co., 1971), 163.

103. Ernst, *Immigrant Life*, 163.

104. Ibid.

105. Spann, *Metropolis*, 74; M. J. O'Neale, "Patterns of Benevolence," *New York History* (January 1976), 60–62, 65, 67.

106. Diane Ravitch, *Great School Wars* (New York: Basic Books, 1974), 12, 21–22.

107. Ibid., 33.

108. Ibid., 35.

109. Ibid., 83.

110. Ibid., 89.

111. Selma Berrol, *Getting Down to Business* (Westport, Conn.: Greenwood Press, 1989), 1–5.

112. Spann, *Metropolis*, 53.

113. James Richardson, *New York Police* (New York: Oxford University Press, 1970), 26, 30, 43, 48.

114. Richardson, *Police*, 44–45.

115. James Richardson, "To Control the City," in Kenneth Jackson and Stanley Schultz, eds., *Cities in American History* (New York: Knopf, 1972), 45; Richardson, *Police*, 45, 49.

116. Lankevich, *Brief History*, 164.

117. Seymour Mandelbaum, *Boss Tweed's New York* (New York: John Wiley, 1965), 66; Lankevich, *Brief History*, 149.

118. Mandelbaum, *Tweed*, 67.

119. Ibid.; W. R. Werner, *Tammany Hall* (Garden City, N.Y.: Doubleday, 1980), 26, 28–29.

120. Mandelbaum, *Tweed*, 75.

121. Homberger, *Atlas*, 88.

122. Lankevich, *Brief History*, 110.

123. Paul Weinbaum, *Mobs and Demogogues* (Ann Arbor: University of Michigan Press, 1979), 59.

124. Ivor Richardson, "The Draft Riots and the Industrial Revolution in New York," typescript of a paper delivered at the New York and the Rise of Capitalism Conference, New York Historical Society Conference, May 18, 1984, 1.

125. Richardson, *Police*, 130; Page Smith, *Trial by Fire* (New York: McGraw-Hill, 1982), 477.

126. Roger Lane, *Roots of Violence in Black Philadelphia* (Cambridge, Mass.: Harvard University Press, 1986), 49.

127. *Richardson*, Police, 131.

128. Joel Tyler Headley, *Great Riots of New York, 1712–1873* (New York: Bobbs Merrill, 1970), 153, 169, 175, 179–180; Homberger, *Atlas*, 99.

129. Richardson, *Police*, 137–139; Smith, *Fire*, 478.

130. Stanley Feldstein and Lawrence Costello, *Ordeal of Assimilation* (Garden City, N.Y.: Doubleday, 1974), 162–163; Homberger, *Atlas*, 97.

131. Feldstein and Costello, *Ordeal*, 162–163.

132. Lankevich, *Brief History*, 168; Rischin, *Promised*, title page.

3

A New Metropolis: New York and Its People, 1870-1920

In the decades following the Civil War, New York City continued to grow in size and importance. By every significant measure—economic strength, population growth, physical size, ethnic diversity, and political complexity—it is clear that the late nineteenth and early twentieth centuries was the time when New York became a metropolis.

In 1874, for example, nearly 61 percent of all American exports passed through the port of New York; a decade later, most of the coffee, tea, sugar, clothing, precious jewelry, and wine entering the United States came first to the New York Customs House. The city between the Hudson and East Rivers became the world's busiest port, and the duties collected there "bogged down the United States treasury with unwanted surpluses." Until 1910, New York continued to be the gateway for 50 percent of the nation's imports.[1] Foreign trade, however, important as it was, was only one aspect of the city's flourishing economy. By the 1880s New York was also the nation's leading jobber and distributor and boasted more department stores, large "emporia," as well as smaller specialty shops than any other city in the United States.

A. T. Stewart's, founded in 1846, was the city's first department store. It moved several times in the next thirty years, but by 1876, when it was taken over by John Wanamaker, it was located at Tenth Street and Broadway. At that point, New York's main shopping district, the "Ladies Mile," ran from Eighth Street to Twenty-third Street. Its boundaries were Broadway on the east and Sixth Avenue on the west. Macy's was at Fourteenth and Sixth, and Altman's was four blocks farther north.

The most elaborate of the stores was Siegal Cooper, which had a "fountain just past the columned entrance" and was located across the avenue from Altman's. Lord & Taylor began life at Broadway and Twentieth Street, close to Arnold Constable, which was a block south. The last store on the "Ladies Mile" was Stern Brothers, at Twenty-third Street and Sixth Avenue.[2]

In addition to trade, the city was home to the most powerful investment banks, and its stock exchange was the busiest in the nation. "In 1886 over a million shares changed hands in a single day." The strength of the New York banking houses enabled the city and state to survive the panics of 1873 and 1893. They dominated Wall Street and, from that vantage point, much of the nation's economy, including its rapidly growing industrial sector.[3] By 1900, 69 of the 100 largest American corporations had their headquarters in New York City. Between 1870 and 1890, the city's plants more than doubled in number, and their total capitalization went from $181 million to $426 million. During those years, fed by heavy immigration, the labor force increased by 49 percent and the value of what they produced jumped by 50 percent.[4]

The city's factories continued to turn out fine furniture, jewelry, and cigars, and New York maintained its leadership in the printing and publishing industries. In 1890, New York had 25,399 factories dealing with 299 different products and producing goods valued at $777 million. Much of this was the result of growth in the textile and clothing industries, and that, in turn, was the result of New York's excellent river, canal, and rail connections with New England, which, when combined with its southern and European trade, added up to an enormous market.[5]

It was expensive to do business in New York; suitable land was scarce and costly, it required a large amount of capital to build a plant, taxes were high, and there were exorbitant transportation charges. As result, only light industry and processing could be profitable. Factories and, even more so, shops were to be found in clusters according to the products they made or the goods they sold. Retail dry goods shops lined Fourteenth Street, Twenty-third Street, Broadway, and Sixth Avenue to catch customers who shunned the more impersonal department stores nearby. The leather district was farther downtown; jewelry shops could be found on Maiden Lane, where, two centuries earlier, Dutch women had done their laundry; the Fulton Fish Market was located at the port on the East River; and Newspaper Row, home to eleven publications, was near City Hall.[6]

Physical growth had more than kept up with economic expansion and, as a result, many important improvements in the city's infrastructure were required in the years following the Civil War. An English visitor, George Fox, making his second trip to New York in 1868, noted that "the general features of the city were the same [as the one he had known earlier]; there was Governor's Island, the Battery, the North River and its wharves and Trinity Church, but the rest of New York was all changed."[7]

Actually, Fox had seen only the beginning of the renovation. Some of the most important steps were yet to be completed, and others had not yet begun. Central Park, for example, was in process but was not finished until 1875. Just the planning for the park, however, had considerable impact on the area above Fifty-seventh Street, where the rough topography, cliffs, and valleys had prevented the building of anything but cheap wooden tenements or squatter shanties. Gas and water mains, available in lower Manhattan, were absent north of Sixtieth Street. The area had not yet been laid out in the grid system that prevailed elsewhere in the city and, except for Broadway, none of the west side avenues reached Sixty-fourth Street; "most trailed off into marshes and ravines" at that point.[8]

Arguments for building the park stemmed from the unsuitable terrain. It was impractical to build housing there, but the rugged yet scenic land, if developed into a park, would lead to residential construction in the surrounding area. This is exactly what happened. Expectation that living near a lovely natural setting would attract owners and tenants sparked real estate speculation in the lots north of Fifty-ninth Street long before the park itself was completed. Similar anticipation led the city to lay street pavements, sewers, and water and gas mains to attract investors and expand the area's tax base.[9]

The far East Side also got a park in the 1870s. This area paralleled the East River from Eighty-fourth to Ninetieth Street, passed the Mayor's residence, Gracie Mansion, at Eighty-eighth Street, and included a walkway along the river. As had been true for Central Park, this development also had a salutory effect on property values and stimulated the building of brownstone houses for the middle class in an area that had previously contained only the mansions of the very rich, such as the Astor, Rhinelander, and Schermerhorn families. By 1890, it was fair to say that on both sides of the island, Manhattan had moved uptown.[10]

Further northward, movement had to await transportation improvements—a need that became more pressing after 1874, when Manhattan annexed the southern portion of Westchester County, which included the towns of Morrisania, West Farms, and Kingsbridge. The easterly portions of lower Westchester were annexed twenty years later and the two sections were named the Bronx in honor of the patron who first settled there, Jonas Bronck. In spite of these developments, the companies who owned the street railways and horse-drawn omnibuses described in the previous chapter made no plans to expand.[11]

The street railways, where they were operative, were very uncomfortable. "People were packed in and silks and broadcloths were ruined in attempts to enter or exit. In addition, pocketbooks, watches and breast-pins vanished via pickpockets." On the other hand, riding on the street railways was an improvement over being a passenger on the rattling omnibuses because the rails were placed flush with the street surface. As a result, passengers received a smoother ride at speeds of six to eight miles an hour. Smoother, yes, but street railways were not adequate for a growing city, even when the arrival of the telephone in the 1870s permitted businessmen to communicate while remaining in their offices and partly relieved the problems of distance and congestion that had previously hampered entrepreneurs.[12]

For various reasons, then, additional ways to traverse the island and reach its developing northern villages needed to be built. There were several choices: a subway running underground, such as London already had, or elevated trains running above the streets. The latter system was chosen, although not without opposition, for technological reasons. Subways in New York had to await the invention of the electric motor because smoke from steam-driven trains would cause problems in the long tunnels that would be needed in Manhattan. By 1883, therefore, there were "els" (short for elevated trains) on Second, Third, Sixth, and Ninth Avenues, and in the next ten years they and other lines were extended into the Bronx and carried 200,000 passengers a year. At the same time, Brooklyn was building its own els. As was also true for the other transit lines in the city, the Brooklyn lines were built and owned by private companies and charged a flat rate.[13]

Arguments that had been heard against the els before they were built—that they would be noisy, spread dirt, and darken the streets they traversed—proved to be true and, as a result, property values on the selected avenues fell and only cheap tenements for the working poor were built there. The els remained a fixture in New York (more were erected in Brooklyn, Queens, and the Bronx in the 1890s) until after World War II, but they could not meet the needs of the constantly increasing population and were, therefore, supplemented by subways, the first of which was opened on Broadway in 1904.[14]

Proposals for a subway line in Manhattan had been discussed by businessmen, investors, and politicians since 1864, a year after London had opened its first steam-driven "underground." Nothing had come of these discussions because of the tunnel problem as well as political impediments. The various groups who wanted a subway faced off those, such as the investors in existing transit facilities, who did not and the State Legislature, which had to grant the necessary franchises, was besieged by lobbyists for both sides. As a result, there was no action until 1894, when the legislators finally passed a Rapid Transit Act, which allowed New York to build subways. The city would sell bonds to raise the money and lay out the route but leave the actual construction to a private company, which would hold operational rights for a given period of years. By 1900, the newly organized Interborough Rapid Transit Company (IRT) began to build the first segment of the subway line, from City Hall to 145th Street and Broadway, and eight years later New Yorkers could travel underground on speedy, electric-powered trains from lower Manhattan to the Bronx.[15]

But this was not enough to make much of a dent in the congestion that continued to grow in poorer areas, such as the Lower East Side, where in certain sections there were 900 people living on one acre of land. Overall, in 1905, the Tenth Ward, which included the Lower East Side, held 643.8 people per acre in contrast to 71.7 for Manhattan as a whole.[16] The city fathers faced a "chicken and egg" problem: Private developers would not build inexpensive housing in the upper reaches of the island and the Bronx until they were sure that enough people could live there and still get to work downtown. On the other hand, the city was unwilling to encourage additional subway lines until they were sure that working-class housing would be available. After 1910, following a decade of the heaviest immigration ever, the dilemma was resolved: Inexpensive housing was built by private developers when additional subway lines were constructed and large areas of the city, such as Yorkville, East Harlem, and the South Bronx, became home for low-income New Yorkers, who could live in newer tenements and still get to work in forty-five minutes or less.[17]

They could also live in a nearby city founded by the Dutch 200 years earlier and named Breuklyn. By the end of the nineteenth century, the spelling had been Anglicized to *Brooklyn* and the area had grown far beyond the original small community on the heights looking west over the East River. It was, in some ways, a collection of villages making up a suburb of New York, mostly inhabited by people who worked in Manhattan but chose to live in a less congested area. In other ways it was "a city unto itself with its own professional fire department, police and schools."[18] In 1869, close to 400,000 people called Brooklyn their home. Its population was less than half that of New York's, but it was a larger city than Boston, Chicago, St. Louis, and San Francisco and growing fast. The reasons behind this expansion were, as one would expect, economic. "It was a major manufacturing center—for glass, steel, tinware, marble mantels, hats, buggy whips, whiskey, beer and glue."[19]

Five well-patronized ferry lines connected Brooklyn to its more populous neighbor. Each left from a different stop in Brooklyn and docked at a different point on the east side of Manhattan Island. "Thirteen boats were kept steaming back and forth, night and day, making something like a thousand crossings in 24 hours."[20] Many Brooklynites, of course, never left home at all because, in addition to jobs, there were many advantages to living there. It cost less to light and heat a home because gas rates were lower than in New York, the schools were of a higher quality, streets were better lighted and, except for the slum area around the Navy Yard, safer. Their politicians were as corrupt as New York's but apparently more efficient because streets were laid out and paved before the need was demonstrated.[21]

Based on all this, when serious discussion of a proposed bridge began, one would not expect Brooklynites to be eager to be connected to Manhattan, but they were. Their reasons were practical: The many residents who had to cross the river to work in Manhattan would have a safe and reliable alternative to the ferries because the plans for the bridge called for both a roadway and a pedestrian walkway. The bridge would be most valuable in the winter months, when the river froze and the ferries stopped running. In addition, the leading newspaper, the *Brooklyn Eagle*, was very much in favor of a bridge, as was the Brooklyn political leadership, who saw opportunities to enrich themselves by collecting pay-offs from the many contractors and suppliers involved in building the bridge.[22]

As a result, on April 16, 1867, the New York State Legislature authorized the New York Bridge Company, a private corporation established by a small group of Brooklyn politicians, to purchase any needed land and to fix tolls. John Roebling, a well-known engineer, was hired to build the bridge, but he and his son Washington could do little until New York supported the idea. That required the approval of Tammany Boss William Marcy Tweed, the master of the city in 1869, who favored the project but would not say so until he was certain that he and his henchmen would profit from it. Making the proper arrangements took time, and so did the building of the bridge, but that was just what Tweed wanted. The longer graft was available, the richer he and his associates would become.[23]

Ordinary New Yorkers were impatient to see the bridge erected because they, like the Brooklynites, saw many advantages from its completion. Shoppers from across the river would increase to the benefit of New York merchants; middle-class recreational areas on the Brooklyn shore, such as Coney Island, would be more accessible; and the prospect of an easier trip to and from work might encourage working-class residents of the most congested parts of Manhattan to move across the river.[24]

The idea of a bridge over the East River had been talked about since the beginning of the nineteenth century, but nothing was done because construction posed several very serious engineering problems. The East River (really a tidal strait and not a river at all) was both turbulent and congested, requiring a bridge that would "make one grand soaring leap from shore to shore over the masts of the ships below." Roebling, therefore, planned for a suspension bridge that would have "one uninterrupted central span, held aloft by huge cables slung from the top of two colossal stone towers and secured on either shore by masonry piles called anchorages," which would lie in the bedrock of the river. Construction began in 1870, followed by many difficulties in the ensuing years, but on May 24, 1883 the bridge was finally opened to traffic, vehicular and pedestrian. The former paid according to size and weight; the latter paid one cent.[25]

The bridge, as we shall see, was one of the major forces leading to the consolidation of the cities of New York and Brooklyn, portions of Westchester and Nassau counties, and all of Staten Island in 1898, but there were also other pressures that led to the same end. One of these was a unified school system, the result of the "second school war" of 1895 to 1896. In response to pressure from a group of anti-Tammany progressives, who had banded together first as a Committee of Seventy to elect a reform mayor, William J. Gaynor, and later as the Public Education Association, headed by Nicholas Murray Butler (the President of Columbia University), the ward trustee system was abolished.[26]

Instead, the schools of what was shortly to become greater New York were united in a centralized system governed by a city-wide Board of Education, with a professional staff led by a Board of Superintendents and a powerful Superintendent of Schools. In place of the corruption, gross inefficiency, and favoritism that had resulted from the decentralized arrangement established after the first school war, teacher selection was now to be done from an eligible list established from written examinations. Decisions on what to teach and where to build badly needed new schools were to be made by a professional staff, working under the Superintendent of Schools.[27]

Thirty-eight new schools were built between 1899 and 1914, primarily in the older sections of the city. This was a massive undertaking led by the Superintendent of Buildings, C. B. Snyder, who developed the "H"-style school, which was built in two wings to allow light and air into all the classrooms.[28] Interestingly, the men and women who had organized the Public Education Association and worked so hard to reform the schools were not the people whose children would benefit from an improved educational system. Their offspring, who attended private schools before the "war," would continue to do so. It was rather the children of the immigrants who were pouring into the city who were their concern. In another example of the symbiosis that has marked the history of New York, the need to make Americans out of "little aliens" resulted in, as we shall see, much improved schools.

In 1897, the various areas that constituted greater New York had unified schools and a unifying bridge but continued to operate as separate governmental units. The great bridge and the centralized schools, however, strengthened the arguments of those leaders, such as Andrew Green, who urged consolidation for the metropolitan area. For much of the 1890s, the forces that favored consolidation, the mercantile élite, battled with those who opposed it in fear of higher taxes and neighborhood change. This became clear after Green, with some difficulty, arranged for a consolidation referendum to appear on the ballot prepared for the New York and Brooklyn municipal elections of 1894, the results of which showed that a majority of New York voters were in favor but that Brooklyn voters were uncertain; 64,744 favored joining New York, 64,467 did not.[29]

The other areas involved, Queens and Richmond counties and the towns of lower Westchester (all of which needed public works but could not finance them), strongly favored unification. Only the tiny town of Eastchester, like Brooklyn, was unsure. The lack of a strong majority for unification in Brooklyn is puzzling because a Consolidation League had been organized to bring it about soon after Green had proposed the idea and had attracted considerable support. The background of the League members, however, makes it clear that they did not represent the people of Brooklyn as a whole but rather spoke for "the mercantile, financial and real estate elites . . . in the metropolitan area." [30]

From their point of view, a unified city government, with more resources, could do much more for the port—maintain channels of navigation, improve docks and warehouses, and control all the owners of waterfront property. It could also "promote a unified . . . development of shipping, railroads and related facilities in such a way as to aid both merchants and property owners." The improvement and maintenance of the port, defined as including southern Westchester, western Queens (including Little Neck and Jamaica Bays), as well as all of New York and Brooklyn, was central to all the groups that favored unification because, as we have seen, New York's magnificent harbor was basic to the prosperity of the entire metropolitan area.[31]

There were also other reasons, especially among Manhattanites, to favor a unified city. Some saw the possibility of using greater resources to increase the efficiency of municipal services; others believed that a single municipal government might make Brooklyn and Queens more attractive to those who needed space and that this would decrease the housing density and consequent social problems of lower Manhattan. To reinforce this argument, a Brooklyn newspaper described free-standing houses that could be rented for $25 a month and two-family houses that cost only $10 per family. The *Manhattan Real Estate Record and Builder's Guide* said that "improved access to inexpensive single family housing would help to separate the industrious poor from the degenerate people by whom they are surrounded." [32]

There were, however, doubters on both sides of the river; in both

Brooklyn and Manhattan, for example, many people feared the prospect of higher taxes and the likelihood that their resources would be used for other than their home area. Reform-minded New Yorkers hoped that unification would reduce Tammany's power; but Brooklynites feared that the organization's activities in their county would be strengthened. Actually, by the mid-1890s, Tammany was less important in Manhattan; Boss Tweed had been convicted and jailed in 1871 and his "Ring" had been exposed and weakened by the Lexow Committee hearings in 1894.[33]

There was enough opposition in Brooklyn to organize a League of Loyal Citizens within a week after passage of the referendum. The membership was as elite as that of the Consolidation League: merchants, property owners, and men of wealth. Their concerns, however, were cultural, not economic. "All of them were deeply devoted to Brooklyn's Anglo-American Protestant Institutions and way of life" and believed that a huge "alien, impoverished tenement house population," would overwhelm them. A Brooklyn minister spoke for many when he made his objections to consolidation clear, saying that good government would not be possible if a large proportion of recent immigrants composed of the "political sewage of Europe" were to settle in Brooklyn.[34]

In the end the unifiers won, mostly because Thomas Platt, the head of the New York State Republican Party, decided that a consolidated city would be more amenable to Republican control and pressed his cohorts in Albany to vote for unification. A Charter Commission was then established, which produced a basic framework for the consolidation of all the territory surrounding the port, for uniform rates of taxation, and for a strong central government "to promote the complete and rational development of the metropolis." The Charter also established five separate boroughs, with elected presidents, as well as a Board of Public Improvements which would coordinate public works projects throughout the city. Provision for an elected City Council and a strong mayor completed the framework, which was modified in 1901 and several times thereafter, although much of the original structure remained.[35]

The economic and physical growth of New York City, as described in the preceding pages, was both the cause and effect of more basic growth—population. By 1900, only London, of all the world's great cities, contained more people. As we have seen, basic growth had been going on throughout the city's history, but it was a series of surges between 1870 and 1920 that placed New York in this position. In 1870, 942,292 people lived on what was then New York (that is, Manhattan Island). In the next twenty years, the population increased by 31.5 percent and in the following decade by 37 percent, bringing about a total of 3,437,000 after consolidation and 5,047,221 by 1915. Ninety-seven percent of these millions were white, 2.5 percent were black, and 33 percent were Asians. The growth did not stop there. The 1920 census showed that 5,620,048 men, women, and children lived in the unified city.[36]

As had been true for all of the nineteenth century, immigration was a major reason for the expansion. Government statistics show that of the 21,130,475 men, women, and children who came to the United States from foreign countries between 1884 and 1919, the largest number—almost 16 million—came to New York. A severe depression in the 1890s caused a 44 percent decrease, but the numbers picked up again at the turn of the century; indeed, the largest single number, 1 million, came in 1907. The 1920 census indicated that almost 17 percent of the city's population had been born abroad or had at least one foreign-born parent.[37]

Manhattan had the largest number of residents (405,996); Brooklyn was next, with 315,904; the Bronx and Queens held many fewer (101,503 and 71,519, respectively); and Richmond had the least (23,173). The number and proportion undoubtedly would have been larger if the preceding decade had not witnessed a world war, but even with the limitation imposed on the statistics by that war, in 1920 New York had the most varied population in the United States. This was not a new development; from 1880 onward, census statistics showed that from 76 to 78 percent of New York City inhabitants were of foreign stock.[38]

A very large segment of the immigrants who came after 1870 continued to come from the British Isles; the 228,824 Irish were the most numerous among them. This group of newcomers was enlarged by more than 49,000 English-speaking Canadians, 1,597 Australians, and almost 4,000 Newfoundlanders. French-speaking Canadians also lived in New York, as did small numbers of Asians, but the largest European group was composed of Russian, Polish, and Austrian Jews. There were almost as many Italians as English-speaking immigrants, and there were somewhat fewer Germans and Slavs from various areas in Central Europe. Italians and Jews made up 32 percent of the foreign-born population of New York and represented over 61 percent of all the Italians and Jews in the United States. All things considered, it is not surprising to find that New Yorkers in the 1890s heard more foreign languages than English when they walked on Broadway.[39]

The kaleidoscope of languages that marked New York City as different from most other American cities during the period from 1870 to 1920 was further accentuated by differences in color. The city on the Hudson did not have the most nonwhites; the West Coast was home to many more Asians, and the South continued to be the place where most black Americans lived. There were, however, enough nonwhites in New York to be noted. In 1870, 19,512 blacks lived in Manhattan and Kings counties; in 1890, 35,872 did so.[40] Those two areas together contained 78 percent of the city's industry and therefore offered the largest number of jobs for unskilled workers. At the latter date, the largest part of the black community was comprised of native-born New Yorkers, but another 5,675 came from other states and 5,000 were foreign born (mostly from the British West Indies). Twenty years later, reflecting the impact of the boll weevil on cotton and the discrimination that left Southern blacks poor and without opportunity, the numbers were much larger. New York City was home to 83,242 blacks, almost 4,000 of whom were from the Caribbean. At the end of the period discussed in this chapter, a total of 141,000 blacks, constituting 2.7 percent of the population, lived in the five boroughs of greater New York.[41]

The immigrants from the West Indies left their island homelands because, although they had been legally free since 1836, their economic position in the underdeveloped economy of the islands was very low. As was also true for the native-born black migrants, more women than men came from Jamaica, Trinidad, Barbados, St. Kitts, Nevis, and the Bahamas because there were more jobs for them than for black males. Regardless of gender, most did the same work as native-born blacks: They were menial laborers, servants, porters, waiters, waitresses, teamsters, dressmakers, and janitors.[42]

By reputation, the West Indians were thrifty and had "business acumen" and, as a result, members of the second generation were more likely than their native-born black peers to open small shops. Those with skills might have preferred to move into higher-paid industrial positions instead, but the arrival of millions of Europeans as well as the racist preferences of employers prevented this. The impact of European immigration was even more damaging on unskilled native-born blacks, who competed on unequal terms with laborers from Italy and eastern Europe. A chart in Herbert Gutman's *The Black Family in Slavery and Freedom* shows that in 1905, the overwhelming majority of black males, twenty years and older, living in Manhattan were laborers and only a tiny number were in white-collar occupations. An even smaller group were entrepreneurs, and a handful were professionals.

New York State had ended institutionalized racism before the Civil War, and the Federal Civil Rights Act of 1873 offered blacks further protection. By 1890, theaters, restaurants, transportation, schools, cemeteries, and voting booths were open to all races. In spite of this, New York City black residents suffered mightily from housing and job discrimination. At the start of the twentieth century, the largest black communities in Manhattan were the rowdy Tenderloin district, around West-Forty-first Street, and the west Sixties. The latter area was called San Juan Hill because the frequent interracial battles that occurred there reminded New Yorkers of the fighting that was going on in Cuba during the Spanish-American War. There were a greater number of episodes in the San Juan Hill area than anywhere else in the city, but the most serious anti-black disturbance since the Draft Riots took place in the Tenderloin during a very hot August in 1900.[43]

The upper Manhattan area known as Harlem, which was destined to become the most famous black community in the United States, had been home to blacks since the Dutch days when, as slaves, blacks worked on the farms located there. Some continued to live in the village after they were freed. The small community grew somewhat larger later in the nineteenth century, as servants who worked for the wealthy families who now lived in the area began to move into the neighborhood. They were concentrated in small enclaves on both the east and west sides of the area above Ninetieth Street and up to 148th Street, but their numbers were scattered and few. A chart of Harlem's population in 1900 showed that only one block had as many as 100 blacks living there.[44]

What changed this picture was the projected expansion of the subway into Harlem. This set off a wave of real estate speculation and the building of luxurious apartment houses, most of which were occupied by wealthy German Jews. The inevitable "bust" came in 1904 and 1905 when, faced with delays in completing the subway, prospective white tenants refused to move into the new buildings. Rather than be ruined, developers opened their property to blacks, using the black-owned Afro-American Realty Company as their agent. During the next twenty years, Harlem became the largest and most famous urban black community in the United States.[45]

Less affluent German Jews moved into tenement apartments east of Fifth Avenue when the Second and Third Avenue els were extended to East Harlem in the 1880s. Their move out of the Lower East Side was a fortunate development because it coincided with the arrival of the Russian and Polish Jews, who might otherwise have had nowhere to go. The German Jewish movement from the slums of the Lower East Side to much improved housing uptown made room for their newly arrived coreligionists (a person of the same religion) and also provided them with an example of what was possible for Jews in America. Although 450,000 Russian and Polish Jews were still on the Lower East Side, by 1910 80,000 of the cohort that arrived after 1880 were living in Harlem.[46]

Almost as famous was another segment of the city inhabited by non-whites, Chinatown, which grew from a tiny nucleus to a substantial size in the last third of the nineteenth century. In 1870 there were a mere handful of Chinese in New York; in 1890 there were 1,970. By 1900, 6,321 Chinese, mostly men, were living in the city and had added another culture to the New York mosaic. Their numbers continued to grow after the turn of the century, and by 1920 there were over 8,000 Chinese living in the city, with the largest number in lower Manhattan.[47]

Chinatown had its origins in the defection of some sailors from a silk ship anchored in New York Bay in 1835. As we have seen, in the 1850s more Chinese arrived; somewhat later, a third group came to the East Coast when the transcontinental railroads they had been imported to build were completed. The growth of the Chinese community was achieved in spite of the passage of the Chinese Exclusion Act in 1884, which barred the entry of laborers and denied naturalization to those already here. Six years later, the barred categories were broadened to include all Chinese except officials, teachers, students, and merchants. The resulting shortage of wives kept the bachelor society small and encouraged the growth of prostitution in Chinatown. The community was very insular: Its members found housing and entertainment among their own people and earned their income as cigar makers, laundrymen, or by supplying their fellow bachelors with the necessities of life. After 1930, women began to enter the United States more easily and it became possible to start a family.

During the period of exclusion, various devices were used to bypass the laws. Since merchants were assumed to be self-supporting and thus welcome, entering Chinese would present "ornate books declaring the bearer to be a shareholder in a Chinatown company." An even more widely used device was the creation of "paper families." A man who was a legal resident of the United States would sell his papers to an unrelated youth and testify that the youth was his child. The "son" had been carefully briefed to give the right answers to the immigration inspectors; in spite of such preparations, admittance did not come easily. Many applicants were held in detention and questioned for more than a year, and a good number were deported. Those who managed to settle in the city turned the streets, such as Mott and Pell (which had been named after the wealthy WASP families who lived there in the eighteenth century), into a teeming community that contained five-story tenements, herbal and tea shops, restaurants, oriental groceries, and fish stores.

There were also some less wholesome enterprises. According to somewhat prejudiced observers, such as journalist Jacob Riis, "Chinatown [in the 1890s] was honeycombed with gambling houses, opium joints, and brothels"—not surprising in a community deprived of family life.[48] Other more objective observers spoke of the close family and clan relationships of the "sojourners" who went back to China, some permanently and others for brief periods to marry and start a family.[49]

Adjacent to Chinatown, and close by to the earlier Irish settlement at Five Points, was the area between Bayard, Park, Mulberry, and Baxter Streets, known as the Mulberry Bend. It was home to a large portion of the Italian immigrant community and, as a result, came to be called Little Italy. Jacob Riis described it as a "district [where] there is scarce a lot that has not two, three, or four tenements upon it." Riis went on to say that, as a result, "when the sun shines the entire population seeks the street."[50] One of the characteristics of this jammed neighborhood was the clustering of families from the same area of Italy. Designated by sociologists as "campanilismo" and derived from the Italian word for bell, *campana,* the term reflects the immigrant's decision to remain not only with other Italians but with natives from their home village or at least within the area in which the ringing of the *campana* in their parish church could be heard.

The streets of Little Italy, therefore, were segregated by hometown geography. People from western Sicily lived on Elizabeth Street, those from the eastern part of the island lived on Catherine or Monroe Streets; Baxter Street had a colony of Genoese; and Bleecker Street was home to northern Italians. The pattern was less obvious as time went on and the immigrants moved out of Little Italy because, now more at home in America, they were willing to share their neighborhoods, as long as the neighbors were from somewhere in Italy. In one of their earliest second-ary settlements, East Harlem, most of the population came from south-ern Italy and Sicily; but later communities in the Bronx, in the Navy Yard area of Brooklyn, or in Williamsburg were quite mixed and more divided by class and income than by "campanilismo." A neighborhood church was present in all these communities and had, as soon as possi-ble, an Italian-speaking priest.[51]

Before the dispersion in the 1880s, when Little Italy was home to the vast majority of Italian immigrants, it had the highest infant mortality rates in the city. Riis, among others, blamed this on the unspeakable housing conditions in the community. As late as 1898 and in spite of the existence of a Metropolitan Board of Health and the efforts of settlement house workers in the districts which were home to the poorest New Yorkers, at the turn of the century, 12,861 dead horses, 7,239 spoiled barrels of fish, and 3,406 barrels of offal from live horses marred the streets.[52]

Crowded, neglected, and dark, the tenements were perfect breeding places for disease. Both Riis and other nativists did as the critics of the Irish had done and saw the people whose poverty forced them to live in terrible housing as a threat. A Columbia University professor said, "Huddled together in miserable apartments in filth and rags, without the slightest regard to decency and health, they [are] a menace to the health of the whole community."[53]

The professor said this in 1890, but it would also have been applicable in 1907, 1910, and 1916, when serious infantile paralysis epidemics af-flicted New Yorkers. Even earlier, when Dr. Antonio Stella conducted a study entitled "Effects of Urban Congestion on the Italians in New York City," he found that the city-wide death rate for children under age five in 1905–1906 was 51.5 percent, but for youngsters who lived in Little Italy, it was 92 percent. Not only children died early and often; their parents suffered from heart and kidney diseases as well as tuberculosis and had a relatively short life span: 41.7 years for men, 43.5 years for women. By 1914 there was some improvement: 54.5 years for men and 56.8 years for women.[54]

The grim facts regarding health conditions in the immigrant districts prompted the organization of a Visiting Nurse Service and the construction or expansion of four hospitals: Bellevue, St. Vincent's, the Eye and Ear Infirmary, and the New York Infirmary for Women and Children. In addition, concern that an inadequate diet was a major cause of poor health among the indigent led the Board of Health to establish twenty-seven milk stations in the area below Canal Street. Also, many of the settlement houses had "well-baby" clinics, to which mothers could bring infants to be weighed and examined.[55]

In spite of the difficulties they experienced in New York, Italians, who began coming in 1870, continued to arrive in increasingly large numbers. Many came via the padrone system, which was similar to the indentured servant arrangements used for various ethnic groups in the previous century. Originally, the padrone system had been used to take children from families in Greece and Italy whose parents could not support them. Once in America, the young boys were hired out as bootblacks and street musicians. In the 1870s, a similar system was extended to adult males. Until the passage of the United States Contract Labor Law in 1885, which forbade these arrangements, the padrone, essentially a labor agent, contracted with a prospective emigrant to work as he directed for one to three years. The padrone deducted the cost of the worker's passage from his wages and controlled his life in other ways as well.[56]

This labor system had an effect on the settlement of Manhattan. In the late 1870s, a padrone arranged for a group of immigrant Italians to work on the extension of the First Avenue trolley tracks in the northern part of the island. As a result, "an Italian workers shanty town developed along the East River around 106th Street" and soon became the destination for other Italians, eager to escape the congestion of Little Italy. Real estate developers quickly moved to erect five-story tenements and thus created a secondary area of Italian settlement, uptown, in East Harlem.[57]

The majority of the Italians who settled in New York, did not come with a padrone but rather as individuals or with members of their family. Some left from Genoa, but most left from Naples because it was easier for the southern Italians and Sicilians, who greatly outnumbered emigrants from other parts of Italy to reach Naples. They followed a trade route established by sailing ships in the mid-1850s, which brought "citrus fruits, sulphur and sumach" from Southern Italy to New York. By 1887, the movement out of Italy was so heavy that it made Naples almost totally dependent on the "emigrant trade." Nineteen million Italian men, women, and children left their homeland between 1861 and 1914, many to Latin America but most to the United States, where, although some people called them "birds of passage," that is, seasonal residents, like birds, the largest number remained.[58]

The reason for this vast migration of people was their extreme poverty. When the peasants of southern Italy began to emigrate, they left behind abysmal conditions. Most had been living in a one- or two-room hovel, which was shared by husband, wife, three or four children, and sometimes a donkey, a goat, or a pig. This home was usually located several miles away from the rented land they farmed, which added to their hardship. If there was enough rain and other weather conditions resulted in a good crop, a large share of the crop went to the absentee landlord as rent.

Matters grew worse as the nineteenth century proceeded and the pressure of a growing population led to lower wages for artisans, who joined their farmer brothers in abject poverty. In short, most of the founding fathers of New York's Italian community emigrated because they could not make a living from the land or from household industry. The new arrival who told the American immigration officials that if he and his family had remained in Sicily they would have ended up eating each other was probably overstating his case, but there can be no doubt that conditions were very grim.[59]

Italian peasants and artisans could and did earn a living in New York. One estimate said that that an unskilled worker could make five to six times the income earned by the best-paid laborers in Italy. In 1880, three out of four Italians were also laborers in New York, but they were much better paid. Those with skills, a smaller number, worked as confectioners, tailors, shoemakers, and masons. Much to the anger of the black community, Italians captured one service occupation—barbering—but most Italian men worked on the wharves and construction sites of the growing city. By 1905, the census figures indicated that the Italian community had experienced some upward mobility; instead of the more than 53 percent who were doing unskilled work in 1890, only 42 percent were doing so in 1905. Ten years later there was other evidence of improvement: The percentage of Italian skilled workers had increased from 13 to 21 percent and semiskilled from 7 to 16 percent. Another route upward was street peddling, which, by the early twentieth century, had led to small shopkeeping. Still another path was the clothing industry. By 1911, Italians held 12 percent of the industry's jobs. Some of the garment workers were not laboring in a factory; many labored in family operations conducted in their homes.[60]

Children, some quite young, were often part of these family factories. A young boy might bring the unfinished goods to his mother and sisters and make the return trip after they had basted and/or sewn them into garments. Even the littlest girl could be used for taking out basting stitches. Not all the work done at home was associated with clothing. A contemporary essay on homework in an Italian household described the tasks of making artificial flowers, which were much in demand for the large hats that were then in fashion: "Only the father and two infants were exempt; the three year old worked on petals, her older sister separated stems and dipped them into paste while the older women [mother and grandmother] placed the petals on the stems."[61]

Settlement workers and school officials were horrified by the use of children, who, by law after 1871, should have been in the classroom. In spite of all their efforts, including the use of truant officers, the officials made little headway. From the point of view of Italian immigrant parents, working children were part of a family effort from which all the members would benefit; to make the family poorer by allowing some to attend school instead of working was opposed to all that they believed. Thus, violation of the school attendance laws, even if they knew of them, was not considered a sin. One modern commentator has explained the importance of the Italian family in historical terms. "Vulnerable to frequent invasions and domination of strangers for much of their history, they endured and built their culture by sealing out the influence of strangers," including truant officers.[62]

During the early years of settlement, these strong feelings led Italians to underuse formal education as a road to upward mobility. As a modern student of the Italians has pointed out, some Italian parents recognized that socioeconomic gain might result from schooling, but most "subordinated unrealistic social aspirations to immediate economic gain." Historical experiences outweighed the arguments of the settlement workers and school personnel and led Italian parents to undervalue education for their sons and daughters. There was, for example, no reason to respect intellectuals or want their children to emulate them because they had been shunned by the Italian intelligentsia for generations and feared that educated children might do the same to them in America.[63]

Poverty, of course, was the single most important reason for low school attendance, demonstrated by the changes that occurred in later generations' school usage. A table constructed from 1950 census data shows that 31 percent of Italian-American males born between 1925 and 1944 had completed four or more years of high school, in contrast to only 6 percent of those born before 1925. The percentage was lower for females (29 and 10 percent, respectively), reflecting once again Italian beliefs in home and family taking precedence over formal education.[64]

The relative paucity of Italian youngsters in the city's classrooms was a great disappointment to the Progressive school reformers active in the first two decades of the twentieth century. The Progressive school reformers wanted to use the schools to Americanize the thousands of poor and foreign children pouring into the city at the turn of the century. Due to their influence, the new schools had well-equipped cooking class-rooms, in which immigrant girls could learn to cook American style; workshops in which boys could learn a trade; rooftop "sanitariums" for pretubercular youngsters; adjacent playgrounds, on which slum children could learn to play American sports, such as baseball; and even school gardens, in which the children might come to realize that the new world was not composed entirely of gray concrete.[65]

What somewhat assuaged the reformers' disappointment was the fact that Jewish immigrant children, arriving in New York at the same time as the Italians, were more likely to attend school. In the lower grades, especially kindergarten, all the little aliens—Italians, Poles, Irish, as well as Jews—were well represented because they were too young to work. After the primary years, however, more Jewish children remained to complete at least the fifth grade, as required by the compulsory educa-tion law. As their family income grew, more grammar school graduates would have Jewish surnames; and after high schools were built in the first decade of the twentieth century, Jewish names were prominent on the lists of graduates.[66]

It is clear that as a group, Russian and Polish Jewish parents favored formal education for their children more than other immigrants did, but the qualifier *as a group* is important. Regardless of the respect religious Jews had for their learned men, the poverty they faced upon arrival and for many years thereafter prevented thousands of first- and second-generation Jewish immigrant children from having an extended educa-tion. Truancy and early dropout were problems in the schools where Jewish children were in the majority. As was true for all groups, there were Jewish dullards as well as able students. A combination of eco-nomic need, distaste for learning, and the availability of other nonaca-demic opportunities led many eastern European Jewish youngsters to end their schooling after the eighth grade.[67]

Another reason for this was the scarcity of high schools. Brooklyn had established one secondary school for boys and one for girls prior to consolidation, but until the early years of the twentieth century, when De Witt Clinton, Wadleigh, and Morris High Schools were opened in Manhattan and the Bronx, post-eighth-grade free education was avail-able only at two very selective preparatory schools attached to the Col-lege of the City of New York and the Hunter Normal College, both of which were outgrowths of the Free Academy, which was established in 1842.[68]

As a result of the unification of the city and the reorganization of its educational system, more secondary schools became available and, at the same time, Jewish families were increasingly able to keep their children off the labor market. In another example of symbiosis, a fortunate match between the skills the newcomers from eastern Europe brought with them and the opportunities offered by the expanding economy of New York when they arrived led to a sizable number of educated men and women whose talents could be used for greater good of the city and its people.

The massive emigration of 2.5 million Jews from eastern Europe between 1870 and 1920 and the fact that most of them, unlike their German Jewish predecessors, chose to remain in New York made them a prominent part of the foreign-born community. Most shunned the hinterland, ignoring the advice of the existing Jewish community, who, alarmed at the influx of their poor and foreign coreligionists, tried to resettle them in agricultural colonies as far from New York as possible. The newcomers made an understandable choice; relatively few had been farmers, almost none successful, in Russia, Poland, and Galicia (part of the Austro-Hungarian empire), and New York was clearly a place where their background in commerce and skilled trades would be useful.

A number of "push" factors had stimulated the movement of millions of Jews out of eastern Europe. In the 1870s, a cholera epidemic in Lithuania (a province of Russia), a famine in Poland (also part of Russia), and a pogrom (riots and attacks on Jews) in Odessa led to the emigration of 40,000 Jews. They were the advance contingent of 200,000 more, who came as a result of the violence and repression that followed the assassination of Czar Alexander II in 1880, the 300,000 who arrived in the 1890s, and the million and a half who left Russia, Poland, and Galicia before World War I.[69]

More important than the crisis provoked by internal problems in eastern Europe as a whole were the worsening economic conditions experienced by the 5 million Jews living in *shtels* (small towns) that made up the Pale of Settlement into which Jews had been herded after Poland was dismembered by the Congress of Vienna in 1815. The Pale consisted of twenty-five provinces, "stretching from present day Lithuania and Poland thru White Russia, the Ukaine and Moldavia." The population of this area grew from 1 million in 1800 to 4 million in 1880, partly because young men married and became fathers as early as possible to avoid twenty-five years of military service, which was designed as much to remove them from their Jewish roots as to provide the Czar with manpower.[70]

The occupations by which most of the Jews in the Pale had managed to eke out a meager living became overcrowded, and uncounted numbers were reduced to beggary. One part of the Czar's mandate to his ministers—that a third of the Jews should die from starvation—seemed possible to achieve, especially when Jews were blocked from previously successful occupations, such as innkeeping. In 1897, the government nationalized the liquor industry and hundreds of thousands of Jews lost their livelihood.[71]

For most of the nineteenth century, an overwhelming percentage of Jews living in the Pale had earned their living as middlemen between farmers and processors of agricultural products; but by 1897, that sector had reached a saturation point and the manufacturing of garments became more important, occupying more than 60 percent of those employed between 1899 and 1914.

Agriculture never attracted more than 3 or 4 percent, commerce no more than 5 percent. Since most Jews were barred from the universities, the professional segment was very small, only a fraction over 1 percent. Laborers and servants constituted the second largest employment category after manufacturing and ranged from 18 to 23 percent of the total Jewish population between the end of the nineteenth century and World War I. Except for a tiny portion (1.6 percent) of the total Jewish population in 1897 who were wealthy, the men who made up the bulk of the manufacturers and traders operated on a small scale in a very competitive market, paid low wages, earned small profits, and, as a result, were mostly poor. In 1898, for example, almost 20 percent of the Jews in the Pale needed charity in order to buy food for the Passover holiday.[72]

In spite of small monetary returns for their labor, however, Russian and Polish Jewish traders and factory workers had gained something that would prove to be more valuable than money when they decided to emigrate: experience in occupations that prepared them to take advantage of opportunities in New York. This was also true for those who came from Galicia.

It is clear that the eastern European Jews, as a group, were better equipped than other immigrant groups to take advantage of the opportunities available in the Empire City. In addition to prior commercial experience, although few understood English, 75 percent of the males were literate in some language and a large number had lived in urban areas. There had been extensive migration within the Pale, to Lodz, Odessa, and other cities as the poor searched for a way to survive. In a sense, the longer trip they took to America (usually from Poland through Germany, embarking from Hamburg or Bremen and landing in New York) was only an extension of their earlier search. The difference, however, was that it was much more successful.[73]

This was not immediately apparent. After inspection and admittance, they went from Ellis Island to the tenements of the Lower East Side, originally *Kleindeutschland* and now, as Jacob Riis labeled it, "Jewtown." Like the housing of their Italian neighbors to the west, their small apartments were very crowded and inadequate. The 25×100 lots on which the Lower East Side tenements rested were originally meant for single-family houses; however, as we have seen, they had been converted and divided into housing for the poor in the 1840s or earlier. The best apartments were in the newer dumbell tenements, which had toilets and running water; the worst were in the older buildings, which the landlords and municipal authorities had neglected. The passage of a stronger housing law in 1901 prohibited some of the worst conditions and forced owners of the older building to make some alterations. At the turn of the century, typical Lower East Side housing consisted of five- to six-story buildings, each of which housed twenty families in three-room apartments, two in the front of the building and two in the rear.[74]

One reason for the resulting crowding was the fact that many needy immigrant families rented space to boarders, who were sometimes relatives needing temporary shelter but could also be strangers whose $3 would help pay the rent (which, at the start of the twentieth century, ranged between $10 and $20 a month). The boarders slept on the floor atop baled garments or on three chairs placed together and their presence made life difficult for the primary tenants. Discomforts, however, were overlooked because the money they contributed made it possible for a family of low-paid workers to manage on an average monthly salary of $36 a month.[75]

The crowding, of course, made it almost impossible to keep the tiny apartments clean and, as a result, rats, mice, and roaches abounded; thus many families kept a cat (never a dog, which would eat too much) to control the "wildlife." Another kind of problem for tenement dwellers on the Lower East Side involved crime, drunkeness, and prostitution because many of their buildings were also home to saloons and brothels, located in the basements. A different kind of business was conducted above ground in apartments that were used as workshops for making clothes.[76]

These homeworkers, in combination with those who took jobs in clothing factories, resulted in Jewish immigrant domination of the garment industry. Many of those who did not make clothes became door-to-door peddlers or rented a pushcart, creating the famous Orchard Street "Mall," a mecca for bargain hunters. Better off were those who brought artisanal skills: "Glaziers, jewelers, shoemakers and carpenters dotted the occupational landscape."[77]

Skilled or otherwise, Jewish workers, as well as Italians, were at the mercy of larger economic conditions, such as depressions, as well as intense competition for jobs. During the first three decades of eastern European Jewish settlement in New York, for workers and peddlers, wages were low and profits small. The irregularity of employment in the garment industry (crash seasons followed by slack times, combined with paltry wages—$6 to $10 a week for men, $3 to $5 for women), led to the formation of the Dress and Clothing Makers Union in 1883. After two spectacular strikes, by shirtwaistmakers in 1909 and machine operators in 1910, the International Ladies Garment Workers Union was formed and remained a powerful force in the garment industry. As their anthem, "Solidarity Forever," stated, the union made millions of garment workers a stronger force in the industry and the city.[78]

As would be expected, the union tried to improve the abysmal physical conditions in the factories, but it took a terrible tragedy to bring about municipal attention. On March 25, 1911, 147 young immigrant women died as a result of a fire which broke out on the eighth and ninth floors of a building on Washington Place. The deaths were the result of carelessness on the part of the owners and neglect by the municipality. As often happens, New York State "locked the barn door after the cows were stolen" by enacting a law in 1913 which greatly strengthened the safety requirements for garment factories.[79]

Many of the victims of the Triangle Shirtwaist Fire were little more than children. In 1911, over 29,000 of the factory workers in New York were under age sixteen, and their numbers were augmented by those who worked at home. All told, the latter group added no more than a dollar a week to the family income, but every cent counted when that income, due to the absence through death or desertion of a male breadwinner, was very small.[80]

It seems clear that the labor of immigrant women of all ethnic backgrounds was needed for family survival and, as a result, they worked as servants, laundresses, ragpickers, peddlers, and, most of all, in the needle trades. After 1900, however, the growth of corporate headquarters and banking and investment firms created a need for clerical workers. These positions were originally filled by the daughters of German and Irish immigrants who had received an eighth-grade education but by 1920, Jewish women filled 22 percent of the clerical positions in the city.[81] Italian women were slower to enter the city's offices, partly because, as we have seen, they did not remain in school long enough to learn the necessary skills but also because their traditional workplace continued to be the home. In southern Italy and Sicily, "they had knitted fringes and sewn military uniforms around their kitchen tables as well as doing agricultural labor."[82]

If they did work outside of the home in New York, they were most likely to be in the garment or garment-related trades; however, by 1920, there was less reason for married Italian women to be working at all because their husbands were bringing more money into the household. The men had become shopkeepers and skilled or semiskilled workers and had improved their position among the unskilled workers by building the New York City subway system, among other construction projects. The same phenomenon was even more pronounced for Jewish workers, who also strengthened their positions in the skilled trades and shopkeeping. As Stephen Steinberg has pointed out, Jews chose the latter occupation not only to make more money but, even more important, to be insulated from antisemitism. An independent businessmen, no matter on how small a scale, was a "balabuss vor selbst"—his own boss.[83]

One of the best measures of Italian and Jewish economic improvement was the movement of Italians to East Harlem and Jewish migration into Yorkville, East and West Harlem, the lower Bronx, and, following the construction of the Williamsburg and Manhattan Bridges and additional subway lines, across the East River to Williamsburg and Brownsville in Brooklyn.

The arrival of new ethnic groups affected the city's political life. Wherever they settled or resettled, the newcomers were the target of Tammany Hall, which had suffered a major blow in 1871 when exposure of its corrupt machinations and the imprisonment of Boss Tweed forced subsequent leaders—John Kelly, Richard Croker, and Charles Murphy— to find ways to maintain the machine under changed circumstances. One of the changes was ethnic: the presence of Italians and Jews, whose numbers grew as the former supporters of the organization, the Irish, began to leave Manhattan for greener pastures in the outer boroughs.[84]

An even greater problem for the Tammany sachems was the growth and strength of the Republican Party in New York, which, in 1902, managed to get one of the leading reformers in the city, Seth Low, elected as mayor. Rigid and pedantic, Low alienated enough working-class voters, naturalized immigrants, and native-born alike to permit Tammany to reclaim the mayor's office in the next election; however Tammany leaders had learned a lesson. Subsequent mayors elected with Tammany support, such as George McClellan, kept Tammany patronage to a minimum and as the twentieth century moved on, the machine became less important to New York politics.[85]

Tammany leaders tried to maintain their former position. They contributed to organized sports—baseball, boxing, and horse racing—because these activities were very popular with working-class New Yorkers. They also went to ethnic group celebrations and emulated Tweed by attending Jewish bar mitzvahs, Italian weddings and eating Irish corned beef. Struggling Italian parishes benefited from their largesse, as did the Hebrew Orphan Asylum. Of considerable importance, to keep up their image as the friend of the working man, they kept the 5¢ fare on the growing transportation system.[86]

When it seemed essential to win immigrant support at election time, they appointed Jewish and Italian district leaders, but the most famous leader of the Lower East Side was Big Tim Sullivan. He organized and paid for picnics on holidays and made sure that Tammany appointed judges who did not enforce the Sunday closing laws and thus allowed the Lower East Side pushcart trade to make up for business lost on

Saturday, the Jewish Sabbath. According to one commentator, "Sullivan ate corned beef and kosher meat with equal nonchalance and it was the same to him whether he took off his hat in church or pulled it down over his ears in the synagogue." [87]

The machine had been accustomed to using "market basket liberalism" to keep the Irish loyal and tried to extend it to the newer immigrants but it did not work as well, partly because of the ethnic emnity between the groups. The Irish were seen as antisemitic by the Jews, and the Italians competed with the Irish for unskilled jobs. Furthermore, when some Tammany members violated Sullivan's policy and asked for payoffs from the Jewish pushcart owners in order to do business on Sunday, they wasted whatever goodwill they had earned by sending Passover baskets to Jewish homes.

Italians presented less direct opposition to the machine, but their political power was also less important, limited by illiteracy, campanalismo, apathy, transience, and, most important, slow naturalization. The Jewish community was less transient and quicker to become citizens, but its members were, except for issues such as the Sunday closing, more inclined to vote Republican out of affection for Theodore Roosevelt, who was in the White House during the peak years of immigration. Furthermore, they wanted to emulate the German Jewish community, which had voted Republican from the time of Tweed into the next century.[88]

The outbreak of World War I in 1914 was a matter of interest and concern to New Yorkers because so many of them had relatives in the warring nations. The majority of citizens hoped for an Allied victory, and many participated in the anti-German hysteria which led to changing street names (DeKalb Avenue in Brooklyn, named after a German military man who had assisted the colonists during the Revolution, was now named Liberty Boulevard). Most, however, favored neutrality and wanted to limit U.S. participation to supplying the Allies, which, as had been true in earlier wars, meant good business for the city. After April 1917, when the United States became a participant, business was even better. New York factories made uniforms and repaired and outfitted the ships needed to carry munitions and other supplies across the Atlantic. The port became busier than it had been for many years.

Immigration, of course, was halted during the war; this caused a labor shortage, which, in turn, led to an increase in migration from the South as blacks moved north to profit from the wartime expansion of industry. Their success, however, was short-lived because soon after hostilities ended, European immigration became heavy again. After being bottled up for four years and seeing a bleak life ahead in their war-ravaged and unstable countries, Russian Jews, Italians, and Slavs poured into New York, enlarging existing communities and competing with blacks for jobs.[89]

The new immigrants were, in general, welcome, partly because their arrival meant family reunions with parents and siblings. Other New Yorkers, without ties to Europe, also viewed the new arrivals favorably because a generally successful relationship between the newcomers and the city had been developed during the years considered in this chapter. Eastern and southern European immigrants had been able to improve their lives in New York, and the city, without planning to do so, had been improved as a result of their presence.

NOTES

1. Moses Rischin, *The Promised City* (New York: Corinth Books, 1962), 5, 6; Thomas Kessner, *The Golden Door* (New York: Oxford University Press, 1977), 9.

2. Jennifer Dunning, "Browsing in the Phantom Empire," *New York Times* (November 5, 1976), B2.

3. Kessner, *Golden Door,* 9; George Lankevich with Howard Furer, *A Brief History of New York City* (Port Washington, N.Y.: Associated Universities Press, 1984), 180.

4. Rischin, *Promised City,* 6.

5. Lankevich, *Brief History,* 179; Eugene Moehring, *Public Works and the Patterns of Urban Real Estate Growth in Manhattan, 1835–1894* (New York: Arno Press, 1981), 26–37.

6. Rischin, *Promised City,* 8.

7. Albert Fein, "Centennial New York, 1876" in Milton M. Klein, ed., *New York: The Centennial Years, 1676–1976* (Port Washington, N.Y.: Kennikat Press, 1976), 75.

8. Moehring, *Public Works,* 41.

9. Ibid., 42.

10. *New York Times,* April 2, 1995, C2.

11. Peter Derrick, "Rapid Transit in New York: Its Development and Impact on the City," *New York Affairs* (May 1986), 3.

12. Robert Daley, *The World Beneath the City* (Philadelphia: Lippincott, 1959), 60; Derrick, "Rapid Transit," 7.

13. Fein, "Centennial New York," 84.

14. Derrick, "Rapid Transit," 15–16.

15. Ibid., 10–11, 20.

16. Ibid., 27.

17. Charles Lockwood, "Quintessential Housing of the Past: Tenements Built for the Poor," *New York Times,* April 8, 1995, Sec. 4, 3.

18. David McCulloch, *The Great Bridge* (New York: Simon & Schuster, 1972), 103.

19. Ibid., 104–105.

20. Ibid., 110.

21. Ibid.

22. Ibid., 116–117, 119.

23. Ibid., 128–135.

24. Lankevich, *Brief History,* 171.

25. McCulloch, *Bridge*, 24, 28; Lankevich, *Brief History*, 172.

26. Diane Ravitch, *The Great School Wars* (New York: Basic Books, 1974), 139, 147.

27. Selma Berrol, *Immigrants at School* (New York: Arno Press, 1978), 6.

28. Ibid., 143.

29. David Hammack, *Power and Society: Greater New York at the Turn of the Century* (New York: Russell Sage, 1982), 206.

30. Ibid., 197.

31. Ibid., 182–185.

32. Ibid., 203.

33. Lankevich, *Brief History*, 155, 195, 172.

34. Hammack, *Power*, 210–211.

35. Ibid., 133.

36. Ira Rosenwaike, *Population History of New York City* (Syracuse, N.Y.: Syracuse University Press, 1972), 72, 133.

37. Rosenwaike, *Population*, 95; U.S. Bureau of the Census, *Fourteenth Census of the United States, 1920* (Washington, D.C.: Government Printing Office), II, 98.

38. U.S. Department of Labor, Reports of the Commissioner General of Immigration, Appendix G, *Arrival of Immigrants at the Principal Ports of the United States, 1884–1919;* Rosenwaike, *Population*, 133.

39. Cities Census Commission, *Statistical Sources for Demographic Studies of Greater New York, 1920* (Washington, D.C.: Government Printing Office), xxiii, xxv; U.S. Bureau of the Census, *Statistical Abstract of the United States: Foreign Born and Foreign Stock in New York City, 1910* (Washington, D.C.: Government Printing Office), 55.

40. Rosenwaike, *Population*, 77.

41. Ibid.

42. Gilbert Osofsky, *Harlem: The Making of a Ghetto* (New York: Harper & Row, 1965), 4–5.

43. Henry Gutman, *Black Family in Slavery and Freedom* (New York: Vintage Press, 1976), 119; Osofsky, *Ghetto*, 133, 146.

44. Osofsky, *Ghetto*, 83.

45. Jeffrey Gurock, *When Harlem Was Jewish* (New York: Columbia University Press, 1979), 14.

46. Ibid., 36.

47. Rosenwaike, *Population*, 78; H. S. Tsai, *Chinese Experience in America* (Bloomington: Indiana University Press, 1986), 64.

48. Jacob Riis, *How the Other Half Lives* (New York: Hill & Wang, 1957), 69.

49. Paul Siu, *The Chinese Laundryman* (New York: New York University Press, 1987), 135.

50. Riis, *Other Half*, 43, 47.

51. Antonio Mangano, "The Italian Colonies of New York City," M.A. thesis, Columbia University, 1903, 7, 38, 42.

52. John Duffy, *History of Public Health in New York City* (New York: Russell Sage, 1968–1974), vol. 2, 515.

53. Allen Kraut, *The Huddled Masses: Immigrants in American Society* (Arlington, Ill.: Harlan Davidson, 1982), 109–110.

54. Antonio Stella, "Effects of Urban Congestion on Italians in New York City," paper delivered at the Conference on Congestion of Population held at the Museum of Natural History, New York City, March 10, 1908, 12, 14.

55. Kraut, *Huddled Masses,* 110–111, 126.

56. Humbert S. Nelli, "The Italian Padrone System in the United States," *Labor History,* V (Spring 1964), 153–167.

57. Robert Orsi, *Madonna of 115th Street* (New Haven, Conn.: Yale University Press, 1985), 14.

58. Francisco Cordasco and Eugene Bucchioni, *The Italians: Social Background of an American Group* (Clifton, N.J.: Augustus Kelly, 1974), 26.

59. Joseph Lopereato, *Italians in America* (New York: Random House, 1970), 27, 33.

60. Mangano, *Italian Colonies,* 42; Kessner, *Golden Door,* 52–53.

61. Thomas Kessner and Betty Boyd Caroli, "New Immigrant Women at Work: Italians and Jews in New York City, 1880–1905," *Journal of Ethnic Studies* (Winter 1978), 19–32.

62. Richard Gambino, *Blood of My Blood: Dilemma of Italian Americans* (Garden City, N.Y.: Doubleday, 1974), 32.

63. Richard Varbero, "Philadelphia's South Italians in the 1920's," in Allen Davis, ed., *The Peoples of Philadelphia* (Philadelphia: Temple University Press, 1943), 255–274.

64. Miriam Cohen, "Changing Economic Strategies among Immigrant Generations: Italians in Comparative Perspective," *Journal of Social History,* 15 (Spring 1982), 446–448.

65. Berrol, *Immigrants,* 149, 153, 176.

66. Selma Berrol, "Education and Upward Mobility," *American Jewish Historical Quarterly,* LXV (March 1976), 3, 260–261, 263.

67. Ibid., 260–261, 263.

68. Berrol, *Immigrants,* 146.

69. Rischin, *Promised City,* 20, 23–24, 31.

70. Richard H. Rowland, "Geographical Patterns of the Jewish Population in the Pale of Settlement of Late Nineteenth Century Russia," *Jewish Social Studies* (Summer/Fall 1986), 207–234.

71. Arcadius Kahan, "Economic Opportunities and Some Pilgrim's Progress: Jewish Immigrants from Eastern Europe in the United States, 1890–1914," *Journal of Economic History,* 38 (March 1978), 236–237.

72. Simon Kuznets, "Immigration of Russian Jews to the United States: Background," *Perspectives in American History,* 9, 78.

73. Stephen Steinberg, *The Ethnic Myth* (New York: Atheneum, 1981), 84; Caroline Golab, "Impact of the Industrial Experience on the Immigrant Family," in Richard Erlich, ed., *Immigrants in Industrial America, 1880–1920* (Charlottesville: University of North Carolina Press, 1977), 16.

74. "Tenement Times," Lower East Side Tenement Museum, January 1993, 1–2.

75. Louise More, *Wage Earners' Budgets: A Study of Standards and Cost of Living in New York City* (New York: Henry Holt, 1907), 124, 130.

76. "Tenement Times," 3.

77. Kessner, *Golden Door*, 61.

78. New York Times, *Out of the Sweatshop: Struggle for Industrial Democracy* (New York: Quadrangle, 1977), 33.

79. "Big Apple Newsletter" (Typescript), June 1982, 3.

80. Jeremy Felt, *Hostages of Fortune* (Syracuse, N.Y.: Syracuse University Press, 1965), 40–41.

81. Kathy Peiss, *Cheap Amusements* (Philadelphia: Temple University Press, 1986), 141; Sharon Strom, *Beyond the Typewriter* (Urbana: University of Illinois Press, 1992), 273–275.

82. Kessner and Caroli, "New Immigrant Women," 20.

83. Miriam Cohen, "From Workshop to Office," Ph.D. dissertation, University of Michigan, 1978, 71; Kessner, *Golden Door*, 113; Steinberg, *Myths*, 78, 80; United States Congress, Senate, Immigration Commission, *Abstract of the Report on the Occupations of First and Second Generations of Immigrants in the United States*, 1911, 57; Berrol, "Education and Mobility," 264.

84. Lankevich, *Brief History*, 198–203.

85. Ibid., 205–206.

86. William Henderson, *Tammany Hall and the New Immigrants* (New York: Arno Press, 1976), 115.

87. William Riordan, *Plunkitt of Tammany Hall* (Boston: Bedford Books of St. Martin's Press, 1994), 39.

88. Henderson, *Tammany and Immigrants*, 48–49, 127.

89. U.S. Immigration Commission, *Abstract of the Statistical Review of Immigration to the U.S.* (Washington, D.C.: Government Printing Office, 1931), 8–9.

4

Boom Times, Bad Times: New York and Its People, 1920–1945

During the three decades that separated World War I from World War II, the United States went from boom to bust, from isolation to war, and the volume of immigration went from a flood to a trickle. All of this, of course, had a great impact on New York City. In one instance—activity on the stock market—New York was the site of both the speculative boom and the collapse that followed. Because it was also the nation's largest immigrant receiving city, drastic restriction of immigration in the 1920s affected all aspects of New York life. Although many people wanted to isolate themselves from events in Europe, the rise of Franco, Mussolini, and Hitler had repercussions on all ethnic groups in New York City, leading to increased bigotry and conflict.

Even earlier, in 1917, when tensions connected to U.S. participation in World War I led to an increase in nativism, the first step to limit the number of European immigrants allowed to enter the United States was the passage of a literacy act. (Asians had been almost completely barred in 1882.) New arrivals were taken to the Immigration Center erected on Ellis Island in New York Bay in 1891, to be screened for contagious illness or obvious inability to support themselves. There they were tested to see if they could read and write in any language, including Yiddish or Hebrew. The Act did little to reduce immigration, which, due to the war in Europe, had already decreased. Furthermore, as Roger Daniels points out, "rising standards of literacy in Europe had vitiated the impact of the law, which, if it had been passed in the Nineties or earlier, would have had more effect."[1]

Partly as a result of its limited impact, but even more the result of a dramatic increase in anti-immigrant feeling that followed World War I, Congress enacted a much stronger law, the National Origins Act, which remained the basis of American immigration policy until 1965. Even earlier, the House of Representatives had agreed to a suspension of all immigration for a year. The Senate, however, had reacted to "frenzied protests" from employer groups, fearing a labor shortage when there was a great need for labor. Responding to this, the Senate ignored the proposed bill. Not for the first time, nor the last, when more hands were needed, immigrants were welcome.[2]

Restrictionists continued to press for a law that would keep out most of the millions, it was assumed, who wanted to leave postwar Europe and its problems. As a result, first in 1921 and more drastically in 1924, the United States adopted a quota system, limiting total immigration and basing the number who could enter on the percent of people of a given national origin who were part of the American population in 1890. The choice of date was of considerable significance to New York because in 1890, the number of people from southern and eastern Europe was much smaller than it would have been if the base had been 1920. In spite of the opposition of the New York Congressional delegation (which included Congressmen Fiorello LaGuardia and Emanuel Celler), the law passed. As a result, the quota for Sicilians and Polish Jews, to use just two examples, was much smaller than it would have been if a later date had been used for the base.[3]

When the counting necessitated by the new law was completed, the figures revealed that in New York City "the German element was larger than in any German city other than Berlin [and] there were nearly twice as many Irish as there were in Dublin, about as many Jews as in Warsaw and more Italians than in Venice or Naples." The 1924 Act, however, prevented many others from leaving the economic hardships and political persecution that made life in Europe so difficult in the 1930s. If immigration had not been restricted, millions who became victims of totalitarianism could have found refuge in America, especially in the city that was most attractive to immigrants, New York.[4]

The National Origins Act was effective. "Of the 35.9 million immigrants who came to the United States between 1820 and 1975, 32 million came before 1927 when the act was fully implemented." As demonstrated by the arrival of 600,000 just before the door was shut, more people would have come to New York if the door had been left open. But since the quota for Italy was less than 6,000 a year and even smaller for Russia and Poland, home to most of those Jews who wanted to leave, "the major sources of immigrants during the previous thirty years were . . . virtually closed off." At the point that the National Origins Act went into effect, 73 percent of New York City's population was foreign born or of foreign stock. The two largest groups were 1.75 million Jews and over a million Italians. Together they constituted 40 percent of the total population of almost 7 million.[5]

It is difficult to predict what the makeup of the population of New York would have been if immigration had not been restricted. The Depression would surely have made New York less attractive. Furthermore, it was difficult to leave fascist Italy and Communist Russia, and the outbreak of World War II made it impossible for people to emigrate. Until 1939, when the war began, German Jews were free to leave since the Führer wanted to make the Third Reich *Judenfrei* (free of Jews) and because Americans of German stock made up so large a proportion of the population that the German quota was large. As a result, enough German Jewish refugees came to New York to establish colonies in Washington Heights and the West Side of Manhattan. Jews living in the countries occupied by Hitler's armies, however, were barred by American immigration laws; the Czech quota, for example, was very small.

In the years following World War I, New York superseded London as the financial center of the world. Money flowed into Wall Street for investment in stocks and bonds, and the city was home to the managers of 70 percent of the corporations listed in the *Standard and Poor* statistics. Continuing the entrepôt pattern first established in the seventeenth century, New York exported clothing, jewelry, furs, perfumes, tea, and coffee and sold them to the rest of the nation and to many parts of the world. As a result, "all types of agents, brokers, jobbers, buyers, assemblers and warehousemen were employed in more than 24,000 wholesale establishments," serving customers from outside the city. Since these men needed to be fed, housed, and amused, restaurants, hotels, and theaters enjoyed a flourishing business. By 1929, for example, the city's hotels "had 42,000 employees [and took in] 165 million dollars a year."[6]

Manufacturers continued to turn out clothing, machine and foundry products, processed foods, printed materials, and chemicals; but, beginning in the 1920s, this portion of New York's economy underwent a relative decline. Many factories moved to nearby areas, where rents were lower. Wherever they relocated, however, they found that labor costs were higher than in the past, partly because of increased unionization but also because immigration restriction, beginning in 1921, reduced the supply of cheap labor.

The smaller number of unskilled immigrants who came to New York in the 1920s found fewer factory jobs awaiting them but, until the onset of the Depression, they were rarely unemployed. As we shall see, the physical landscape of the city was enormously changed between the two world wars, and it was the availability of unskilled immigrant labor that helped to make this possible.

As a result, the loss of some manufacturing plants was not a serious blow to the city but does, once more, illustrate the symbiotic nature of European immigration to New York. When fewer unskilled workers were available to work for low wages, some factories moved away, but the need for laborers in other areas of the economy kept new arrivals employed.

There were also other adjustments. As we have seen, the port of New York had been of the greatest importance to the life of the city, but by 1920, it could no longer cope with the demands of trade. Railroad yards and pier facilities were grossly overcrowded, leading the states of New York and New Jersey, in 1921, to create an administrative body called the Port of New York Authority to make improvements that neither state could make alone. The Authority was "charged with developing the terminals, transportation and other facilities within the port district, a territory extending roughly twenty miles in all directions from the Statue of Liberty." It was supported by bond sales and tolls from the Holland Tunnel and the George Washington Bridge, when they became operational. Because of the Port Authority, until the Depression, New York was able to continue its healthy trade with European, South American, and domestic ports.[7]

Further links between New York and New Jersey were forged later in the 1920s under the direction of Othmann Ammann, the chief engineer for bridges in New York. He was also the top operations officer for the Port Authority and its "copy cat" organization, the Triboro Bridge Authority, which was organized in 1933. The latter organization was responsible for both the magnificent bridge, completed in 1937, that connects the Bronx, Queens, and Manhattan and the Bronx Whitestone Bridge, another link between the Bronx and Queens, which opened in 1939. Adding to the bridge connections were the Holland and Lincoln Tunnels, completed in 1927 and 1937, respectively, and the Queens Midtown Tunnel, which in 1940 established an additional link between the boroughs.[8]

Air transportation was not of great importance in New York in the 1920s, but by the end of the next decade, North Beach airport (renamed LaGuardia for the man who was largely responsible for its creation) was opened. Nine years later, a much larger international airport began operations on Jamaica Bay. The building of bridges, tunnels, and airports required further construction, such as access roads, which helped fill another need of New York: easier movement of people and vehicles within the city.[9]

Traffic congestion in New York was nothing new but had been worsened by the use of half a million automobiles, which competed with street cars, elevated trains, and 29,000 horse-drawn vehicles (some of which, until 1929, were used for mail deliveries). Absence of parking regulations and insufficient stop lights made matters worse. The heaviest traffic was on north-south avenues because of people's desire to live in the northern part of Manhattan Island while continuing to work in the southerly districts. "In 1926, an estimated 859,600 people commuted daily to areas of Manhattan below 58th Street from the Bronx or Upper Manhattan." The subways built earlier carried most of the commuters, but the fact that in 1925, 2.3 million people lived and worked in Manhattan, led to surface congestion severe enough to "reduce the city's competitive advantage." [10]

Several partial solutions, such as one-way streets, were helpful, but the strangulation of commerce continued. So did the proposed solutions, one of which was building limited access highways on the east and west sides of the island. The Regional Plan Association suggested various ways to do this, and by 1928 the Board of Estimate had approved an elevated highway for the West Side. Plans for the East Side ran into more opposition from property owners and residents of some of the areas involved with what was to be a highway running from South Street to 125th Street, parallel to the East River. Because it was so difficult to get agreement among the various interests involved with such a large undertaking, the East River Drive, as it was called, was built in pieces. Construction of the first portion, leading to the Triboro Bridge, was begun in 1934.[11]

This represented a change from earlier plans, which had been to begin the highway on the Lower East Side. Robert Moses, the most important urban planner of his era, was responsible for the new decision. Moses—the Yale, Oxford, and Columbia University educated scion of a wealthy New York Jewish family—left a greater mark on New York City and its environs than any previous or subsequent administrator. Beginning as a staff member on the New York State Reconstruction Commission, which had been established by Governor Alfred E. Smith to make changes in New York State government, Moses went on to become president of the Long Island State Park Commission and began a forty-year career during which, according to his biographer, Robert Caro, "he reshaped New York." [12]

The reach of projects Moses was involved in was enormous. He wore many hats: New York City and New York State Parks Commissioner, Construction Coordinator, member of the City Planning Commission, Chairman of the Emergency Public Works Commission when the Depression struck, the strongest member of the Triboro Bridge Authority, and the "sole member of the Henry Hudson and Marine Parkway Authority." Thanks to the design talents of his chief architect and federal money available to reduce joblessness, New York was enriched with playgrounds (their number quadrupled by 1942), twenty swimming pools (indoor and out), more usable beaches, and a parkway system extending into eastern Long Island at one end and Westchester County on the other. Moses was also responsible for a less permanent event, the 1939 World's Fair.[13]

In view of all this, Moses should be considered one of the great heroes of New York history, but an authoritarian and manipulative personality tarnished his image. As detailed in Caro's book, Moses rode roughshod over opponents who decried the destruction of neighborhoods to build parkways (the Cross Bronx Expressway is a well-known example). When criticized, he adopted a statement attributed to Italian dictator Benito Mussolini: it was not possible to make an omelette without breaking some eggs.[14]

Powerful as he was, there were some aspects of physical growth in the city which Moses did not control. The subway system, which was inaugurated in 1904, for example, continued to expand into Brooklyn, the Bronx, and Queens. In November 1939, the existing privately owned lines, the Brooklyn-Manhattan Transit (BMT) and the Interboro Rapid Transit (IRT), were joined to the newly built Independent lines to create a unified underground and elevated transit system. As Charles Garrett says in his book, *The LaGuardia Years*, "unification did not usher in a transit millenium," but it did lead to several improvements because it enabled the city to gradually remove the els. As a result, property values on the liberated avenues rose, as did the flow of traffic. Furthermore, the BMT and IRT Companies were bankrupt and, as a result, the systems they operated had deteriorated. Some of the worst deficiencies were corrected by the city; overall, unification presented New York with more advantages than disadvantages.[15]

This could be also be said, more strongly, of another change in the physical landscape of Manhattan during the 1920s and 1930s. Under the aegis of the enormously wealthy Rockefeller family, a collection of limestone-sheathed skyscrapers (called Rockefeller Center) were erected between Fifth and Sixth Avenues, encompassing the area of Forty-eighth to Fifty-first Streets. Among other advantages Rockefeller Center brought to the city, it hastened the demolition of the Sixth Avenue el and created an elegant and useful "city within a city" in midtown Manhattan. Most of the tall buildings were occupied by corporate offices, but the Center also included an elegant and imposing theater, the Radio City Music Hall, which offered movies and a high-quality stage show that became a great favorite with tourists and residents alike. According to the *Historical Atlas of New York*, the Center is "regarded as the finest urban complex in the United States."[16]

Skyscrapers, of course, were not a new phenomenon in New York. One of the first, the forty-seven-story Singer Building, was begun in 1905 and "launched a thirty year period in which great companies commissioned architects to design taller and taller buildings," culminating in the one hundred and two-story Empire State Building in 1931. The adaptation of the steel girder made skyscrapers possible, and it was their appeal to service rather than manufacturing companies that led to their construction in New York. The financial and insurance companies that proliferated in Manhattan required above-street-level office space with good windows, elevators, and electric power. Unlike manufacturing firms, their floors did not need to bear the weight of heavy machinery. As a result, "Manhattan could be home to thirty, fifty or even higher story buildings and still accomodate the spatial needs of hundreds of service sector companies on relatively small plots of land." [17]

More mundane building also took place in the period discussed in this chapter. Before 1933, the city's sewage emptied directly into the Hudson and East Rivers, leading to contamination of beaches, especially Coney Island. Using federal funds allotted by the Public Works Administration (PWA), the city erected a sewage treatment plant at the much used Brooklyn resort and followed this with six more plants in various parts of the city, putting about 46 percent of municipal sewage under treatment. Along the same lines, new incinerators were built and landfill operations increased, ending the dumping of garbage and rubbish in the Atlantic Ocean, from which it had washed up on the Jersey shore.

Some of the garbage came from the pushcarts that dotted the city. Their low prices enabled poor families to make ends meet, but they snarled traffic and created sanitation problems. To remedy the situation, nine enclosed municipal markets were built by 1945, lessening traffic problems and ensuring the distribution of cleaner food. A different kind of waterfront improvement resulted from the construction of new docks; fourteen new piers were built between 1934 and 1942, three on the Hudson River to accomodate super liners such as the *Normandie* and *Queen Mary*.[18]

All of these physical changes were important to the residents of New York City, but housing was basic to everything else. It was especially important to the over 2 million people who had been born abroad, many of whom entered the United States in the two decades before the barriers went up. First of all, building the row houses, tenements, and apartment houses provided work for the thousands of newcomers who knew the construction trades. Furthermore, the availability of newer housing made it possible for established New Yorkers to improve their living quarters, leaving older and cheaper dwellings to the new arrivals. The construction boom resulted in another welcome development: Competition between the builders of public works or office buildings and the developers of residential housing kept wages high for thousands of workers, skilled and unskilled.

The prosperity of the 1920s led to the construction of over 650,000 apartments and row houses, the former mostly in Manhattan and the Bronx and the latter in Brooklyn, Queens, and Richmond. The boom in new housing, however, did not empty the "dumbell" and "railroad" apartments in the "old law" tenements of lower Manhattan until the effects of immigration restriction reduced the number of newcomers who needed cheap apartments. When that happened, sections of the city, particularly the Lower East Side, became much less congested. By 1925, the density had decreased by half: 500 persons per acre, compared to 1,000 in 1918.[19]

A continued bull market for new housing, stimulated in part by the simultaneous bull market on the Stock Exchange, led to the construction of limited dividend apartment housing based on state and municipal tax remissions. Several were begun in 1926. One of the first, the Knickerbocker Houses in lower Manhattan, was completed in 1934. The rents were not low enough for manual workers, however, and as a result, only a few such developments were built at that time. Instead, in the 1930s, the city (using federal funds) began a program of slum clearance and building of low-rent housing projects under the auspices of the Municipal Housing Authority. "First Houses," located, as one would expect, on the Lower East Side, was opened in 1936; by 1944, thirteen projects had been completed and many low-income families had moved into spare but infinitely better living quarters.[20]

At that point, still another kind of project, this time for the middle class, was about to come on the market. When interest rates on its other investments declined, the Metropolitan Life Insurance Company decided to put its money into a development called Parkchester, a series of apartment buildings in the Bronx, "covering 129 acres and housing 40,000 people," which opened in 1940. Somewhat later, the company purchased and demolished eighteen blocks of depressed housing on the East Side between Fourteenth and Twentieth Streets and built several thirteen-story apartment houses, known as Stuyvesant Town. Still another version of sponsored housing was the Amalgamated Houses, a large cooperative development in the Bronx, backed by the Amalgamated Clothing Workers Union, which opened in 1927. Familiarly called the "Coops," it was home to Jewish garment workers and their families and, among other things, was known for the many varieties of "Reds," ranging from socialists to anarchists, who lived there.[21]

Communists, living the "Coops" or elsewhere, were not an important element in New York City politics. In the 1920s, the heavily Irish Tammany organization controlled City Hall and was able to keep first John Hylan and then Jimmy Walker in the mayor's seat from 1918 to 1932. Tammany also dominated the Board of Estimates, which in 1926 consisted of "six Irish Catholics, a German and a Jew." At that point, Jimmy Walker, "dapper and wisecracking," began his first term as mayor. Governing New York in the mid-1920s was relatively simple. City Hall was less important and had fewer responsibilities because "Boss" Platt, after finding that unification had not strengthened his Republican Party, used his power in the State Legislature to return many municipal functions to the boroughs, "some of which [his party] could hope to rule."[22]

It was a fortunate arrangement for the city because Jimmy Walker treated the mayoralty as a part-time job. This was not for lack of ability; reliable sources indicate that he was quick-witted and decisive when he wanted to be, but most of the time he preferred to be a playboy. During his administration, Irish appointees dominated city jobs, from department heads to clerkships, and were also in the majority in the Police and Fire Departments. Partly for these reasons, Walker was elected and reelected, defeating Fiorello LaGuardia in 1929.

He did not, however, complete his second term. In 1939, Governor Franklin D. Roosevelt appointed Judge Samuel Seabury to head a commission whose assignment was to investigate rumors of corruption in the city government. Two years later, Seabury and his commission members were able to expose extensive malfeasance by the mayor and his associates. Faced with prosecution and jail, in September 1932 Walker resigned. Joseph McKee, the president of the Board of Aldermen, took over until November, when Tammany's choice, John J. O'Brien, was elected to complete the remaining portion of Walker's second term. O'Brien's caliber was made clear by his response to the question "Who will be your police commissioner?" "I don't know, they [Tammany leaders] haven't told me yet!"[23]

The stock market had crashed on Walker's watch, but the full impact of the Depression struck when O'Brien occupied City Hall. At that point the mayor was forced to sign the so-called Banker's Agreement, under which the clearinghouse banks agreed "to finance part of the city's operating expenses through 1937 and the city . . . accepted certain limitations on its financial powers." The Agreement staved off immediate bankruptcy but did little to improve conditions for the people of the city. In 1934, 232,000 New Yorkers were unemployed and 16 percent of the population was dependent on relief. The budget was unbalanced by more than $30 million, and the city, due to a low credit rating, was unable to market its long-term securities and was "barred from Federal loans and grants, which forced work to stop on several long term improvements, including the Queens Midtown Tunnel."[24]

It would seem that no one but a magician could cope with such a disaster, but such a man was elected to occupy City Hall in November 1933 and remained there for twelve years, during which the city not only survived the Depression and war but was also greatly changed, mostly for the better. Fiorello LaGuardia, who was the son of a Jewish Mother and Italian father and known as the "little flower" with a loud voice, released New York from the bondage of Tammany Hall, alleviated the suffering brought about by unemployment, and brought about the entry of two ethnic groups, Italians and Jews, into the political life of the city.

According to Charles Garrett, the author of one of several excellent works on LaGuardia and his era, this latter change occurred when he was able to establish "a broad public welfare program [which] loosened the machine's hold on immigrant blocs." He did this with the help of Franklin Roosevelt's New Deal and Governor Herbert Lehman's equally liberal state government. In many ways, the "Tinkers to Evers to Chance" alliance between Washington, Albany, and New York in the 1930s provided the Empire City with the very best government it has ever had.[25]

In addition to protests from the Irish, who were almost totally displaced from power in these years, LaGuardia did not govern without criticism. Some of his support came from the American Labor Party (ALP), a left-wing political group consisting of a variety of radicals; the Amalgamated Clothing Workers; the Transport Workers Union; and the International Longshoremen's Association. The ALP was the object of hostility from conservative New Yorkers, especially the Catholic Church. In addition, one of LaGuardia's closest advisors, Vito Marcantonio (nicknamed "Marc"), was a well-known leftist and this, too, gave the mayor's image a pinkish hue.[26]

In reality, however, LaGuardia was basically a talented politician who used ideas and experiences acquired in campaigns dating back to the 1920s, when he was president of the Board of Aldermen and later congressman from East Harlem, to initiate needed programs and policies as well as to appoint gifted and honest men and women to municipal positions. Although he asked Marc to manage his Congressional campaigns and designated him as his political heir, LaGuardia was more liberal than radical. The basis for both men's strength was ethnic preference on the part of the Italians of East Harlem, which in 1930 "contained the largest Italian population in the nation."[27]

Several commentators have seen the LaGuardia years as a political coming of age for the children of the Italians and Jews who had populated the Empire City at the turn of the century. Many more entered city government than was the case when Tammany was in power. Always cognizant of ethnic sensibilities and aware of the need for their votes, LaGuardia spared no effort to mold and hold an Italian-Jewish constituency. One well-known incident demonstrates this point. During a tight Congressional election campaign against a Jewish opponent, Henry Frank, LaGuardia challenged Frank to a debate "entirely in the Yiddish language," which he had learned as a clerk in the consular service years earlier. He knew that Frank did not speak the language and, just as he had hoped, the "debate" turned into a one-man show, during which LaGuardia made a speech in "quite passable Yiddish."[28]

At the same time, although he was a Protestant, LaGuardia often emphasized his roots in the Roman Catholic Church. One of the reasons he did this was to reassure Italian voters who were somewhat alienated by his strong attacks on Benito Mussolini. With the same purpose in mind, he appointed Italians to city jobs, albeit at low levels, and appeared at their social functions. As a result, in 1937, 64 percent of Italian-American New Yorkers voted for him. In general, he was superbly attuned to ethnic interests. His most recent biographer, Tom Kessner, has said that "if New York had a solid group of Chinese Mohammedans, LaGuardia would doubtless have discovered strong ties to them."[29]

Although those who knew him well report that the "little flower" had a fierce temper, it is his image as a warm and cheerful leader that has remained, partly due to his reading of the comics, with appropriate flourishes, during a newspaper strike. This was a Sunday afternoon activity much appreciated by the children of the city and their voting elders.

LaGuardia was also responsible for more permanent changes and deserves credit for many physical improvements in New York City as well as for rebuilding municipal politics. Elected on a Fusion ticket, and therefore not obligated to either the Republicans or the Democrats, he was able to say that there was "no Democratic or Republican way to clean the streets." In this area as well as others, he brought nonpartisan and honest government to a city that had known neither for many decades.[30]

LaGuardia's first task was to deal with the wreckage of city finances, and to this end, as soon as he took office in January 1934, he sent the State Legislature a bill that would enable him to balance the budget by eliminating various city offices, dismiss municipal employees, and require an annual one-month payless furlough for those still employed, now on lower salaries. After a difficult battle with the civil service unions and many legislators, he got most of what he wanted and was able to cut the budget by more than $11 million.[31]

This achievement, in addition to the imposition of new taxes on businesses, brought the 1934 municipal budget into balance and enabled the city to market its bonds. Also, with a balanced budget, the city could now ask for and receive federal help to complete several capital projects abandoned when the crisis began. With money received from the Public Works Administration (PWA), for example, men were hired to complete the Independent subway system and the Queens Midtown Tunnel; this somewhat reducing the unemployment statistics and improved transportation. LaGuardia's severest critics were the owners of real estate because taxes on their properties were increased to build capital projects, such as schools, hospitals, health centers, playgrounds, and sewage disposal plants. Increased taxation also led a number of manufacturers to leave New York, but LaGuardia believed that improvements in the infrastructure were of greater long-term value to the people of the city than lower taxes on real estate and businesses.[32]

Prior to LaGuardia's arrival in City Hall, evidence of the hardships that came with the stock market crash and the ensuing Depression could be found in the "Hoovervilles" (shanty towns) erected by the homeless in the parks and vacant lots of the city. This was also apparent in the "long lines of unemployed men and women who waited for handouts at soup kitchens, while apple sellers" stood nearby. Welfare rolls rose higher and higher, approaching 900,000 in 1932. A Depression-era song entitled "Brother, Can You Spare a Dime?" demonstrated the need for charity in a city in which as many as one-fourth of the workers, especially in the construction trades, were unemployed. White-collar workers were not spared but, in general, were more likely to keep their jobs, albeit at lower salaries.[33]

An interesting byproduct of this was the rise in the number of children remaining in school longer, hoping to become eligible for office jobs upon graduation. As a result, and because they could not find work if they dropped out, the number of students attending high school increased by 45 percent between 1930 and 1935. If jobs had been available, fewer might have stayed to graduate because their parents, in many cases, were having a very hard time avoiding eviction for nonpayment of rent, enduring cold and darkness when electricity and gas were turned off because payments were long overdue, and suffering the embarassment of accepting free meals from the Salvation Army or other charitable organizations.

Few New Yorkers escaped entirely, but some, because of the nature of what they made or sold, felt relatively little impact. Paint store proprietors, for example, held their own because unemployed householders took the opportunity to improve their dwellings. Similarly, auto repair shops kept their heads above water because, unable to afford a new car, owners scraped up enough money to keep an old one running. The tides of unemployment rose and fell in the 1930s, eased by New Deal measures, but jobs did not return in pre-Depression numbers until World War II broke out in 1939.[34]

Chinese New Yorkers were only a tiny proportion of the total New York City population (12,753 in 1930) because the absence of women had prevented natural increase. Small or not, the Chinese community also felt the impact of the Depression. Unemployed Caucasian New Yorkers did their own laundry and cooked at home. As a result of the loss of customers, in 1934, 30 percent of Chinese workers in Manhattan were without an income. Most managed to survive with aid from their savings and loan associations and by sharing jobs, thus shunning relief money from the city.[35]

The Chinese lived apart from Caucasian New Yorkers, and other ethnic groups were also quite separatist. As was true in the early days of New York, every ethnic nationality created boundaries. Ethnic groups, large and small, had carved out niches in Manhattan and Brooklyn. In Brooklyn, Williamsburg (just across the river from the Lower East Side) was heavily Russian and Polish Jewish; nearby Greenpoint was mostly Polish and Italian. Bay Ridge housed the relatively small number of Norwegians; and many of the Irish, who continued to emigrate to the United States, peopled Flatbush and Crown Heights. They also lived in the Bronx, where enough well-to-do Irish families had settled along Alexander Avenue to allow the street to be called "the Irish Fifth Avenue." Working-class Irish tended to settle in areas they knew because of their jobs as railway, subway, or bridge builders. This led the Inwood section north of Washington Heights in Manhattan, Woodlawn in the Bronx, and Woodside in Queens to become Irish settlements.[36]

Neighborhoods were constantly changing as new buildings attracted those who could afford better housing, but ethnic concentration remained a constant. The Lower East Side lost its Jewish population all through the 1920s and 1930s, but its former inhabitants reconstituted similar Jewish neighborhoods elsewhere in Manhattan and in the Bronx and Brooklyn. Income and occupation usually determined location. Williamsburg, for example, was home to families only slightly better off than those who remained on the Lower East Side; this was also true for the South Bronx. Jews who had reached middle-class status, however, chose the West Bronx (especially an apartment on the Grand Concourse) because husbands could easily reach their places of business via the elevated portion of the East Side IRT or the underground Independent line.

Higher-income Jews chose the west side of Manhattan, and by 1930, they comprised a third of the population living between Seventy-ninth Street and 110th Street from Broadway to the Hudson River. Real estate tax abatements, the pressure of black Harlem on Jewish Harlem, the existence of a subway link to their work place, the garment center at Seventh Avenue and Thirty-fifth Street, and the substantial income of many East European Jewish entrepreneurs prior to the Depression created the Jewish West Side.[37]

Some of the German Jewish refugees from Nazism who arrived in the 1930s also settled on the West Side, but more congregated in Washington Heights. To a greater extent than other groups, Jews seemed to prefer apartment living to home ownership, living in tenement walkups when that was all they could afford or in the elegant apartment houses on the West Side or along the Grand Concourse in the Bronx when their income rose. Some authorities have said that due to their past experiences, Jews wanted to move quickly if antisemitism made it necessary.

Although their fears had a basis in reality, such worries did not keep

Jewish New Yorkers from earning a livable wage and achieving considerable upward mobility. The results of a study made by the Welfare Council in 1935 indicated that the largest number of Russian-born Jews (31 percent) were proprietors, managers, or officials. Semiskilled workers came next, at 29.8 percent, and skilled workers constituted 23.1 percent. Only 3.8 percent were professionals, but an even smaller group were engaged in unskilled or service occupations. Their sons and daughters were doing even better. The same survey indicated that 56 percent of employed Jewish youths aged sixteen to twenty-four were in proprietary and management work, 43 percent were in clerical and sales occupations, and 37 percent were in the professions. Some (24 percent) were working at skilled and semiskilled trades and 5 percent were in service occupations, but the large proportion who were wearing white collars was clear proof that their parents or grandparents had been wise to settle in New York.[38]

This does not, however, mean that all New York City Jews came through the Depression unscathed. A different study done by the Committee on Economic Adjustment of the American Jewish Congress, three years later, supported the earlier data but also revealed that 13.5 percent of Jews able to work were unemployed. Also, many proprietors were merely the owners of small "Mom and Pop" stores whose customers faded away as unemployment spread; many a lawyer became a civil service clerk when clients did not appear.

Even the owners of some of the thousands of garment factories had to close shop when demand for clothing diminished. As was true for all ethnic groups, Jews during the Depression were forced to change career goals, and many chose to become teachers instead of one of the more prestigious professions. This had a wondrous effect on public education in New York as increasingly more of the best and brightest young Jews, male and female, took the rigorous examination given by the Board of Education, passed muster, and were placed on the list that emerged, waited their turn, and finally became licensed, tenured professionals.[39]

As Diane Ravitch has said in *The Great School Wars*, the New York City public schools were often a "battleground for social change," demonstrated in this case by the efforts of the Irish examiners to keep Jews out of the system. The written examination posed few difficulties for Jewish candidates, but the oral test and, to a lesser extent, the classroom performances and interview portions were hurdles that many could not overcome. The aspiring teachers were, in most cases, the children of immigrants who were accustomed to hearing and often speaking Yiddish, which made it easy for hostile examiners to find evidence of "foreignisms" and heavy d's and t's and decide that the Jewish man or woman before them was not fit to be a teacher.

The practice of eliminating Jewish candidates on these grounds was well known and led the municipal colleges to test students who wanted to enter the education program and exclude those whose speech was not perfect before they had gone too far. Many a potential teacher was thus forced to follow a different vocational path. Gradually, however, Jewish instructors replaced the Irish and Germans in the city's classrooms. Between 1930 and 1939, Jews constituted more than 30 percent of those entering the school system, while the percentage of Irish appointees dropped from 30 to 12.5 percent and Germans from 31 to 8 percent.[40]

Most of the children they taught were members of ethnic groups who had arrived in New York between 1880 and 1924. Italian teachers began to appear in 1920, but they were never a large number. Those who were employed were likely to be the children of northern Italians because, as we have seen, poverty and family traditions had resulted in abbreviated schooling for most of the youngsters in southern Italian families. As time went on and their economic position improved, more Italian children went to school and remained to complete the eighth grade or more. They also became aware that civil service jobs were a useful way to make a living and therefore tried to obtain more schooling, and to pass the tests required for positions in various governmental departments. The occupational profile of the community, however, remained mostly blue collar; the sanitation department, for example, was heavily Italian.[41]

The Depression years were difficult for most Italian New Yorkers. They had achieved some upward mobility during the prosperous 1920s (mostly by skilled and semiskilled labor in the construction trades), but since that industry was at a virtual standstill after the crash, many of the carpenters, roofers, plumbers, and pipefitters who made up so large a proportion of the community had to turn to private or public charity. In 1934, about 50 percent of workers on relief were from the trades in which Italians had formerly been employed.[42]

As a result, the Italian communities of the city were sad places in the 1930s. East Harlem, in the best of times no garden spot, deteriorated badly. Among other problems, the peddlers at the large open-air market at 116th Street could not sell their squid, eels, zucchini, and finoccio, much as the housewives would have liked to buy them. Owners of coffeehouses, although the seats were still occupied, could not make a profit from the unemployed men who sat there day after day. From all the evidence, however, it seems that what had been the Italian way of life in New York remained in place, particularly campanalismo (their desire to live among people from their home village). Sicilians lived on 104th Street, Neapolitans on 106th. Other traditions were also continued. The largest church, Our Lady of Mount Carmel on 115th Street, where the annual parade in honor of the "jewel laden statue of the Madonna" was held, continued to be in place even in the darkest years. So did the importance of the family. Increasing nativism and the consequent need for solidarity may have been one of the reasons for this.[43]

As John Higham has pointed out, nativism and bigotry flourish during periods of crisis in a nation's life. On those grounds the Depression years, which were surely a very bad time, were, not surprisingly, marked by extensive interethnic hostility. A prime example was the friction between Irish and Jewish New Yorkers. One issue was the entry of Jews into municipal positions, including, as we have seen, the schools, which led to displacement of the Irish. Neighborhood change was another source of trouble. Washington Heights and the South Bronx were "battlefields where ethnic conflicts became street brawls between warring tribes." The Heights was a desirable part of the city in which to live, and middle-class Irish families had settled there between 1900 and 1910. Upper-class German Jews began moving in shortly after World War I, followed by a much larger migration of eastern European Jews later in the 1920s. By 1930, 22 percent of New York City Jews lived in Washington Heights; by 1940, they constituted 33.8 percent of the people living there.[44]

As much as possible, Irish Catholics and Jews tried to avoid each other, but this was not enough to curb hostility. As in many areas of the city, there was better and worse housing in Washington Heights, and the fact that most of the Jews could afford the higher-grade apartment houses while many of the Irish remained in tenements did nothing to improve relations. Neither did LaGuardia's appointment of Italians and Jews to positions formerly held by the Irish. The entry of German and Austrian Jewish refugees after 1933 exacerbated existing tensions. Furthermore, as the prewar decade moved on, the radio preaching of Father Coughlin as well as the organization of the violently antisemitic Christian Front and the equally hostile Christian Mobilizers led to vandalism of synagogues, "including stonings, painting of swastikas on doors, breaking of windows and interruptions of services by boys shouting 'kill the Jews.' " Among other charges, Irish antisemites said that Jews were responsible for the United States' entry into World War II. Not until 1944, when Catholic, Protestant, and Jewish leaders joined together in a Washington Heights Interfaith Committee, was the interethnic conflict subdued.[45]

A somewhat similar situation existed in the South Bronx, which was first settled by Irish and Germans in the late nineteenth century followed by Jews and Italians in the first decade of the twentieth. By 1923, Jews constituted 48 percent of the population of the southeast Bronx, a number that constantly decreased as upwardly mobile families left for better housing in the west Bronx or in adjacent areas, such as Hunts Point. The South Bronx as a whole was ethnically more diverse than

Washington Heights because Italians and Germans continued to live there, along with the Irish and Jews.[46]

There was, however, ethnic segregation based on income. As Ronald Bayor's study shows, residents of Jewish areas had higher incomes and were less likely to be unemployed. Once again, the Christian Front and Christian Mobilizers, this time joined by the pro-Nazi German-American Bund, precipitated vandalism and violence. One of the main charges of the antisemites was that the Jews owned everything and had all the money. The same complaints were heard in Flatbush, Brooklyn and any other area of the city in which Jews and Irish were unwilling neighbors.[47]

Clearly, the 1930s were not a period of goodwill, although matters improved somewhat after the United States entered World War II and the worst bigotry went underground. The German-American Bund, never popular with those Germans who remembered their difficulties during World War I, ceased to exist after Pearl Harbor. Although Italy was also America's enemy and Italian and Jewish competition for jobs in the garment industry and for housing in East Harlem had caused some difficulties in the past, most of the time there was minimal hostility between them. Mussolini's fascism was deplored by many New Yorkers, Italian and otherwise, but since the Italian government did not persecute the Jews until the German occupation began, it was easier not to criticize Italian-Americans.

There was one group of New Yorkers, however, who did dislike Italians enough to require Mayor LaGuardia to post 1,500 police officers at Madison Square Garden when Primo Carnero fought the black hero Joe Louis for the heavyweight title in July 1935. One of the reasons for the hostility between Italians and blacks was Mussolini's invasion of Ethiopa and the defense of this act by many Italian New Yorkers. Even without this foreign event, about which neither group could do much, friction between the two communities was certain. The men of both groups were equipped to work as unskilled laborers, as was true for Poles and other southeastern European immigrants. They competed for jobs during the interval between the end of World War I and the onset of restrictions, but once the entry of new arrivals was limited, it was easier for blacks to keep the jobs they had held during the war years.[48]

It is difficult to draw a straight line between immigration restriction and the movement of southern blacks to the North, but the fact that southern Congressmen voted enthusiastically in favor of restriction might indicate that they "saw the immigrant as first cousin to the Negro." It might also demonstrate that they wished to accomplish what actually occurred: fewer blacks living in the South, more in the North. By design or inadvertently, the enactment of immigration restriction made more work available for unskilled blacks during the prosperous

1920s. In any case, between 1920 and 1930, when fewer Europeans arrived, there was a 46 percent increase in New York's black population. Some of the new arrivals came from the West Indies, but the largest number were from the South.[49]

They came to a de facto segregated city with several black ghettoes, but most chose to settle in Harlem. As we have seen, delay in completing the Lenox Avenue subway line had deprived developers of white tenants, for whom they were erecting substantial apartment houses. To prevent further loss, they opened these houses to blacks, albeit at higher rentals than they would have asked of whites. "Between 1920 and 1930, 118,792 whites left Harlem and 87,417 blacks arrived."[50]

During the same period, landlords raised rents anywhere from 15 to 75 percent. In 1919, the average Harlemite paid "twenty or twenty-one dollars a month; by 1927, these rents had doubled." This led to "doubling up"; to pay the rent, two families shared apartments intended for one or took in boarders. The use of the "repeating" or "hot bed" system (i.e., "as soon as one person awoke and left, his bed was taken by another") was also widespread. In 1925, 32 percent of the black families in Harlem took in lodgers, and the population density reached 336 per acre compared to 223 in the white West Side of Manhattan. In addition, landlords divided up the spacious apartment and brownstone houses so that the population of a given building might treble, with resulting terrible wear and tear on the facilities, which were rarely repaired.[51]

A combination of poverty, overcrowding, inexperience with urban living, and landlord neglect made Harlem a slum, and the people who lived there suffered accordingly. "Undertaking was a most profitable Harlem business" because in the 1920s the death rate was 42 percent higher than in the rest of the city. Residents died at birth or from tuberculosis, venereal disease, and various infectious illnesses. There were also other harmful developments. Even when parents survived, they seemed unable to keep their children in school.

The reasons for this were multiple: As had been true for the "little aliens" from Europe who had come earlier, black children in the South had received little or no schooling. The difficulties of catching up were accentuated by the shortage of school buildings, which led to classes of forty or fifty. Schools were de facto segregated; white parents transferred their children when blacks entered, or the Board of Education adjusted district lines to separate the races. In addition, teachers in Harlem schools were often teachers-in-training or substitutes, waiting to get a permanent license. They might also be people who had placed low on the examinations. Candidates who had placed highest were appointed to schools in which the children were considered easier to teach.[52]

Different historians described different Harlems in the 1920s. Most, including Gilbert Osofsky, in his *Harlem, the Making of a Ghetto*, portray a Harlem tragedy. Another book, however, *Terrible Honesty: Mongrel Manhattan in the Twenties,* by Ann Douglas, gives a brighter picture, one in which blacks were confident that they "could use white models and channels of power" to bring "their gift of story and song" to the larger society. As a result, Douglas says, the black metropolis in Manhattan "hosted a dazzling array of black talent . . . celebrated by blacks and whites as the Harlem Renaissance." As the old story of the elephant and the three blind men tells us, the view depends on what part of the picture you study. Harlem was a mecca for blacks and whites, drawn by speakeasies and brothels as well as night club talent, but the proliferation of bootlegging and prostitution shows a darker side.[53]

Blacks had moved North for economic opportunity, and in some cities, such as Detroit, they achieved their goal. In New York, however, the "predominance of trade over industry . . . offered proportionally fewer opportunities for skilled work." As a result, most blacks did unskilled, poorly paid work when they could get it. Some did better and opened barber shops, hairdressing salons, tailoring stores, funeral parlors, and restaurants for their own people. By 1920, there were also a small group of professionals in Harlem: 176 clergymen, 96 dentists, 50 lawyers, and 95 doctors. Black women, although still primarily engaged in domestic work, increasingly found jobs in garment, paper box, and leather factories. In 1930, 22.6 percent of employed black women were working in factories, an increase of 13.4 percent over 1910, and the 86 percent who had been doing housework in 1910 had decreased to 71.5 percent a decade later.[54]

For several reasons, New York was spared some of the interracial riots that scarred other American cities in the 1920s. Residential and school segregation was a "safeguard against white violence . . . and Harlem was the only . . . fully developed, large scale black community in the United States."[55] However, Harlem could not entirely escape pressures in the larger society. In March 1935, police were erroneously accused of killing a black youth who had tried to steal a knife at an E. H. Kress store on 125th Street and crowds began smashing the windows of white-owned stores, none of which had any black employees, and looting them. Another riot occurred in August 1943 when rumors that a black soldier had been shot by a white policeman caused a fracas that left five blacks dead and many others injured. This riot was caused, in part, by resentment toward the Metropolitan Life Insurance Company, which, although it had received tax concessions and other kinds of help from the city, refused to rent Stuyvesant Town apartments to blacks.[56]

Housing discrimination remained a fact in New York City after World War II, but the war years brought many other changes to the inhabitants of the city, black and white. The war, by drawing personnel to the armed forces and defense factories, had created a labor shortage. This was accompanied by many other shortages: some kinds of food, all kinds of housing, automobiles, and telephones. As a result, ration stamps were distributed to prevent hoarding, and rent control was instituted to prevent gouging by landlords.

Although the shortages made money difficult to spend, the substitution of full employment for the unemployment of the previous years was good news for New Yorkers. Other healthy changes resulted from the need for labor; a Presidential order and various state and city actions made it more difficult to discriminate against blacks. As a result, black women became nurses, while men, after a Harlem boycott of the Fifth Avenue Bus Company, got jobs in transportation and were admitted as members of the all-white, mostly Irish Transport Workers Union. The ice was broken in several fields; black telephone operators and department store clerks began to be hired.[57]

Decreased discrimination and economic prosperity were only part of the good news for New Yorkers. As was true for the rest of the United States, New York City was spared the bombing that scarred European and Asian cities. Other developments (e.g., Broadway shows and the entertainment industry as a whole) flourished. The first television station in America, WNBF, began operations in 1941. Less well-known activities, such as the Manhattan Project (which split the uranium atom) and the breaking of the secret Japanese code, were occurring behind closed doors. There was also plenty of bad news: 891,923 New Yorkers left to enter the armed services; 16,106 did not live to see V-E or V-J day.[58]

The war was followed by the establishment of an international organization, the United Nations, which, it was hoped, would prevent further military struggles. The United Nations was born on the campus of Hunter College in the Bronx and then moved to the former World's Fair grounds in Queens. Finally, with the cooperation of two major New York realtors, the Rockefellers and Zeckendorfs, a permanent home for the world organization was erected on the East Side of Manhattan at Forty-second Street, bringing a physical presence to what New York, in terms of its people, had always been: a world city.[59]

NOTES

1. Roger Daniels, *Coming to America* (New York: HarperCollins, 1990), 278–279.

2. Ibid., 180.

3. Ibid., 281–282.

4. Eric Homberger, *Historical Atlas of New York* (New York: Henry Holt & Co., 1944), 144.

5. Ann Douglas, *Terrible Honesty: Mongrel Manhattan in the 1920s* (New York: Farrar, Straus and Giroux, 1995), 306; Frederick M. Binder and David Reimers, *All the Nations Under Heaven* (New York: Columbia University Press, 1995), 152.

6. Thomas C. Cochran, "The City's Business," in Allan Nevins and John Krout, eds., *New York, the Greater City* (New York: Columbia University Press, 1948), 147, 150, 154, 182.

7. Homberger, *Atlas,* 144.

8. Cochran, "City's Business," 141–142.

9. Binder and Reimers, *Nations,* 184; Cochran, "City's Business," 146.

10. Owen D. Gutfreund, "The Path of Prosperity," *Journal of American Urban History,* 21 (January 1995), 149.

11. Ibid., 151, 157.

12. Laura Rosen, "Robert Moses and New York: The Early Years," *The Livable City* (December 1988), 5–7.

13. Robert Caro, *The Power Broker: Robert Moses and the Fall of New York* (New York: Alfred A. Knopf, 1974), 5–6.

14. Ibid., 11.

15. Cochran, "City's Business," 140; Charles Garrett, *LaGuardia Years: Machine and Reform Politics in New York City* (New Brunswick, N.J.: Rutgers University Press, 1961), 218–219.

16. Homberger, *Atlas,* 142–143.

17. Eugene P. Moehring, "Space, Economic Growth and the Public Works Revolution in New York," Pamphlet, n.d., 52.

18. Garrett, *LaGuardia Years,* 182.

19. Binder and Reimers, *Nations,* 153; Cochran, "City's Business," 175.

20. Cochran, "City's Business," 176; Garrett, *LaGuardia Years,* 185–186.

21. Cochran, "City's Business," 177; "U.S. Journal: The Bronx," *New Yorker* (August 1, 1987), 49–55.

22. Binder and Reimers, *Nations,* 161; Warren Moscow, "Jimmy Walker's City Hall," *New York Times Magazine* (August 22, 1976), 31, 33.

23. Moscow, "Walker," 34; Herbert Mitgang, *The Man Who Rode the Tiger: Life and Times of Judge Samuel Seabury* (Philadelphia: J. B. Lippincott, 1963), 245; George Lankevich with Howard Furer, *A Brief History of New York* (Port Washington, N.Y.: Associated Universities Press, 1984), 220; Binder and Reimers, *Nations,* 182.

24. Lankevich, *Brief History,* 226; Garrett, *LaGuardia Years,* 143.

25. Garrett, *LaGuardia Years,* 254.

26. Binder and Reimers, *Nations,* 187.

27. Anthony Gronowicz, "Review of *Vito Marcantonio: Radical Politician,* by Gerald Mayer," *New York History* (September 1989), 101–103.

28. Leonard Chalmers, "Fiorello LaGuardia and Ethnic Politics," Typescript of a lecture given at the Columbia University Seminar on the City, January 15, 1977, 1.

29. Thomas Kessner, *Fiorello LaGuardia and the Making of Modern New York* (New York: McGraw-Hill, 1989), 415.

30. Kessner, *LaGuardia and New York,* 575.

31. Garrett, *LaGuardia Years,* 142.

32. Ibid., 143.

33. Binder and Reimers, *Nations,* 176; Lankevich, *Brief History,* 220.

34. Barbara Blumberg, *New Deal and the Unemployed: View from New York* (Lewisburg, Pa.: Bucknell University Press, 1979), 17.

35. Ronald Takaki, *Strangers from a Different Shore: History of Asian Americans* (New York: Penguin Books, 1989), 250.

36. Homberger, *Atlas,* 163; Lloyd Ultan and Gary Hermalyn, *The Bronx in the Innocent Years, 1890–1925* (New York: Harper & Row, 1985), xiiii; Jeff Kisseloff, *You Must Remember This* (New York: Harcourt, Brace Jovanaovich, 1989), 219.

37. Selma Berrol, "Manhattan's Jewish West Side," *New York Affairs.* (Winter 1987), 20–21.

38. Ronald Bayor, *Neighbors in Conflict* (Urbana: University of Illinois Press, 1988), 19.

39. Deborah Dash Moore, *At Home in America* (New York: Columbia University Press, 1981), 95; Ruth Jacknow Markowitz, *My Daughter the Teacher: Jewish Teachers in the New York City Schools* (New Brunswick, N.J.: Rutgers University Press, 1975), 89–90.

40. Bayor, *Neighbors,* 26–28; Interviews with Elaine Frey, Harriet Pollack, and Norma Crown, May 5, 1995. Frey was not permitted to major in education at Brooklyn College; Crown and Pollack failed the oral examination. Author's personal experience confirms the difficulty of the examination.

41. Kisseloff, *Remember,* 308.

42. Bayor, *Neighbors,* 11, 19.

43. Jerre Mangione and Ben Morreale, *La Storia: Five Centuries of the Italian American Experience* (New York: HarperCollins, 1992), 148; Kisseloff, *Remember,* 339.

44. Lee Lendt, *A Social History of Washington Heights, New York City* (New York: Columbia University-Washington Heights Mental Health Project, 1960), 73, 76; Bayor, *Neighbors,* 195.

45. Bayor, *Neighbors,* 31, 155.

46. Ibid., 161.

47. Ibid.

48. William Scott, *The Sons of Sheba: African Americans and the Italian-Ethiopian War, 1935–1941* (Bloomington: University of Indiana Press, 1993), chapters 9–11, *passim.*

49. Gilbert Osofsky, *Harlem: The Making of a Ghetto: Negro New York, 1890–1930* (New York: Harper & Row, 1968), 128–129; Louise Venable Kennedy, *The Negro Peasant Turns Cityward: Effects of Recent Migrations to Northern Centers* (New York: AMS Press, 1968), 34; Douglas, *Honesty,* 306.

50. Douglas, *Honesty,* 311.

51. James Weldon Johnson, *Black Manhattan: The Negro in New York: An Informal Social History, 1626–1940* (New York: Frederick A. Praeger, 1969), 153; Osofsky, *Harlem,* 136; Thomas A. Woofter, *Negro Problems in Cities* (New York: Doubleday, 1928), 79, 87.

52. Osofsky, *Harlem,* 141–142; Kennedy, *Negro Peasant,* 193.

53. Osofsky, *Harlem,* chapter 9, *passim.*

54. Douglas, *Honesty,* 315.

55. Kennedy, *Negro Peasant,* 86, 90.

56. Binder and Reimers, *Nations,* 195.

57. Lankevich, *Brief History,* 144–145; "The War Years: How New York Changed," *New York Times* (July 30, 1995), 10–11.

58. Binder and Reimers, *Nations,* 194; Lankevich, *Brief History,* 246.

59. Lankevich, *Brief History,* 247.

5

Postwar New York: Bright City, Dark City, 1945–1970

In the summer of 1945, the people of the "World City," delighted to see the end of World War II, joyously celebrated V-E and V-J days, welcomed home General Dwight D. Eisenhower and other military leaders with ticker-tape parades, and paid tribute to the survivors of the force they had contributed to the war effort. That done, their attention turned to relieving the shortages that had plagued the city during the war years.

It was this market, avid for housing, to name only the most important demand, and fueled by savings accumulated during the war when jobs were abundant and wages were high, that helped prevent the return of a dreaded depression. It had been feared that the end of the war and the concomitant end of wartime production would lead once more to breadlines and relief payments. Instead, New York's harbor bustled, the city continued to be the nation's leading financial center, and its factories expanded to meet pent-up demand. "In 1945, the wealth and power of the giant [city] on the Hudson was envied, respected and conceded." The respect was particularly true for cultural matters: The "tastes, images and assumptions of its cultural leaders were adopted throughout the world." [1]

In 1948, when greater New York marked its fiftieth birthday, there was much to celebrate. New retail and wholesale enterprises opened every year, unemployment was low, and the struggles of the depression-ridden prewar years receded into memory. The economy grew even stronger in the next decade; in 1954, the city was home to 40,000 manufacturing firms and 104,000 retail outlets and sold $10 billion worth of goods a year. The Port of New York continued to handle a substantial portion of the East Coast water trade, aided by twelve railroads and 750 trucking firms. Each year the city's two airports served 37 percent of all U.S. domestic travelers, and a half million workers commuted to Manhattan from New Jersey, Connecticut, and Long Island every day.[2]

They came to work in the great glass-walled office towers erected on Third Avenue, newly freed from the el that had darkened the avenue for years, as well as on Park Avenue. Between 1947 and 1963, more than 58 million square feet of office space was added to the city, many with plazas. Structures such as Lever House, the Time-Life and Equitable buildings, and, most of all, the thirty-eight-story Seagram Building added additional interest to the city's famed skyline. There were also other additions to the urban landscape; in 1956 a massive Coliseum, intended to attract trade shows, opened at Columbus Circle, and preparations for the erection of a large arts complex (the future Lincoln Center), at what was formerly the San Juan Hill battlefield (where the black and Irish poor had struggled for turf), proceeded apace.[3]

All of the foregoing explains why, at the end of World War II and in the 1950s, New York appeared to be a "swaggering, optimistic city that taught the nation about good times, about being on a roll."[4] Closer examination, however, would give alert observers some reasons for concern about the future of the city. The office building boom, for example, was a response to a basic change in the city's economy; it signified more white-collar employment and fewer factory jobs. Furthermore, the opening of the Verrazano Narrows Bridge connecting New York with New Jersey and the addition of a third tube to the Lincoln Tunnel portended the movement of middle-class people (who could afford to own a car), out of the city.

Although they were brief, three nation-wide recessions during the generally prosperous 1950s hurt New York City factories much more than its service industries, and the increased use of automatic machinery in the manufacturing process enabled factory owners to reduce the size of their labor force. As a result, "the lowest rung of the job ladder, unskilled labor, narrowed as the city lost 227 manufacturing firms and 87,000 factory jobs between 1958 and 1965."[5]

The loft buildings in which "raw materials went in at the top and finished products came out at the bottom," which once had been the mainstay of New York City industry, were now abandoned as manufacturing moved out to the suburbs and beyond. One of the reasons this happened was connected to transportation changes. When boats and railroads carried raw materials to factories and took finished goods away, manufacturing plants tried to locate near rivers or railroad sidings. The great highways constructed in the 1950s freed New York manufacturers from their ties to the city's waterways and railroad freight yards and in this way played a significant role in changing its economic profile.[6]

The industrial sector was still an effective economic machine as late as 1963, when 33,000 manufacturing establishments employed 927,000 workers and the city's clothing workers created 28 percent of the apparel worn in the United States. At the same time, however, the number of law, accounting, advertising, and financial firms was growing faster than the city's factories.[7]

During the same postwar years, 1945 to 1970, the population of the city (7.5 million when the war ended) did not increase much, but it changed in many other ways. The 600,000 blacks, 245,000 Puerto Ricans, 4,000 Chinese, a small number from the British West Indies, as well as Haitians, Dominicans, and Colombians living in New York were joined by compatriots and newer groups, both immigrants and migrants. The number coming from what came to be called the Third World was to grow much larger in the later postwar period because economic and political conditions in their home countries grew worse and because of changes in U.S. immigration laws. Immigrants from the Western Hemisphere, for example, had never been barred from the United States because they were a source of cheap labor for southwestern farmers; however they did not become a significant element in the New York population until after World War II.[8]

Many Chinese had wanted to come to New York but, as we have seen, were prevented from doing so after 1882. Because of this, Chinatown had remained a small district in lower Manhattan. Change began to come in 1943, when Congress repealed the Exclusion Act and assigned a quota to China, now our ally in the war against Japan. As a result, the bachelor society in lower Manhattan gradually became a thing of the past; instead young wives and children joined husbands and fathers in an expanding Chinese community.

Postwar Congressional action on immigration, however, notably the McCarren-Walter Act of 1952, kept the number of Asian New Yorkers relatively small. The Chinese quota remained at 105, and a new provision of the Act created an "Asia-Pacific Triangle," consisting of South and East Asia, which limited the number of immigrants from South and East Asia to 100 a year. Even fewer actually came because Asians living elsewhere in the Western Hemisphere were charged to the already tiny quota.[9]

Another provision of the McCarren-Walter Act limited immigration of blacks from the West Indies because it removed the provision of the 1924 act, which had allowed island natives to come in under the quota of the European nation that owned them. This had been very useful to would-be emigrants from the British West Indies because Great Britain had been assigned a large quota, which was often not filled. With the passage of the new act, only 100 immigrants from a colony could legally enter the United States each year. Numerically, immediate postwar Third World immigration did not greatly alter the New York ethnic mix, but it did lay a foundation for what occurred after 1965, when more significant changes in the immigration laws were made. The earlier contingent formed the basis for future communities and sent news and money home to enable others to follow them when American immigration laws were revised.[10]

In the same postwar years, black and Puerto Rican communities also expanded. Most Brooklyn blacks continued to live in Bedford Stuyvesant, but the housing shortage in that area led many to find apartments in Bushwick and Brownsville. Many Puerto Ricans who moved out of East Harlem settled in the Morrisania district of the Bronx. These changes led to a general shifting of population because whites moved out of neighborhoods that bordered on the expanding ghettoes as soon as they could find housing elsewhere.[11]

Politically, in 1945, New York was poised on the cusp of change. A few months after V-E and V-J days, Mayor LaGuardia would be succeeded by William O'Dwyer, returning a much weakened Tammany presence to City Hall. In spite of his questionable political backing, the new mayor seemed ready to cope with the unbalanced budget, dirty streets, and overcrowded schools that awaited him. In addition, due to a shortage of money during the Depression and a shortage of workers during the war, city departments were understaffed; pollution and sewage problems, ignored in previous years, threatened the harbor; the subways were falling apart; and returning veterans could not find a place to live. They also could not find an automobile, a radio, or any kind of household appliance.[12]

O'Dwyer could not supply consumer goods, but he could and did take steps to relieve the housing shortage. Between 1946 and 1956, an unprecedented number of rental apartments were built by the New York City Housing Authority and private builders. This did not happen all at once, and many a married ex-serviceman spent his first few years as a civilian doubled up with his parents or in temporary Quonset huts erected in the East Bronx and Queens.

Other ingenious ideas helped the veterans who were using benefits awarded to them under a federal program known as the GI Bill of Rights to attend graduate school. Those enrolled at New York University, for example, lived in a remodeled hospital on North Brothers Island in the East River. It was better than living with mom and dad but far from luxury housing. At a gathering in one of these makeshift apartments with thin walls, the hostess asked "Who wants coffee?" and received answers from her guests as well as people living in the apartments on either side. Seeking greater privacy and taking advantage of low interest rates and federally guaranteed GI mortgages, other young families moved into single-family houses in the counties bordering on the city.[13]

The mayor also continued and expanded wartime rent controls, thus protecting veterans who wanted to remain in the city from extortion by greedy landlords. This was only one of several ways in which O'Dwyer, a former policeman and district attorney, was "in tune with and adaptable to the changing human face of the city he governed." Just prior to his taking office, the New York State Commission Against Discrimination had been established, to be followed, at O'Dwyer's instigation, by a City Commission on Human Rights, which would prevent discrimination in housing, employment, public accomodations, and education.[14]

All of this was intended to benefit black New Yorkers, but at the same time the mayor, by threatening to remove the tax exemption given to the two largest universities in the city, Columbia and New York University, brought to an end the discriminatory policies that had long prevented more than a few Jews from enrolling. Unquestionably, the time was right for such a move. Increased knowledge of Hitler's racism had shocked most New Yorkers, which made it possible for an Irish mayor to take a stand against antisemitic practices. Furthermore, pressure from City Hall led the two universities to go a step further and appoint Jewish faculty members, including some very distinguished men and women who had fled the Nazis and found safety in New York.[15]

Still other problems were addressed early in O'Dwyer's administration. Traffic congestion and air pollution were to be reduced by a new bureau; a threatened smallpox epidemic was averted by an inoculation campaign; and several strikes, including one by the tugboat workers, were settled by mayoral intervention. A threatened shutdown of the municipal transit system was averted by a salary raise to Transport Workers Union members, and a doubled subway and bus fare (from five to ten cents) after July 1, 1948 would pay for it.[16]

Not his doing but on his watch, O'Dwyer presided over the opening of Idlewild International Airport and the Brooklyn-Battery Tunnel; furthermore, he watched as the cornerstone of United Nations Plaza was laid and welcomed the opening of Stuyvesant Town. As a result of his efforts, he was reelected by a landslide in 1949 but was not to remain mayor for much longer. What brought him down was his refusal to punish the police involved in a scandal concerning the protection (for money) of bookmakers—notably Harry Gross, who told the Kefauver Committee (a Congressional body investigating organized crime) of making a $20,000 contribution to the mayor's reelection fund. O'Dwyer resigned and was appointed Ambassador to Mexico, leaving City Hall and Gracie Mansion to the President of the City Council, Sicilian-born Vincent Impelliteri. A short time later, "Impy" was elected as an Independent and won the distinction of being the "best dressed, best rested Mayor since Jimmy Walker" because he did so little during the two years he served to complete O'Dwyer's unfinished term.[17]

Some developments did not require mayoral attention. Robert Moses continued to build bridges and expressways; indeed he spent over $2 million on postwar road building within the boundaries of the city. Impelliteri was not totally inactive: He expanded two moves that O'Dwyer had made. The sales tax was raised to 3 percent and the subway fare to 15 cents. Both of these steps were necessitated by the perennial shortfall of funds that plagued the postwar city regardless of who sat in the mayor's chair.[18]

Impelliteri's defeat of the Tammany candidate in the special election that followed O'Dwyer's resignation was one signal, among others, that the power of Tammany Hall was fading. Edward Costikyan, himself a Tammany leader at the time, suggested several reasons for this. "After the war, people were more mobile and their long term relationships with their district . . . leaders disappeared."[19] Moreover, in the late 1940s and 1950s, young upwardly mobile people did not need to serve an apprenticeship with Tammany to become a success. Perhaps most important was that the New Deal and the Fair Deal (the latter Harry Truman's social welfare program) had obviated the need for the "market basket liberalism," (such as gifts on special occasions, help with expenses, etc.) which had been used by local politicians to gain votes in the past. Most important of all was the demographic change that took place in the postwar years.

To put it in the simplest possible terms, whites (both working class and middle class) moved out of the city and blacks and Puerto Ricans moved in. By 1952, there were 775,516 black and Spanish-speaking people, 10 percent of all the city residents, living in New York. Migrants from the South and Puerto Rico continued to pour into the city during the next decade. At the same time, there was a surge of whites moving out, mostly to the nearby suburbs of Nassau, Suffolk, Westchester, and Rockland Counties. Some of the older communities were products of the 1920s, the result of an enormous increase in automobile use and parkway building in that decade. For example, the Hutchinson River Parkway, opened in 1928, and the Sawmill River Parkway, operative in 1929, had stimulated commuting from Scarsdale, Mount Vernon, New Rochelle, and Bronxville.[20]

Even without an automobile, it was possible to commute to New York by railroad. "Grand Central Terminal at Forty-second Street and Park Avenue had no rivals as a commuter hub" and led to the development of Westchester County, "the first large suburban area in the nation." It was more difficult to travel in from Nassau and Suffolk Counties because the Long Island Railroad terminated at Atlantic Avenue in Brooklyn and therefore required a subway ride into Manhattan. For this reason, the Long Island suburbs remained small until after World War II.[21]

Commuters in the prewar years, whether they traveled by railroad or auto, were generally well to do; but during the period following World War II a different kind of settler made the move out of the city. Higher wages in the prosperous postwar years, government assistance (especially to veterans), high birthrates (these were the baby-boom years), the desire to avoid living in racially integrated neighborhoods, the availability of low-cost mass produced housing (such as Levittown on Long Island), the desire for better schools, and Robert Moses' highways (which destroyed city neighborhoods and improved access to the suburbs) caused almost a million and a half people, mostly middle class, to leave New York City for a house outside of the city between 1945 and 1970.[22]

The population loss for the city was somewhat cushioned by the arrival of more than a million European immigrants, who entered between 1946 and 1970. In terms of income, however, the city suffered a serious tax loss. Neither the Holocaust survivors nor the Italians, Greeks, and Irish (who were pushed out of their home countries by postwar economic problems and pulled to New York by new immigration policies enacted in 1965), nor the thousands of blacks moving to the North or the islanders from the Caribbean (especially Puerto Ricans) could be as large a source of city revenue as the middle-class families moving out. The latter now paid their property taxes to Westchester, Nassau, or Suffolk County, shopped at suburban malls and supermarkets, and thus avoided paying New York City sales tax. The Long Island counties gained almost a million white residents in the postwar years; Westchester and Rockland added 200,000 in the same period.[23]

The new European immigrants who arrived in the 1950s and 1960s included ultraorthodox Hasidic Jews, most of whom entered under the Displaced Persons Act. A small number (85,000) compared to the millions of Jews who had come earlier in the twentieth century, they settled in the Brooklyn communities of Williamsburg, Crown Heights, and Borough Park, which grew rapidly as a result of fertility that produced families of seven and eight children. An additional number came as a result of the family unification provisions of the Immigration Act of 1965, which also resulted in the addition of 6,000 Italians, Greeks, and Irish to the New York City ethnic mix. Most joined compatriots who had come earlier and who helped the newest arrivals find homes and jobs. Both groups differed from earlier European immigrants: They were more likely to come as families, were literate if not well educated, and came with urban experience and skills useful in New York. The Italians mostly settled in Queens, Brooklyn, and Staten Island, and the Greeks enlarged the existing Greek community in Astoria, Queens.[24]

The legislation (the Hart-Celler Act) that made their arrival possible represented a great change in American immigration policy. It was proposed during the administration of John F. Kennedy (1960–1963) and became law in 1965 when Lyndon Johnson was in the White House, a time when Great Society programs of various kinds were attempting to correct injustices of the past. Essentially, the new law abandoned the numerical quotas that had been designed to keep the ethnic proportions of the American population as they had been in earlier centuries and chose instead to encourage family reunification and attract people with skills needed in the United States. Thus, quotas were abolished and preference categories were established based on family relationships and skills. The doors were not completely opened; there were numerical limits for each hemisphere and each national group.[25]

The number of Europeans coming to New York during the early postwar years was not large and, as a result, the number of foreign-born residents decreased from 1,784,206 to 1,463,821 between 1950 and 1960. There was an increase in the next decade, but by themselves the newly arrived Italians, Greeks, Jews, and Irish could not have kept the population figures at prewar levels. Nonwhites, however, made a significant contribution to the demographic statistics. As a result of the changes made by the Hart-Celler Act, "old Asian communities were transformed and a multitude of new ethnic Asian colonies" were formed in New York. This development, together with a generally higher birth rate and the continued entry of southern blacks and Puerto Ricans, caused the total population of the city to increase by more than a million, reaching 7,781,984 in 1960.[26]

The arrival of the people who came to be called minorities led to considerable demographic change in the five boroughs. In 1960, there were more blacks and Puerto Ricans living in every borough than there had been in 1940. Four years later, a school census showed that children from these two groups constituted the most rapidly growing portion of the city's school population. Manhattan showed the biggest increase, reflecting the takeover of Italian Harlem by Puerto Ricans and the movement of black newcomers into Harlem. Both minority groups were poorly represented on Staten Island, which added only 41,000 people. The Bronx and Brooklyn received 140,367 blacks and 3,500 Puerto Ricans between 1940 and 1960, while 120,000 whites left the former borough and 342,292 left the latter. Many of the Brooklynites and Bronxites who deserted their home boroughs moved to Queens, which gained 384,228 white settlers in the postwar years as well as a much smaller number of blacks and Puerto Ricans.[27]

By 1960, when blacks constituted 13.6 percent of the city's population, they made up only 4.8 percent of the people living in the outlying counties. Even fewer Puerto Ricans moved to the suburbs; in the same year, they accounted for 7.8 percent of New York City's population and only 0.5 percent of the people in the adjoining communities. Both groups might have been better off if they had been able to follow the migration of blue-collar jobs to the suburbs rather than staying in New York as the city became less of a manufacturing center and more service oriented. Unfortunately, it appears that the minorities were "captive casualties of suburbanization" because most could not afford the expenses of home ownership as well as the other costs of suburban life and therefore could not live where the manufacturing jobs were. At the same time, they were too unskilled and undereducated to work at the white-collar jobs that came to dominate the economic profile of the city.[28]

Given the limited opportunities New York offered them, why did the migration from the South and the Caribbean continue? The black men and women who came to New York were following a migration pattern that had begun in the nineteenth century and increased in the twentieth, but the arrival of large numbers of Puerto Ricans was something new. In the broadest terms, both groups came for the same reasons that had motivated Europeans and Asians in the earlier centuries. In Puerto Rico and the American South, greater medical knowledge had led to longer life and lower infant mortality, thus increasing a population that could not acquire land or find factory jobs in areas where industry was sparse.

The details of the "push and pull" factors might be different, but the underlying motives were the same. The migrants came because they wanted to escape the poverty they had endured as sharecroppers in the South or as farm laborers in Puerto Rico. The "pull," as for earlier immigrants, was the expectation that they would earn more money in the Empire City. In these respects, the new arrivals were much like their predecessors. However, there were other characteristics, such as skin color, that made it more difficult for them to achieve their goals in a city that, unlike the years when European unskilled workers were arriving, was losing the kinds of jobs they were equipped to do. The result of the breakdown of symbiosis led to a variety of social and economic problems that continue today.

There had been a flourishing trade between Puerto Rico and the United States prior to 1898, when the island was still a Spanish colony. The Puerto Ricans exported molasses and sugar to the United States, and American factories sent them agricultural and processing material for harvesting sugar, coffee, and tobacco. When, after the Spanish-American War, the United States began to import sugar from its other new possessions (Cuba, Hawaii, and the Philippines), many small Puerto Rican farmers became a part of a landless proletariat who moved to the island's cities. They were very poor and, as the twentieth century went on, they became poorer still because the population doubled and the pressure of numbers and absence of work made emigration an attractive alternative.[29]

For some time, wealthy members of the creole class had been sending their sons and daughters to the United States to study and, as a result, some 6,500 persons of Puerto Rican birth came to New York between 1900 and 1920. Skilled and semiskilled workers as well as underemployed professionals began coming in the 1920s, most working at factory positions that, due to the limits placed on European immigration, were then open to them. Just before the onset of the Depression, there were 45,000 Puerto Ricans living in New York, constituting 62 percent of all the Puerto Ricans living on the mainland. Before there could be additions to the stable working-class community that was forming in East Harlem, however, the Depression arrived. The economic disaster hurt Puerto Rico in two ways: It limited the United States' market for luxury items, such as cigars and sugar, at the same time as it virtually eliminated jobs on the mainland, including in New York.[30]

As was true for workers everywhere in the United States, the outbreak of World War II offered renewed opportunities for employment in New York. Beginning in 1942, the War Manpower Commission established an office in San Juan and recruited unskilled workers for both factory and farm work in various communities, including New York. The contract labor arrangements were usually failures; the workers were abused and quit but represent an important aspect of the Puerto Rican migration.

The men who came became aware of the opportunities available on the mainland and transmitted the information, as earlier immigrants had done in "America letters," to their friends and relatives at home. This stimulated many to come to the mainland, especially New York, which, as the size of the community grew, "became the chief magnet for new arrivals." By 1947, there were enough Puerto Ricans in the city for newspapers to protest the "airborne diaspora" and criticize the Puerto Rican provincial government of "shoveling their poor out," as the British had done with the Irish suffering from famine a century before.[31]

The peak years of the migration were 1952 to 1953, when 58,500 men, women, and children settled in New York, but migration tapered off thereafter. In 1960–1961, for example, only 8,000 arrived. They, like most of their kinsmen, stayed in New York, where, in 1970, they constituted 70 percent of the 820,000 Puerto Ricans living on the mainland. In spite of the slowdown in the migration, a high birthrate increased the Puerto Rican population of the city. By 1970, there were more Puerto Ricans living in New York than in San Juan.[32]

Because New York was so close to Puerto Rico and the airfare was an affordable $50, the migration was of a "to and fro" nature and a recession in New York would quickly change the numbers. Until the use of jet planes on the routes between New York and the Caribbean, the trip in propeller planes took six hours—unpleasant but a far cry from the trip endured by European immigrants earlier. Because the journey was relatively cheap and brief, arrivals and departures were acutely sensitive to news of jobs; when more work was available, more Puerto Ricans came; when mainland workers were laid off, fewer made the journey and more returned home.[33]

From the foregoing, it is clear that Puerto Ricans have been part of the fabric of New York for most of the twentieth century, but the people who came and their impact on the city varied greatly. The small number who came in the early years of the migration did not grow rich but found employment in the garment industry, in restaurants, and in various kinds of unskilled work. According to Jack Agueros, the son of two migrants and an author who grew up in East Harlem in the 1920s, until the huge migration of the late 1940s and 1950s, Puerto Rican families lived in a "clean and open world" in East Harlem and other parts of the city, such as the area around the Brooklyn Navy Yard. In East Harlem, as long as their numbers were relatively small, Puerto Ricans shared their turf amicably with Jews and Italians. At La Marqueta, a huge open air market under the Third Avenue el, they purchased the food of their homeland from Jewish merchants (who learned enough Spanish to make sales), and conflicts between Puerto Rican and Italians (notwithstanding Leonard Bernstein's modern version of Shakespeare's *Romeo and Juliet* tragedy, *West Side Story*) were minimal.[34]

In Agueros's opinion, East Harlem deteriorated because "four to five times more people" came running to an ancient neighborhood designed to hold half as many and to an economy that had fewer and fewer jobs to offer to the unskilled. The neighborhood recalled by Agueros was replaced by one in which children ran wild and gangs, drugs, wine, and zip guns drove the Jews and Italians out. The Catholic Church, well established in East Harlem to serve the Italian community, did not seem welcoming to the Puerto Ricans, many of whom became less observant as they lived in New York or chose to worship in evangelical storefront churches that they established themselves.[35]

East Harlem was the largest Puerto Rican community but not the only one; there were *colonias* in the South Bronx, Washington Heights, the lower East Side, and various other areas in lower Manhattan as well as in Williamsburg, Brooklyn. However, wherever Puerto Ricans lived, life was hard. Residential discrimination forced them to live in slums that deteriorated year by year, and their economic condition was often precarious. In 1946, the New York City Commissioner of Welfare said that

Puerto Ricans were the cause of a 54 percent increase in the welfare rolls during the past year. In spite of such news, the picture was not entirely dark; in the garment trades, in restaurants, and at the docks, men and women joined strong unions which protected wages and job security. They shunned politics; although Vito Marcantonio, the "boss" of East Harlem, tried to organize the Puerto Ricans in his district and thus enable them to exert pressure on the municipal government, he did not succeed and most did not vote.[36]

Perhaps because they were the first large group of non-English-speaking people to arrive in New York since 1929, and perhaps because they were racially integrated, were often illiterate, were accustomed to consensual marriage without benefit of clergy, and were seen as a burden on the public purse, Puerto Ricans encountered considerable hostility from the larger community, white and black. Sociologist C. Wright Mills, writing in 1950, included a quotation, originally referring to Irish immigrants a century earlier, to describe the views of Puerto Ricans held by many New Yorkers:

The conditions under which they were born and brought up were generally of the most squalid and degrading character. Their wretched hovels were crowded beyond the bounds of comfort, health or, as it would seem to us, of simple social decency.[37]

One of the causes for the bigotry was the fact, as some community leaders admitted, that many Puerto Ricans were "illiterate in two languages." Education on the island had been brief and inadequate, and parental attitudes to schooling in New York were closer to the early Italian model than to the Jewish and were complicated by their strong desire to keep their children from forgetting how to speak Spanish. Migrant children, aged five and over, were enrolled in school soon after arrival, but "faced with a strange city, a strange neighborhood, a different language and a new way of life, they experienced great difficulties." In contrast to the classification system used in Lower East Side schools a half century earlier, they were "expected to converse in grammatical English" and were assigned to classrooms suited to their age, not the level of their prior education, which in many cases had not gone beyond the third grade.[38]

Many middle-class teachers, speaking only English, were unhappy with their assignment to East Harlem, which certainly added to the children's problems. As Agueros described his eighth-grade class, "Education collapsed. Every classroom had ten kids who spoke no English." Junior High Schools were the most troubled parts of the system and, in many instances, teachers simply stopped trying. "The math class," says Agueros, "was sent to the gym after roll call," homework was not assigned so books were left in school, and he felt that he had learned almost nothing.[39]

The minority of Puerto Rican youngsters who completed junior high were generally counseled to enroll in a vocational high school, where they would be taught a trade. Unfortunately, such schools became merely dumping grounds, mostly because the equipment and machinery were obsolete and the student who enrolled and expected to emerge as an automobile mechanic instead found that he would have been better off with an apprenticeship in a functioning garage using modern equipment. Sometimes the efforts to teach a trade worked well; the Yorkville Vocational High School for Women's Service Trades, for example, taught beauty culture to willing students. Teachers of other subjects, such as literature, mathematics, or social studies, were faced with disinterest compounded by reading difficulties. Some instructors developed unorthodox methods to reach their resistant students; others did not even try.[40]

Innovations were helpful, as were the efforts of the bilingual coordinators appointed to help the teachers, parents, and children to adjust. Nonetheless, the gulf separating the three groups was hard to bridge. Parents saw family matters as taking precedence over schooling. Crowded apartments with radios blaring and visitors coming and going impaired study and, as a result, many children dropped out at sixteen or just stopped going to school earlier. This was not very different from the behavior of many immigrant children of the past, but the times had changed and that made an enormous difference. In the nineteenth and early twentieth centuries, the Irish or Italian or Pole or Greek child who did not complete high school could find employment, albeit low level and poorly paid. In the 1950s and 1960s, however, there were many fewer such jobs in the city, leaving hundreds of thousands of uneducated, untrained young men and women without a future.[41]

When the dimensions of the problem became clear to educators and concerned citizens, the idea of teaching the standard subjects (such as arithmetic, social studies, and science) to the non-English-speaking child in Spanish while in a different portion of the school day he or she was learning English gained favor. The idea behind this plan was sound: The general education of a child whose first language was not English would not be delayed. If all went well, bilingual education, as these programs came to be called, would enable immigrant or migrant children to emerge from high school as well prepared for college or a white-collar job as their English-speaking peers. But all did not go well; a large proportion of the Spanish-speaking teachers who were employed in these programs were not sufficiently prepared in the subject matter they were expected to teach, and many of those assigned to English classes did not set high enough standards.[42]

As a result, by 1992, when a young Puerto Rican woman who was enrolled at Baruch College of the City University of New York received a series of poor marks on her book reports and essays and brought in her diploma from Seward Park High School to show the professor that other educational authorities believed that she had learned enough to graduate from high school, the bilingual programs had become little more than a patronage program in those schools with a large non-English-speaking population. Like many previous patronage programs, they were difficult to dislodge. As of this writing, the arrangement has become an area of vested interests for Spanish-speaking teachers and administrators and seems impregnable in spite of the fact that results, as demonstrated by continuing high dropout rates and the need for extensive remedial English and mathematics programs at the various colleges of the City University, have been very poor.[43]

In addition to these well-publicized school difficulties, other distressing information began coming out of Puerto Rican neighborhoods in the 1960s and 1970s. It involved a different kind of plague than those that had afflicted earlier immigrant communities: drug addiction. Beginning with smoking marijuana cigarettes and moving on to inhaling heroin and then injecting it, many East Harlem youngsters became customers and sellers, turning to crime to finance their habit. They were certainly not the only drug users in the city; as time went on, the problem became a sad feature of urban life that affects all races and levels of New York society.[44]

In spite of the grim picture described in the preceding paragraphs, the Puerto Rican migration to New York was not entirely tragic, and the city did not entirely fail them. Although they had to pay taxes on what they earned (not the case on the island) and living expenses in New York were higher, the median annual income of Puerto Ricans living in the city in 1959 was $2,513, as compared to the average median income of $819 for those living on the island in the same year. In 1970, more than half of the employed Puerto Ricans were operators, service workers, and laborers; over 18 percent were in clerical and sales positions; more than 15 percent were craftsmen and foremen; and 8.5 percent were professionals, managers, and proprietors, mostly of bodegas (the neighborhood grocery stores). All of this meant that many of the migrants had experienced greater upward mobility than would have been possible had they remained on the island.[45]

As earlier portions of this book have shown, newcomers to the city have often come in pairs: Irish and Germans, Italians and Jews, and, after World War II, blacks and Puerto Ricans. The size of both of the last groups markedly increased between 1950 and 1970, with the number of black New Yorkers growing from 458,000 to 1,668,000 and outnumbering the approximately the 1 million Puerto Ricans living in the city by the latter date. The biggest growth occurred in the 1950s, especially for blacks; by 1970 they constituted 20 percent of the city's population.[46]

The same force that led white Americans to move from small towns and rural areas to the major cities—a search for economic opportunity—propelled the movement of blacks in the postwar years. What has been called "the semi-feudal economic and social character of the South" was the push factor; the pull was the availability of jobs during and after the war, the absence of legal discrimination, and the belief that new migrants would not stand out in the mixture of people already in New York. When the civil rights revolution of the 1960s as well as an "economic renaissance" changed the South, the migration was reversed. After 1965, almost all the black newcomers to the city were immigrants from the newly independent English-speaking countries of the Western Hemisphere. They were now included in the 120,000 ceiling allotted to the Western Hemisphere instead of being limited to the much smaller number permitted when they were counted as part of the British quota. Another reason for the increased immigration of English-speaking blacks was a change in British policy. In 1962, when the United Kingdom adopted rules designed to keep West Indian blacks out, New York became a popular destination for them.[47]

Black immigrants from the Caribbean had been coming to New York for a long time, but the number of new arrivals soared after 1965, when the Hart-Celler Act took hold. Over 10,000 came from Barbados, 55,000 from Jamaica, and 24,000 from Trinidad and Tobago. By 1970, they constituted a very large segment of the people living in the Bedford Stuyvesant area of Brooklyn, the largest black community in New York City. Other parts of Brooklyn, such as Brownsville, Crown Heights, East New York, Bushwick, and East Flatbush, lost white population and gained blacks, both native born and immigrants (this was also true for South Jamaica in Queens and, to a lesser extent, the Bronx).[48]

Much of this movement was the result of placing low-rent municipal housing projects in previously white areas. This did not promote the integration that was hoped for but rather established "minority islands in a hostile environment" or stimulated white flight. When whites did not flee (as was the case in Crown Heights, where the Hasidic Jewish community had taken root and would run no more), there was considerable friction between the races. In addition, hostility between blacks and Italians in the East New York section of Brooklyn caused other difficulties. In short, the postwar years saw continuing racial tension in New York.

What did improve was the occupational status and income of many New York City blacks. In 1940, only 14 percent of the blacks (native and foreign born) residing in Brooklyn were earning a living by other than manual labor. In 1950, only 18 percent did so. Twenty years later, 43 percent were white-collar employees in the municipal government, many were working in hospitals, a small number were working as entrepreneurs, and more were working in the entertainment industry. Good news, certainly, but it must be balanced with an awareness that the median income for blacks in 1970 was $6,772 a year as compared to $10,000 for whites.[49]

A better economic situation was acompanied by greater political strength, which was a product of the increase in numbers as well as more political experience. As a result, the Reverend Adam Clayton Powell was elected to Congress, Hulan Jack was chosen to represent Bedford Stuyvesant in the New York State Assembly, and Shirley Chisholm became the first black woman to be elected to Congress. Partly because of their increase in clout but also because of a growing awareness (fostered by the 1965 Watts riots in Los Angeles and the Kerner Report that followed), that all was not well in the black ghettoes, governments, at all levels, made a serious effort to remedy the disparities and injustices affecting the American black population.[50]

On the federal level, Lyndon Johnson's Great Society program produced the Economic Opportunity Act, which included provisions for affirmative action (to open previously closed jobs to minorities); Model Cities (to improve ghetto housing); and new money for schools (including a "Head Start" program for minority children). Efforts on behalf of minorities in New York City had begun even earlier with the elevation to the mayor's seat of Robert Wagner, Jr. in 1953. The son of a much-loved liberal senator, Mayor Wagner, who was also a liberal, appointed a Comission on Intergroup Relations to deal with whatever frictions arose.[51]

And arise they did: In 1962, the mayor changed the name of the Commission from *Intergroup* to *Human* and created a Rent and Rehabilitation Administration to deal with specific complaints from the poor. In spite of such activity, racial tensions persisted and grew worse. In 1964, the death of a Harlem boy at the hands of a white policeman during a July heat wave precipitated the first of many summer disturbances. In addition, the disclosure that in the early 1960s blacks comprised 13 percent of the city's population but received 45 percent of the welfare payments created considerable ill will among the white majority, who also resented the fact that Puerto Ricans (8 percent of the population) received 30 percent of the public assistance payments.[52]

The high cost of welfare, however, was only one of the expenses that increased an already unbalanced municipal budget. When World War II ended, Mayor LaGuardia, expecting continued largesse from Washington, had prepared plans for spending $125 million on improvements for the city. The Truman Administration and the first postwar Congress, however, were not prepared to continue Depression-era programs, and this caused the municipality to begin an era of borrowing money and using fiscal "gimmicks" to balance the city's books.

Matters worsened under LaGuardia's successors because the costs of running the city increased. The municipal hospital system grew in order to meet the needs of the new arrivals from the Caribbean and the South; both O'Dwyer and Wagner had agreed to more generous pensions for city workers; roadways deteriorated more rapidly under the impact of more cars; and certain fixed costs, such as operating the city-owned transit system, could not be lowered. Indeed, on the day that Wagner left office, Mike Quill called an illegal transit strike, which resulted in a substantial raise for the workers and an increase in the fare to 20 cents.[53]

Wagner dealt with financial problems on an emergency basis, authorizing "one-shot" borrowing and disguising the imbalance in the budget by various devices. Near the end of his term in office, however, the State Legislature appointed a Temporary Commission on City Finances, which warned that the city was borrowing too much money, "resulting in enormous debt service charges and high taxes." One of the Commission's solutions was a graduated personal income tax, which, when it went into effect, did produce additional income for the city. Unfortunately, it also accelerated movement out of the city because residents of Westchester, Nassau, and Suffolk Counties as well as those living across the Hudson in New Jersey or Connecticut, although they earned their living in New York City, did not pay this tax. In general, efforts made to stem the flow of jobs and people to the suburbs and nearby states did not succeed, and the financial condition of the city did not improve. Rather, its finances worsened and its unhappy minorities grew more sullen.[54]

After Wagner left City Hall and Republican-Independent John Lindsay (a forty-four-year-old graduate of Yale Law School and former East Side Congressman) came in, racial problems increased in severity, as did attempts at solutions. The new mayor required all his comissioners to read the Kerner Report, informed them of the New York City riot of 1964, and set about establishing antipoverty programs, improving the welfare system, increasing housing options, and reforming the schools, using federal money from one of the Great Society programs: the Economic Opportunity Act.[55]

One notable innovation was the Community Development Agency, which allocated funds to local community corporations, which, in turn "would subcontract to a host of local organizations" to operate programs that, although marred by corruption and inefficiency, accomplished some good. Ghetto youngsters were hired for summer projects, thus averting much-feared street disturbances and even more important, "middle class, civil service, white collar jobs" were provided for "large numbers of blacks and Puerto Ricans." Charles Morris, who has found much to criticize in Lindsay's efforts, points out that this was "a service not unlike that performed for the Irish by an even crasser system of patronage a couple of generations earlier."[56]

Morris is less reasonable in his view of the changes made in the welfare system during Lindsay's years in City Hall. The welfare rolls, as has been noted, had been rising before he took office but during his administration, due to the efforts of Mitchell Ginsburg (his Commissioner of Social Services) as well as pressure from the welfare rights movement, grants were raised and more people were placed on the rolls. More were also placed in public housing, which previously had required that the head of the family have a paying job. The replacement of stable working-class families with unstable welfare recipients led to a rapid decline in the quality of life in the projects.[57]

The welfare load doubled in the 1960s, with about a third of the cost being borne by the city. This was watched with puzzlement and alarm by the taxpayers. Although the second postwar decade was not as prosperous as the first, economic conditions were still good. In 1962, black unemployment had declined to its lowest level in many years. At the same time, funds going to unmarried mothers (mostly black and Puerto Rican), under the Aid to Families with Dependent Children (AFDC) provision of the Social Security Act (passed during the New Deal years), rose increasingly higher.

The problems of the New York black community were also present in other northern cities to which they had migrated. Detroit was one such city which became infamous when its black population exploded in a serious riot. The riots, wherever and whenever they occurred, were contagious. Due to the successful efforts of Mayor Lindsay and his aides, New York was spared, even when news of Dr. Martin Luther King's assassination reached the city. Among other steps, a Summer Task Force, involving several different agencies, took steps to keep the city "cool" by providing summer jobs, busing volatile youngsters out of the city, and responding quickly to complaints about poor housing and crime from the ghettoes.[58]

When John Lindsay moved into City Hall, several reports and articles in newspapers and magazines had spread bad news about the New York City public schools. The buildings, it was said, were dilapidated, due to age and poor maintenance; drugs, mostly marijuana, were being used; and the school system, city wide, continued to be *de facto* segregated. One important report from State Education Commissioner James Allen said that black and Hispanic children constituted 75 percent of the school population, and most of them were not receiving a decent education.[59]

In 1969, more than 33 percent of the pupils attending elementary school in the black districts of Brooklyn were a year or more behind the norm in reading and in Harlem, more than 85 percent were behind. It was generally agreed that integration via busing or redrawing district lines had failed. Between 1954 and 1960, the number of Brooklyn schools with virtually all minority populations had increased from nine to thirty-eight; by 1970, 50 percent of these schools had almost totally black and Hispanic populations. The same was true in Harlem and portions of the Bronx. Whites moved out when blacks and Hispanics moved in, and the neighborhood schools reflected this.[60]

The prospect of having their children attend school with black and Hispanic youngsters did not alarm all white parents. Many wanted to live in the city, enjoy its cultural facilities, and avoid the cost and pain of commuting; they preferred the multiethnic city to the sameness and sterility of the suburbs, but only those who could afford private school tuition could do so. Parents who remembered the excellent education they had received in the public schools and saw, correctly, how that education had enabled them to attain middle-class status feared for their children's future if they did not receive similar training. As experienced teachers left the classrooms and poorly trained ones arrived, as the curriculum was watered down and standards were lowered, that training seemed impossible to achieve. The turmoil in the New York City schools in the late 1950s and 1960s frightened many reluctant families into a move to the suburbs, lured by a real estate agent's assurances about the high quality of the schools in the area in which they were planning to buy a house.

The proposed substitute for the failed integration attempts was decentralization—that is, giving a community control of the schools in its district by empowering an elected local board to make many of the decisions formerly emanating from central headquarters at 110 Livingston Street, Brooklyn. Although people who were aware of New York school history recognized the similarity between the proposed local control system and the ward trustee organization of the nineteenth century (which was abolished, as we have seen, in 1897 because of corruption, favoritism, and educational inadequacy), the change was strongly favored by black leaders as well as, to a lesser extent, the mayor and various researchers and writers.

In September 1966, black militants blocked the opening of a new school, Intermediate School 201 in East Harlem, claiming that white teachers and administrators "reinforced a black child's feelings of cultural inferiority" and demanding the appointment of blacks instead. The Board of Education accepted their views and went further, establishing three decentralized demonstration districts in Ocean Hill, Brooklyn; Harlem; and the Lower East Side. Elections were held for community school boards in these three areas. In Ocean Hill, the new board appointed Rhody McCall, an experienced black teacher and administrator, as superintendent.[61]

The predominantly white United Federation of Teachers unit in Ocean Hill had originally cooperated with plans for the demonstration district, but toward the end of the 1966–1967 school year, militants on the local board said Superintendent McCoy made them feel unwanted. To show their strength, they went on strike in September 1967. The Ocean Hill Board kept its schools open, using substitutes and volunteers. After a short time, most of the strikers returned, but in May 1968 a new crisis erupted. The local board dismissed thirteen teachers and six assistant principals; the City Superintendent of Schools ordered them reinstated; the Ocean Hill Board refused to do so; 350 teachers walked out or were dismissed and the schools were closed. Nothing was settled during the summer or during the three system-wide teacher strikes that followed in the fall of 1968.[62]

At the same time, Mayor Lindsay, responding to the new state law that ordered him to prepare a school decentralization plan, created an Advisory Panel on Decentralization of the New York City schools and appointed McGeorge Bundy, the president of the Ford Foundation (which had shown considerable interest in educational innovation), as its chairman. The result was a report, formally titled "Reconnection for Learning, A Community School System for New York," which was submitted to Albany with the recommendation that the Legislature enact its provisions into law at its next session.[63]

The measure that resulted was signed by Governor Nelson D. Rockefeller in April 1969. It created a City Board of Education, which consisted of members appointed by the borough presidents and the mayor and was empowered to appoint a Chancellor, who would have considerable power over the thirty or more community boards elected by the voters of the district in which they lived. These board members were to have "substantial operating control over all the education in their district," excluding high schools, which were subject to the Chancellor and the central Board of Education. The framework erected by the new law was essentially neutral; depending on who was elected to the local boards and who was chosen to be Chancellor, it had the potential to alleviate some of the problems of the city's schools.[64]

There was one final provision, however, which boded ill. In response to the black community's wishes to have more black teachers instructing their children and in tune with affirmative action measures coming out of Lyndon Johnson's Great Society programs, the law permitted the bottom 45 percent of the schools, as indicated by comparative reading scores, to engage instructors who had passed only the notoriously easy National Teachers Examination, and had given a presentable performance at an interview. The result of the adoption of this thoughtless policy was to have "the blind teaching the blind"; children most in need of skilled instructors would be taught by less well-prepared ones.

Writing in 1974, Diane Ravitch, who has thoroughly explored the Great School War of the 1960s, concludes that decentralization "was neither the disaster that its enemies had feared nor the panacea that its proponents had anticipated."[65] More than twenty years later, however, the educational deficiencies of many of the graduates of the New York City public schools are glaring—nowhere more clearly exposed than in the municipal colleges, which, in 1971, began an experiment in Open Admissions.

Open Admissions, to be discussed in detail in Chapter 6, like decentralization, was an attempt to democratize educational opportunity. Both approaches succeeded in bringing many more blacks and Hispanics into the schools as students, teachers, and administrators. As was the case with many of the Great Society programs, the educational turmoil that scarred the city in the 1960s brought a large segment of the American population, previously left on the sidelines, into the mainstream.[66]

John Lindsay deserves to be praised for his attempts to improve the conditions of life for members of minority groups in New York, but his efforts exacerbated the city's financial difficulties, culminating in a damaging fiscal crisis in the mid-1970s. As we have seen, the problems did not originate with Lindsay. In at least two important ways, New York in the 1960s was adversely affected by events occurring outside its control. One was the financial burden of the Great Society programs, most of which required matching financial contributions from the localities in order to receive federal funds. The other was the war in Vietnam. Protests against the war on college campuses exacerbated other discontents, mobilized radicals to oppose the war itself, and resulted in demonstrations and riots which the police could not always control. Shouts such as "Hey, Hey, LBJ, how many boys did you kill today?" were increasingly heard, and newspapers described campus riots in which administrators were locked into their offices until they agreed to student demands.[67]

In an attempt to ease the racial tensions of the 1960s, the Metropolitan Museum of Art, under the leadership of Thomas Hoving, sponsored a multimedia exhibit called "Harlem On My Mind" to "tell the history of blacks in Harlem [from] the earliest days of the 20th Century . . . [to] the unrest of the Sixties." Before it opened, however, protests began. For one thing, it did not include the work of established black artists, such as Romare Beardon, and for another, Hoving had chosen a Jewish Associate, Allen Schoener, who, many blacks said, "had no expertise about black culture" to work on the exhibit. A recently (1995) published edition of the catalogue shows that it did bring black cultural achievements to the attention of mainstream society, but much that was worthwhile was obscured by the furious storm it created, thus enhancing the racial hostility present in the city.[68]

At the same time as the streets became increasingly disturbed, entire neighborhoods were succumbing to urban blight. Housing inhabited by the poor (usually blacks and Puerto Ricans) was abandoned by landlords who were unable, due to city rent control, to raise rents. Landlords were also unwilling to make costly repairs in areas where vandalism was rampant. Beginning in the 1960s, the abandonment of thousands of buildings in the South Bronx, Harlem, and Bedford Stuyvesant—many of which were set afire—created a landscape that "looked as if it had experienced war time air raids." [69]

The happiness that was described at the start of this chapter had been greatly diminished, if not destroyed, by disappointment and despair a quarter century later. This was not true for all New Yorkers, many of whom had been able to participate in the good life that was also available in the city. There was certainly less institutional bigotry and racism, and consequently members of minority groups had more opportunities for jobs and housing. Technological advances improved the quality of life and offered new careers, and expanded educational openings allowed many young people to aspire to middle-class standing. Nonetheless, as John Lindsay left City Hall and Abraham Beame entered, a dark cloud hung over much of the Empire City.

NOTES

1. David Reimers and Frederick Binder, *All the Nations Under Heaven* (New York: Columbia University Press, 1995), 197; George Lankevich with Howard Furer, *A Brief History of New York City* (Port Washington, N.Y.: Associated Universities Press, 1984), 249; Eric Homberger, *Historical Atlas of New York* (New York: Henry Holt, 1994),147.

2. Lankevich, *Brief History*, 248, 250, 254; *New York Times*, July 30, 1995, 8.

3. Lankevich, *Brief History*, 263.

4. Homberger, *Atlas*, 148.

5. Lankevich, *Brief History*, 264–265.

6. Bayard Still, "Bicentennial New York," in Milton Klein, ed., *New York: The Centennial Years* (Port Washington, N.Y.: Kennikat Press, 1976), 179.

7. Ira Rosenwaike, *Population History of New York City* (Syracuse, N.Y.: Syracuse University Press, 1972), 134, 139; David Reimers, *Still the Golden Door* (New York: Columbia University Press, 1985), 29; Daniel Moynihan and Nathan Glazer, *Beyond the Melting Pot* (Cambridge, Mass.: MIT Press, 1970), 93.

8. Reimers, *Golden Door*, 17, 29.

9. Ibid., 19, 37.

10. Moynihan and Glazer, *Melting Pot*, 94.

11. *New York Times*, July 30, 1995, Sec. 4, 8.

12. David Ward and Olivier Zunz, *Landscape of Modernity* (New York: Russell Sage Foundation, 1982), 326.

13. The author was a guest in Arthur and Ethel Witkin's apartment on North Brothers Island when this incident occurred.

14. Leonard Dinnerstein, "Anti-Semitism in America, 1945–1950," *American Jewish History* (September 1981), 40.

15. Leonard Dinnerstein, *Uneasy at Home: Anti-Semitism and the American Jewish Experience* (New York: Columbia University Press, 1987), 51.

16. Lankevich, *Brief History*, 253–254.

17. Salvatore La Gumina, *New York at Mid-Century: Impelliteri Years* (Westport, Conn.: Greenwood Press, 1992), 22.

18. Robert Caro, *Power Broker* (New York: Alfred A. Knopf, 1975), 843.

19. Edward Costikyan, "Politics in New York City: A Memoir of the Post War Years," *New York History* (October 1993), 422.

20. Caro, *Power Broker*, 858; Kenneth Jackson, *Crabgrass Frontier* (New York: Oxford University Press, 1985), 166–167.

21. Jackson, *Frontier*, 194.

22. Reimers and Binder, *Nations*, 206; Leonard Wallock, "Myth of the Master Builder," *Journal of Urban History*, 17 (August 1981), 347, 349.

23. Solomon Poll, *Hasidic Community of Williamsburg: A Study in the Sociology of Religion* (New York: Schocken Books, 1969), 29–31.

24. Nancy Foner, *New Immigrants in New York* (New York: Columbia University Press, 1987), 17–19.

25. Roger Daniels, *Coming to America* (New York: HarperCollins, 1990), 341–343.

26. Rosenwaike, *Population*, 133.

27. Ibid.; table, p. 64.

28. Ibid.; Wallock, "Master Builder," 349, 351.

29. Virginia Sanchez Korral, *From Colonia to Community: History of Puerto Ricans in New York City, 1917–1948* (Westport, Conn.: Greenwood Press, 1983), 3.

30. Ibid., 26, 28.

31. Ibid., 3; Edwin Maldonado, "Contract Labor and the Origins of Puerto Rican Communities in the United States," *International Migration Review*, XIII 1979, 103.

32. Moynihan and Glazer, *Melting Pot*, 91–94.

33. Kal Wagenheim, *Puerto Rico, a Profile* (New York: Praeger Publishers, 1970), 194.

34. Jack Agueros, "Halfway to Dick and Jane," in Thomas Wheeler, ed., *The Immigrant Experience* (New York: Dial Press, 1988), 93; Sanchez Korral, *Colonia*, 56.

35. Agueros, "Dick and Jane," 93; Sanchez Korral, *Colonia*, 208; C. Wright Mills, *Puerto Rican Journey* (New York: Russell & Russell, 1950), 111.

36. Mills, *Journey*, 81; Sanchez Korral, *Colonia*, 58.

37. Mills, *Journey*, 81.

38. Elena Padillo, *Up from Puerto Rico* (New York: Columbia University Press, 1958), 57, 200, 209.

39. Padillo, *Puerto Rico*, 205; Agueros, "Dick and Jane," 94.

40. This information is based on the author's observations and experiences

as a social studies teacher at Yorkville Vocational High School from 1948 to 1954.

41. Padillo, *Puerto Rico*, 210.

42. Conversations with Rudolph Martinez, Assistant Professor in the Academic Skills Department at Baruch College, CUNY, in 1979.

43. This statement is based on the author's experience as a Professor of History at Baruch College, CUNY; *New York Times*, October 7, 1995, B3.

44. Agueros, "Dick and Jane," 95.

45. Mills, *Journey*, 86.

46. Rosenwaike, *Population*, 174.

47. Charles Morris, *The Cost of Good Intentions* (New York: McGraw-Hill, 1980), 59; Foner, *New Immigrants*, 3.

48. Foner, *New Immigrants*, chart, p. 57; Harold Connelly, *A Ghetto Grows in Brooklyn* (New York: NYU Press, 1977), 135.

49. Connelly, *Ghetto*, 132, 134.

50. Ibid., 192.

51. Edward Levinson, *Black Politics in New York City* (New York: Twayne Publishers, 1974), 88–89.

52. Morris, *Intentions*, 31.

53. Lankevich, *Brief History*, 262, 270.

54. Joshua Freeman, *In Transit: Transport Workers Union in New York City* (New York: Oxford University Press, 1989), 335; Morris, *Intentions*, 84–85.

55. Martin Shefter, *Political Crisis, Fiscal Crisis: The Collapse and Revival of New York City* (New York: Basic Books, 1987), 115–117; Morris, *Intentions*, 29.

56. Nat Hentoff, *Education of John V. Lindsay* (New York: Alfred A. Knopf, 1969), 67.

57. Morris, *Intentions*, 63, 66.

58. Hentoff, *Lindsay*, 68; Morris, *Intentions*, 69.

59. Barry Gottehrer, *Mayor's Man* (Garden City, N.Y.: Doubleday 1975), 52.

60. Reimers and Binder, *Nations*, 122.

61. Connolly, *Ghetto*, 212–218.

62. Morris, *Intentions*, 108–109.

63. Ibid., 110–111; Marilyn Gittell and Maurice Berube, *Confrontation at Ocean Hill Brownsville* (New York: Frederick A. Praeger, 1969), 74.

64. Diane Ravitch, *The Great School Wars* (New York: Basic Books, 1974), 312, 315, 330, 336.

65. Ibid., 387.

66. Ibid.

67. David Lavin, Richard Alba, and Richard Silberstein, *Right Versus Privilege: The Open Admission Experiment at the City University of New York* (New York: Free Press, 1981), 1–5; Ravitch, *School Wars*, 397.

68. Morris, *Intentions*, 213; Lankovich, *Brief History*, 268–269.

69. "Culture and Race Still on America's Mind," *New York Times* (November 19, 1995), B1.

6

Roller Coaster Years: New York and Its People, 1970–1996

In 1976, the United States was 200 years old and there was much to celebrate. New York was even older but had less reason to commemorate the occasion with festivities. As we have seen, population growth had slowed in the 1960s and the central city continued to lose people to the neighboring suburbs in the 1970s. In other ways as well, the decade was a period in which unwelcome trends seen earlier persisted and grew more pronounced.

The white middle class continued to leave the city, and new immigrants from all over the globe continued to arrive. Demands on the city's purse grew while sources of municipal income decreased; neighborhoods and schools deteriorated; racial conflict, although less violent than in the previous decade, did not subside; and the gap between rich and poor New Yorkers grew wider. As a result, much of New York suffered from what one observer called "quiet riots": unemployment, poverty, social disorganization, inadequate housing, and increased crime.[1] By 1980, the form that New York was likely to take for the rest of the twentieth century had appeared: a troubled multiethnic city, frequently on the brink of disaster but somehow managing to survive.

The 1980s saw a major change in the economy. No longer an important manufacturing center, New York became a city noted as a center for finance and technology. This aspect of the city's life has persisted into the 1990s, but there also have been new developments. The outward movement of people has been somewhat reversed by the return of young men and women who were born and raised in the suburbs but who now see New York as the place for opportunity and fun. Some of the fun may be eating at one of the new ethnic restaurants or shopping for exotic foods at one of the new markets that have opened in many parts of the city. Both of these developments resulted from the arrival of new immigrants from various parts of Asia, the Caribbean, the Middle East, and South America. The newcomers increased the attractiveness of an already cosmopolitan city, illustrating, once more, the symbiotic pattern that has marked New York City history.

These strengths were not apparent in the 1970s. The bicentennial year was noted, but celebrations were overshadowed by the worst fiscal crisis in New York history, from which the city had barely recovered from when, on the Fourth of July, a "parade of tall ships came through New York Harbor" and proceeded up the Hudson River. The colorful procession, a reminder of New York's marvelous maritime history, helped to cheer up the people of a city that had just been through a terrible ordeal, but serious problems remained.[2]

For most of the previous decade, the city had been living beyond its means. The causes were varied. Urban services in New York included more than the basics, such as street cleaning and garbage removal, schools and police protection. The city also spent more than other municipalities on higher education, including, as we will see, an expanded City University. In addition, New York had nineteen municipal hospitals, which also offered child health care and home nursing. Welfare, primarily the city's contribution to the federal Aid to Families with Dependent Children (AFDC) program, cost more than in other cities, partly because New York was a mecca for migrants from all parts of the nation, as well as for immigrants from abroad.[3] The municipal treasury also supported cultural life, contributing $96 million in 1974–1975 for the support of Shakespearean dramas and Philharmonic concerts in Central and Prospect Parks. All of these activities, remedial or pleasurable, led to an increase in the number of municipal workers, "from about 150,000 in 1945 to 330,000 in May 1975." Furthermore, they were a greater burden on the municipal purse because unionization in the 1960s had led to higher salaries and pension contributions.[4]

In June 1974, Abraham Beame, the former city comptroller, became mayor of New York. Because of his previous position he knew, better than most, that New York spent twice as much per capita than any other American city. The resulting high operational costs were hidden by creative bookkeeping, such as shifting the expenditures into capital accounts, and by short-term borrowing. All of this had led to a debt of $13.3 billion by May 1975, when the major banks refused to buy or float any more municipal bonds and the city was therefore unable to meet its payroll or make payments on the debt. Beame tried various gimmicks, including laying off some workers, but default loomed with unthinkable consequences for the Empire City. Municipal employees would not be paid and, if they then refused to work, fires would not be extinguished, children would not be taught, and garbage would not be collected. The Big Apple was being squeezed to a pulp from two sides: the bankers and the unions.[5]

One view of the crisis saw the villains as the banks, which had encouraged the city to pile up debt and then refused to roll over the very bonds they had urged the municipality to issue. Help from Washington was not forthcoming. Indeed, as the *New York Post* stated, President Ford told the city to "Drop Dead."[6] Fortunately, Albany came to the rescue. To avoid the oncoming catastrophe, Governor Hugh Carey appointed an experienced banker, Felix Rohayton, to head an advisory committee, which led to the creation of the Municipal Assistance Corporation (MAC) and the Emergency Financial Control Board (EFCB), which would monitor New York City finances. This enabled the city to borrow money from sources which had major stakes in the city's solvency: the state government, commercial banks, and the municipal pension funds.[7]

Because the EFCB was an effective watchdog, these actions gave the city access to outside borrowing by 1980. Damage, however, had been done. The fiscal oversight boards had encouraged (one might even say forced) the "city to slash institutions that served poor people, such as health clinics and day care centers and fire thousands of modestly paid municipal workers while they backed new bonds for which existing bonds could be exchanged and earn higher interest rates for investors."[8]

The State agencies limited the control of elected officials over the municipal government and forced many changes on the city: To begin with, 25,000 city workers were dismissed, previously negotiated wage increases were deferred, "take home pay was reduced by requiring workers to pay a greater proportion of their contributions to their pension funds," tuition was imposed on the students at the city colleges, and the subway and bus fare was raised three times after 1975. As all this makes clear, almost no group escaped some of the fallout from the crisis, but the city's poor suffered the heaviest blows because programs from which they had benefited were eliminated. Furthermore, blacks and Hispanics, because they had been on the municipal payroll only since the Lindsay years, lacked seniority and were the first to be fired.[9]

People who had not been employed anywhere had a different problem: The welfare grant was frozen although the cost of living had increased, leading many poor families to forgo their rent payments. This, in turn, led many landlords to forgo repairs and maintenance on their now unprofitable holdings, and the city's housing stock deteriorated. So did the lives of the people who lived in those buildings and those who were evicted, leading to a problem that was to grow much worse in the 1980s: homeless individuals and families.[10]

Not only lives and housing deteriorated: so did the city's tax base, historically drawn from small and large retailers, many of whom now found it more profitable to follow their middle-class customers and move to shopping malls and highway strip malls in Nassau, Suffolk, and Westchester counties. This was only one of the reasons for the city's predicament; at bottom, the fiscal crisis was an outgrowth of the economic decline of New York that had been going on since the 1960s.[11]

From any point of view, in New York—where economic matters are closely fused with social, political, technological, and ecological concerns—the city was in serious trouble. For one thing, as we have seen, people had been leaving since the 1950s, a trend which continued during the next two decades.[12] Employment figures explain why this occurred. In the 1960s, private employment grew by only 2 percent, in contrast to national growth of 27 percent. Manufacturing employment, in particular, declined by 19 percent but increased nation-wide by 27 percent. Between 1960 and 1973, New York lost over 600,000 jobs; in 1973, 4.4 percent of the city's workers (25 percent of them blacks) were unemployed. As a result, there were 442,000 fewer people living in New York at the time of the bicentennial celebration.[13]

Effective buying income was far below seven other major American cities, partly because 1,174,632 people were being supported by welfare and had only minimal amounts of money to spend. According to *Sales Management*, a magazine devoted to marketing, in 1973, New York households ranked seventh among American cities in "effective buying income" and a study by Chase Manhattan Bank in 1969 showed a drop of $4,000 in middle-class family income during the previous ten years. One result of this was slowing sales and increasing thefts in the great department stores, which encouraged some of them to leave the city.[14]

The construction industry, always sensitive to economic winds, expanded and contracted during the 1970s. When the decade opened, office building projects begun in previous years were completed "in perfect timing with the downward spiral in employment." The result was that "some 30 million square feet of office space . . . stood empty in 1973" and no more commercial towers were built until well into the 1980s. The now idle carpenters, plumbers, and masons who had been employed in office construction could not find alternative jobs building residential housing, which was greatly curtailed by a decrease in state and city support for subsidized apartments. In addition, reinstatement of rent control (after a three-year period of decontrol) made investments in middle- and high-income housing less attractive to developers. Finally, the severe drop in manufacturing curtailed another kind of construction: industrial plants. The resulting unemployment of blue-collar workers, skilled and unskilled, affected the entire economy.[15]

The garment industry had been an important ingredient in New York

City's economic growth since the previous century and was "clustered in a central location where customers could be shared, transport costs minimized . . . accessibility to the labor force maximized, and trade with suppliers facilitated." [16] In the post–World War II years, however, this changed. To begin with, the large, capital-intensive firms making low-price garments began to relocate out of the city in search of cheaper labor, at first to the South and then to the Southwest. Later, firms making higher-priced, trendy garments who had previously employed New York–based designers and merchandisers also began to move out. At the same time, foreign producers "deeply penetrated the American market [placing] severe competitive pressure on even the largest American producers." [17] Between 1969 and 1975, New York lost 81,000 garment industry jobs, and the remaining workers were paid lower wages to keep their employers competitive with companies in other parts of the nation, which were "trying to woo away the city's plants." [18]

In 1977, although much diminished, the apparel industry provided 28.6 percent of all the city's remaining manufacturing jobs. Herbert Bienstock, the regional Commissioner of Labor Statistics, however, was not optimistic about the apparel industry's future, partly because he thought the remaining factory owners had retained techniques appropriate to the pushcart era instead of installing technological innovations. As it turned out, the Commissioner was unduly pessimistic. The passage of the Hart-Celler Act in 1965, which led to the arrival of thousands of workers from the Dominican Republic and China, has kept New York's diminished apparel industry alive. [19]

The causes of New York City's economic distress in the 1970s were mutifaceted. In addition to the factors previously discussed, there was a national recession brought on in part by an energy crisis that resulted from a boycott by OPEC, a consortium of Middle Eastern oil-producing nations. Furthermore, the city lost hundreds of thousands of office jobs as corporations moved out to avoid high energy costs, high office rents, and high crime rates. Many white- and blue-collar jobs shifted to the suburbs: A *New York Times* survey in 1972 showed that the city's share of metropolitan area jobs was down by 7.1 percent since 1960. [20]

In spite of declines such as these, New York certainly was not dead. It was still home to ninety-six of the nation's largest corporations and held six of its largest banks, four of its largest insurance companies, nine out of ten of its most prosperous advertising agencies, and one third of the nation's most prestigious law firms. In addition, it contained 28,000 restaurants, 500 art galleries, and more theaters, museums, and department stores than any other American city. Furthermore, by the end of the 1970s, improvement was in the air because the "fundemental economics of supply and demand began to produce corrections in the underlying imbalances." [21]

In the short term, the corrections were painful, but in the long run, they resulted in at least a partial recovery. The cost of doing business in New York decreased: Wages for both manufacturing and clerical workers did not rise, developers lowered office rents rather than see their buildings remain vacant, and "businessmen, pressured by falling profit margins," took Bienstock's advice and introduced advanced computer systems.[22] In addition, the dollar declined in the 1970s and thereby attracted both foreign investors and tourists, which led money to flow into the previously moribund real estate market and to the opening of international bank branches and expensive retail shops as well as into hotels and restaurants, both old and new.[23]

The net result was considerable economic recovery for the city by 1981, partly due to the posture and rhetoric of Edward I. Koch, who was elected mayor in 1977. At that point, the future of New York was grim enough to make few politicians eager for the job, but not Ed Koch, who defeated Abraham Beame in the Democratic primary election and went on to be elected mayor the following November. His spirited campaign and consequent election provided a welcome tonic to a depressed city. In his inaugural address, for example, Koch told the world that "New York is not a problem. New York is a stroke of genius. From its earliest days, the city has been a lifeboat for the homeless, a refuge for the hungry, a living library for the intellectually starved, a refuge for the oppressed."[24]

Koch's daring paid off. Although he was not directly responsible for the better times of the 1980s, he could bask in the glow that resulted. Many of the changes that occurred, such as real gains in employment during each year of the recovery decade, were predominantly in the service and government areas. By 1983, 28.9 percent of the city's workforce was in the former category and 15.5 percent was in the latter, a considerable gain over previous years.[25] The high proportion of municipal workers was demonstrated in a chart that showed the division of city resources in 1980: Almost a quarter of every budget dollar went to Human Resources, almost as much went to education, 10 percent went to pensions, and the rest went to other municipal agencies, such as the police, fire department, hospitals, and courts. In each case, staff salaries claimed most of the dollars.[26]

The jobs listed in the budget, with some exceptions, were for white-collar workers. This was bad news for unemployed unskilled workers because all the estimates and forecasts that emerged from the worst fiscal crisis in the city's history foretold that as many as three-quarters of the 1,170,000 private job openings to be filled would also be in white-collar occupations. The finance, insurance, and banking industries were expected to grow at a rapid rate, as a result of which clerical workers would find many job openings. Most optimistic of all were the devotees of the new technology, who predicted that "the creation of new jobs as a result of technological advances might be the touchstone for the revitalization of New York."[27] Indeed, employment in the communications industry, which included television, did increase; and, in the late 1970s, finance, insurance, real estate, and retailing companies employed 1.5 million people, a number that grew even larger by 1983.[28]

An econometric model chart predicting average growth rates for 1980 to 1990 appeared in the *New York Times* in April 1979 and indicated a 7.6 percent increase in total output, a 9.6 percent increase in sales, and an 8 percent improvement in personal income, although total employment would grow by only 0.3 percent. The last figure was the result of other data in the chart, such as the fact that the garment industry was not expected to grow because it continued to be cheaper to make items for the mass market elsewhere. The industry, however, was expected to retain its ability to make high fashion clothing, thus selling fewer articles but at high prices.[29]

As a result of all the economic shifts of the post–World War II years, New York never regained its position as a manufacturing center. This was certainly true for Manhattan, although, as mentioned earlier, due to the arrival of immigrants from Asia and South America, by 1995 more garments were manufactured in the city—and not just garments. In Long Island City, in the Red Hook area of Brooklyn, and in Flushing, Queens, a great variety of products are being provided for sale in the city. For example, in Long Island City, a factory produces thousands of pita breads (a Greek specialty) for New York City diners and groceries. Other items include "Indian spices, French bread, theatre costumes, mannequins, picture frames, false teeth and CD-Roms." All of this is, of course, very much related to post-1965 immigration because it is the newest New Yorkers who are producing and consuming much of what is being sold in the city and thus strengthening the New York economy as previous immigrants had done.[30]

The expansion of white-collar and professional jobs that delineated New York's economic profile in the 1980s also strengthened a different side of the city. The cultural and entertainment services that are a unique mark of New York flourished because middle- and upper-class residents, as well as tourists visiting the city for business or pleasure, bought tickets for plays, visited the city's great museums, and shopped in its stores. These welcome developments, however, obscured the continuing problems in the city's economy. The bulk of the new jobs that were created when the economy recovered were filled by middle-class whites, a result of the continuing mismatch between employment opportunities and the abilities of potential workers—a problem that has persisted, although to a somewhat lesser extent, into the 1990s.[31]

If the city government had not continued some of the liberal policies instituted in the 1960s, it would have been an even greater problem. The expansion of municipal activities, however, accompanied by affirmative action policies established in both Washington and Albany, led to the employment of many black and Hispanic men and women who might otherwise have been unable to fit into the city's economy. In spite of these policies, however, in 1979 only 71.3 percent of working-age blacks were employed, a situation that worsened during the following years. In 1983, only 54 percent of black New Yorkers had jobs.[32]

The unemployed were most likely to be new arrivals. Throughout the 1960s, the black migration northward had continued, leading to a 62 percent increase in their number. Harlem's population grew larger and larger; this was also true for Bedford Stuyvesant, Brownsville, Crown Heights, Bushwick, East Flatbush in Brooklyn, and several areas in Queens and the Bronx. Harlem continued to be the cultural center of the New York black community and is the site of the Schomburg Library (a division of the New York Public Library), whose extensive collections present information (historical, scientific, and aesthetic), relating to the black community.[33]

There were also many religious institutions, including the much respected St. Philip's Protestant Episcopal and Abyssian Baptist churches, but in spite of the efforts of agencies such as the Harlem Urban Development Corporation, a state agency, and various antipoverty programs, Harlem remained the home of the poorest people in the city living in some of its worst housing. Those who could, moved out, especially to Bedford Stuyvesant and other Brooklyn communities, but wherever they settled, they lived in "slum ghettoes" and wrestled with familiar problems: single-parent households, welfare dependency, and white flight, which, in turn, led to segregated schools. Many residents managed to move out of the ghetto, but their success did not make an impression on the public at large, because the number who remained very poor continued to grow.[34]

By 1990, non-Hispanic blacks constituted 24.2 percent of the New York City population, an increase of 9 percent in ten years. A similar increase occurred in the number living below the poverty line. In 1969, 25 percent of New York blacks lived below the poverty line; in 1988, 33.8 percent did so. In the latter decade, 40 percent of black families were headed by women, two-thirds of whom lived in poverty. As indicated earlier, one reason for this was the fact that between 1970 and 1980, the city lost 153,000 jobs that required minimal education, making it extremely difficult for undereducated men and women to find work.[35]

In the 1990s, some aspects of the black condition, notably the fact that West Indian blacks were having more success than their American-born brethren, became widely known and led to much speculation regarding the cause. One reason emerged immediately: Black West Indians were "self selected travelers, primed for upward mobility" because they had lived in majority black societies. In addition, they financed their move and resettlement through rotating credit unions and were extremely frugal. There were still other reasons: because the British had been absentee landlords, West Indian black farmers had made important economic decisions, and since Britain abolished slavery twenty-seven years earlier than the United States did, English-speaking Caribbean blacks had more experience as free men and women.[36]

As noted in the previous chapter, Caribbean blacks had been coming to the United States under the British quota for many years, but the Hart-Celler Act made it even easier to enter and more came. By all the usual standards used to judge immigrant achievement, such as education and income levels as well as home ownership, black West Indian immigrants have made a good adjustment to New York. Statistics issued in 1980 showed that most men and women were employed and did not require welfare payments. Although they lagged behind Asian immigrants in this regard, by 1988, between 6,000 and 8,000 had established small businesses, mostly in Brooklyn. Many women were domestic workers and were much prized by families with children because of their elegant British accents.[37]

An article which appeared in the *New York Times* on October 25, 1995, discussed one particular group of West Indian immigrants—those from Jamaica, who have settled in the Wakefield and Williamsbridge districts of the northeast Bronx. The article described a community of more than 14,000 who were "wealthier, better educated, more likely to own their own homes and have greater family stability than those in Brooklyn, where the majority still lived." As was true for the Italians and Jews who had left Little Italy and the Lower East Side for better housing in East Harlem, the northern Bronx is a second area of settlement for Jamaicans. By virtue of hard work and ability to fit into the New York economy, they have achieved what so many immigrants who came before or are coming now have tried to accomplish.[38]

At the same time, because, as a group, their children have done well in school, they have provided workers for white-collar jobs as well as other service industries and their purchases of homes have rescued neighborhoods in many areas of the city, such as Flatbush and Midwood in Brooklyn, which had been in decline. By the late 1980s, the people from Guyana, Trinidad and Tobago, St. Vincent, Grenada, and Barbados, as well as Jamaica, had made their mark on the city, and shops began to sell codfish cakes and "spicy jellied chicken" to the island expatriates.[39]

They also made their mark in other ways. As a result of their good adjustment, they have experienced greater acceptance by the white majority than has been the case for native-born blacks. Sad to say, racism in New York grew by leaps and bounds during the period discussed in this chapter, fueled by increasing crime, drug use, and welfare costs (to mention only a few of the issues). Black ethnocentrism has also played an important role, as has the antisemitism of some black activists. Two prominent leaders, Minister Louis Farrakhan and Professor Leonard Jeffries have encouraged their followers to see Jews as exploiters and worse.

Housing has been a particular problem area. Proposals for building low-income housing in middle-income neighborhoods created protest and bitter opposition in the 1970s when a cooperative development consisting of six towers, each twenty-four floors high, was proposed to occupy a triangular area bounded by Queens Boulevard, the Long Island Expressway, and Flushing Meadow Park. Three of the buildings were to be for low-income tenants, thus injecting a very different population into a heavily Jewish middle-class community known as Forest Hills. As would be expected, opposition was very strong, based on the expectation that the low-income tenants would be blacks. The carrying costs would be too high for families receiving welfare payments, but even self-supporting black neighbors were not acceptable to the people who had settled there in the pre- and early postwar years.

In an October 1995 article published in the *New York Times,* sociologist Nathan Glazer argued that the opposition was based primarily on fear of crime and secondarily on a perception that the neighborhood schools, as well as the neighborhood itself, would deteriorate, not based on race per se. Regardless of how the argument was structured, it was clear that this middle-class white community did not want to share its turf with working-class blacks. After much friction, future Governor Mario Cuomo, then a Queens lawyer, was appointed by Mayor Lindsay to mediate a compromise. What emerged was a much smaller complex: three twelve-story buildings to be purchased only by people who could show that they could afford to pay the maintenance charges.[40]

With the addition of a provision that 40 percent of the apartments were to go to senior citizens, the matter was settled and the buildings were constructed. Two decades later, a court-ordered plan to increase the number of minority tenants revived the controversy. In 1992, the New York City Housing Authority admitted that it had diverted minorities from thirty one of the city's 338 housing projects, including the one in Forest Hills. As result of this a federal court ordered that thirty-eight minority families be placed in the complex.[41]

While housing has been a major area of conflict, it is not the only area of conflict. Blacks and Italians have clashed in Canarsie, Howard Beach, and Bensonhurst, Brooklyn as the constantly growing black population has sought additional room but, in addition, black-Jewish antagonism has developed over other issues. One of the worst disturbances occurred in Crown Heights, which in 1991 exploded in a full-scale riot when an orthodox Jewish Australian student was killed by a gang of black hoodlums. Black-Asian conflict was present elsewhere in the city, and Korean grocers with stores in black neighborhoods have often had a difficult time.[42]

In general, blacks have become more visible in various municipal departments, including sanitation, transportation, and the police. By the end of the 1980s, they occupied a larger share of the city payroll than they did of the population—one-fourth of the latter compared to one-third of the former. This was partly the result of increasing political impact. Black voters, for example, enabled black candidates to become part of a new, more important City Council established in 1991. Prior to that date, the Council shared power with the Board of Estimate, which consisted of the Borough Presidents, the Council President, and the Comptroller. The courts, however, found that this arrangement violated the one-person, one-vote principle and ordered the Board to be dissolved, leaving the Council as the sole check on the mayor.[43]

The Council has not been a very active body, but it has provided more representation for black New Yorkers. By 1991, 40 percent of the members were black. Furthermore, two years earlier black voters had been able to help elect the city's first black mayor, David Dinkins. As a result of increasing black political power, Mayor Koch appointed the first black police commissioner, Benjamin Ward, and Mayor Dinkins followed suit by choosing a second black, Lee Brown, for the post. A different first-time appointment was his choice of another black, Richard Green, to be the Chancellor of the New York City school system.[44]

Green served for only two years and was succeeded by Joseph Fernandez, who was appointed Chancellor in 1990. This was another first and reflected the growth of the Puerto Rican community, which had peaked at just under 1 million in the 1970s, when it constituted 10 percent of the city's population. It remained at that point in spite of considerable outmigration to other cities and states or back to the island during the decade that followed. In 1990, Puerto Ricans represented 50 percent of the 1.8 million Hispanics living in New York but were losing ground to new Spanish-speaking arrivals from Colombia and other South and Central American nations and, most of all, to immigrants from the Dominican Republic.[45]

Four decades after their community was established, Puerto Ricans were living all over the city, albeit it in distinct communities set off from both white and black New Yorkers. Their settlements included the South Bronx, Long Island City, Williamsburg, Sunset Park and Bushwick in Brooklyn, the Lower East Side, and their original core settlement, East Harlem. Wherever they lived, they were poor—according to the 1990 census, they were the poorest ethnic group in the city. The same tabulation showed them to be a youthful group; nearly half were under eighteen and the same percentage lived in female-headed households.[46]

Not surprisingly, these children were dependent on welfare and were subjected to substandard housing and dangerous streets. Their difficulties were due to a number of factors, including racism. A more important reason for their poverty (indeed basic to everything else) was shrinking opportunity as the New York economy changed in the 1970s and 1980s. The industries that had employed Puerto Ricans (metal products, electrical equipment, food packaging, and apparel manufacturing) had automated their plants or left the city and were not being replaced.

As a result, Puerto Ricans moved into the only jobs available: low-wage work as waiters, kitchen help, porters, hospital custodians, and sewing machine operators in nonunion shops. Unfortunately, there were not enough of these insecure and low-paying jobs. With some exceptions, they had only limited access to better paid, unionized occupations. Although they were not immigrants, these underpaid workers have made it possible for many undercapitalized firms to remain in the city, thus performing a service akin to that of earlier immigrant groups, who arrived at a time when the economy was expanding.[47]

As we have seen, jobs for all New Yorkers were not abundant in the 1970s, but when the economy improved in the 1980s, and more white-collar jobs were available, few Puerto Ricans were hired. In 1979, for example, Puerto Ricans held only 27 percent of such jobs, compared to blacks, who held 35 percent. Many of these positions were in government offices, and equal opportunity laws made it clear that some Hispanics should be hired to fill them, but relatively few Puerto Ricans could meet the requirements. The reason for this unfortunate state of affairs was closely related to the fact that although there was an 11 percent increase in Puerto Rican high school graduates between 1980 and 1990, in the same period 60 percent of those who had enrolled had not remained to graduate. Puerto Ricans were also underrepresented at the CUNY colleges except for one in the Bronx (Hostos), in which much of the instruction was in Spanish.[48]

As matters stood in the 1970s, 1980s, and 1990s, it was not unusual for a child whose first language was Spanish to go through bilingual elementary, high school, and college programs and emerge ill equipped for a white-collar position in New York. The court decision of 1974 that resulted from a suit brought by ASPIRA, a Puerto Rican organization organized in 1961 to encourage children to complete high school and college, mandated "a transitional bi-lingual program for all students with limited proficiency in English." Unfortunately, as discussed in the previous chapter, the transitional aspect was forgotten and Puerto Ricans remained less likely than other New Yorkers to complete high school or college. The result was their underrepresentation in manage-rial, sales, or professional positions.[49]

Decentralization and community control, like bilingual education, did not lead to substantial educational or economic gains for black and his-panic children, but after the turbulent 1960s, conditions in the New York elementary and high schools did not attract as much attention. Instead, interest in providing upward mobility for minorities via formal educa-tion shifted to higher education, which in New York meant the various public colleges. These colleges were joined, "after a decade of haggling," into the City University of New York (CUNY) and became operative with the appointment of the first Chancellor, John Everett, in 1960.[50]

One of the factors leading to this step was the establishment, in the 1950s, of the State University System of New York (SUNY), composed of a number of upgraded teacher training colleges and several new uni-versity centers, all of which charged low tuition. Alarmed at the pros-pect of losing middle-class students to inexpensive, more prestigious campuses outside of the city, the municipal colleges pressured their rep-resentatives in Albany to match Governor Rockefeller's initiative with one that would benefit the city.[51]

Beginning in 1950, several reports had foretold the need for expansion of the municipal colleges (Hunter, Brooklyn, City, and Queens) and the creation of several two-year community colleges, three of which (Staten Island, Bronx, and Queensborough) opened their doors in the decade that followed. At that point, as had been true since they were first estab-lished, all of the municipal colleges followed a policy of selective admis-sions. The cutoff average depended on the number of applicants and the seats available, and more space would therefore mean that a lower average could be required. This, in turn, might encourage youngsters who had not done very well in high school to apply.[52]

In 1962, the Board of Higher Education, disturbed by the fact that although 50 percent of the city's high school graduates were black or Puerto Rican they constituted only 10 percent of the students attending the City University, established a committee called "Look to the Future." The resulting report urged further physical expansion to provide a rea-son for more high school students to remain in school, graduate and be eligible to enter one of the units in what would be a much larger university.[53]

History played a role in the Board of Higher Education report and was often cited during the battle that ensued. Because many of those who favored expansion had been children from poor and foreign fami-lies who had moved into the middle class via their education at one of the municipal colleges in the 1920s, 1930s, and 1940s, they argued that formal higher education could do the same for poor minority children in the 1960s, overlooking the fact that the scholastic success of the earlier group followed the achievement of minimum economic stability by their parents. Applying this to conditions in the minority community, it might have been more important for the city to provide blue-collar jobs for their parents than to expand opportunities for higher education for their children. As the following pages will demonstrate, a mistaken assumption led to massive changes in the educational framework of the city.[54]

The Board's report fell on deaf ears at City Hall, and the only expansion that took place was the creation of a College Discovery Program (CDP) in 1963. CDP, funded by New York State with $5,000, was a small experimental program for "disadvantaged" students (two per high school) who could be admitted to one of the community colleges on the basis of a principal's recommendation instead of their high school average. All of the recommended youngsters had to be in their final year of high school and come from families with incomes of less than $1,700 a year. Principals of "ghetto" schools could recommend more than two students. The program was moderately successful—more than a quarter of those who entered college in 1963 graduated with an associate's degree in 1964 and 1965. Even better, three-quarters of those who entered in the latter year, aided by a counseling program set up at that point, completed the course a few years later.[55]

The experiment with CDP was followed, in 1966, by a much larger program, the Search for Elevation, Education and Knowledge (SEEK), which placed students with two handicaps—poverty and low high school grades—into special programs in the senior colleges where, with the aid of counselors, tutors, and special classes, they were expected to join the mainstream and graduate within a reasonable, although longer than the norm, period of time. Like CDP, SEEK was funded by New York State, which encouraged the second chancellor of CUNY, Albert Bowker, to ask for (and receive) more money. This money was used to establish a college construction fund to build another senior college, York, in the heavily black area of Jamaica, Queens and a bilingual two-year college in the Bronx, which was named after the Puerto Rican hero Eugenio Maria de Hostos.[56]

This was only the beginning. Between 1963 and 1983, CUNY added four community colleges: Kingsboro, Borough of Manhattan, Queensborough, and LaGuardia. At the same time, five new senior colleges opened their doors: the College of Staten Island, Lehman (formerly the Bronx campus of Hunter College), Baruch College (previously the business school of City College), John Jay, New York Technical College, and Medgar Evers College. Three additional community colleges, a graduate center, a medical school affiliated with prestigious Mount Sinai Hospital, and a law school completed what was now one of the largest public educational organizations in the United States.[57]

The tremendous expansion, as one can see from the locations and names, was the result of political and ethnic accomodations as well as educational considerations. Legislators in Albany were willing to provide the money, but all of them wanted to please those of their constituents who had children expecting to attend college, and thereby be reelected. The new colleges, some in elegant buildings, now had ample space but not enough students, partly because SUNY continued to lure many away but also because relatively few graduates of the New York City high schools could meet the requirements for admission. Since the colleges' budgets depended on the number of students enrolled, their previous high admission standards had to be thoroughly revised. To accomplish this, an open admissions policy was devised by Bowker and his associates and was endorsed by the Board of Higher Education.[58]

Various groups and individuals had reason to support the idea. They included Governor Rockefeller, who was eager to enhance a liberal reputation that would carry him to the White House in the following presidential election year; labor leader Harry Van Arsdale, who was anxious to provide upward mobility for the sons and daughters of his (mostly white) supporters; and members of the black community, including students already at City College, who took over the South Campus of their college on Harlem Heights to make their views known. The serious disturbances that followed, including temporarily changing the name of the oldest and best-known unit of the City University into the University of Harlem, led the Deputy Chancellor of the University to say "What the hell! Let them all in."[59]

And so it was done. After a hectic year of closings, negotiations, and takeovers, Open Admissions became University policy in July 1969. As stated in the Board of Education resolution, all New York City high school graduates could attend some unit of the City University, and those that needed help would receive remedial and support services. Applicants graduating from high school with an average of 80 or better or who occupied a place in the top 50 percent of their graduating class could attend a senior college; others could enroll in a community college from which they could transfer after earning an associate's degree.[60]

In September 1970, 35,000 students entered the City University, a 75 percent increase over the previous year. In spite of twelve months of planning, none of the colleges was prepared for the entry of such a huge number all at once. Some, such as Baruch College, made hasty arrangements with the Roman Catholic diocese of New York and took over, temporarily, a vacant building that had previously housed Cathedral High School. It was an awkward arrangement that required both faculty and students to become commuters between the Twenty-third and Fifty-first stations of the Lexington Avenue subway line.[61]

The ethnicity of the first crop of Open Admissions students also caught the colleges by surprise. As Van Arsdale had hoped, the majority of the students entering in the early years were whites from working-class families. The increase in the number of Italians, for example, was notable. Until the advent of Open Admissions, they were only a handful; but by 1972, they constituted 20 percent of the student body. Something that was expected and did occur was a substantial increase in the dropout rate, particularly after the first year, when students had to begin taking credit-bearing courses, not just remedial ones. Puerto Rican students had the highest dropout rates unless they were enrolled at Hostos, where, as we have seen, they did not need English in order to pass a course. More than a third of the first Open Admissions class, many of whom had attended private or parochial schools and could have entered before the new policy was adopted, remained to graduate. For those who came from public schools, however, the road to a bachelor's degree was a long and rocky trip.[62]

Why were they so unprepared? Putting aside noneducational reasons for the moment, the curriculum of the high schools had drastically changed in the 1960s and the difficulties experienced by the freshmen entering the City University in the 1970s were the result. High school students could choose (and therefore avoid difficult courses) from a menu of offerings, substituting, for example, black history for the older social studies curriculum which had included civics, geography, and economics as well as Ancient, Modern European, and American history, or opting for business arithmetic instead of geometry.

A survey done in March 1978 showed that this took place even at the most selective high schools in the city, such as Brooklyn Technical, where in 1973 94 percent of the students completed three years of mathematics whereas only 77 percent did so in 1978. At other high schools, such as John Bowne in middle-class Bayside, Queens, only 42.6 percent took the previously required mathematics sequence. At Boys and Girls High School in Bedford-Stuyvesant, only 24 percent did so. The figures for City University entrants overall showed that the percentage of students who had completed the previously mandated four-year English sequence had dropped precipitously during the 1970s.[63]

The end of specific course requirements for high school graduation followed the institution of a single comprehensive diploma, which replaced the previous three: academic, commercial, or general. In essence, the piece of paper awarded to New York City high school graduates after 1973 was merely a social diploma. Many of the young men and women receiving the parchment were being rewarded for sitting through four years of schooling without disrupting their classes but without learning very much either.

Most of the CUNY faculty, although apprehensive about the future and unprepared for a different student body, were ready to give the new approach a try. In a short time, however, many of the doubters turned into opponents when, as was the case at the City College of New York (CCNY), 70 percent of the English department courses had to be devoted to teaching basic writing. After five years of Open Admissions, protests from the CUNY colleges, now spending more and more money on remediation, led the Chancellor (then designated Superintendent of Schools), Irving Anker, to "require that students read at least at the 9th grade level and be able to do arithmetical computations at the 8th grade level in order to graduate from high school." To avoid keeping disruptive students in school indefinitely, the Chancellor also offered a Certificate of Attendance if, after four years, students could not meet the minimal requirements.[64]

Unfortunately, the Chancellor's changes had little impact on the problem of remediation at CUNY. Until the 1990s, and then as a result of budget reductions ordered by Albany and City Hall, remedial English and mathematics remained part of the CUNY curriculum. At this point, however, better news may be on the way. Members of the class entering CUNY in the fall of 1995 were "the best prepared in two decades" as a result of a cooperative program between the University and the Board of Education known as the College Preparatory Initiative (CPI), which imposed "mathematics, English and other academic requirements on high school students considering attendance" at one of the CUNY colleges.[65]

A recent survey of children in the city's lower schools offers even more hope for the future. Tests administered to New York City elementary, middle, and high school students showed that 47.5 percent scored above grade level in reading and 50.3 percent above grade level in mathematics, a better showing than all but one of the nation's urban school systems. This improvement was accomplished in spite of the fact that in 1994, the students in the New York schools came from 188 different nations.[66]

Many school districts with heavy immigrant enrollments offer English as a second language or bilingual classes, but one particular institution—the Newcomer School in Long Island City, Queens—is attempting to do even more. "Because the school's 27 teachers speak a total of 19 languages and dialects and the adolescent students speak 25," the schoool is "Teaching in Many Tongues." The Newcomer School is experimental, and the criteria for entry are based on length of residence in New York (less than one year) and lack of English. The student body of the Long Island City school, of course, is only a tiny fragment of the 153,000 non-English-speaking youngsters entering the New York City schools each year. As a result, more Newcomer Schools are on the drawing boards.[67]

The twenty-five different languages and dialects spoken at the Newcomer School demonstrate that New York is receiving the most varied group of immigrants in its history. In addition to small groups of Albanians, Arabs, Greeks, Indonesians, Irish, Japanese, Filipinos, Vietnamese, Colombians, Portuguese, Poles, Haitians, and Ukranians, a much larger number of Asian Indians, Chinese, Koreans, Dominicans, and Russians have made New York their home. They are present, in varying numbers, all over the city; but in Queens, it is Asians, of all varieties, who have most changed the ethnic profile of the borough.[68]

In spite of the city's economic difficulties, as was true for those who came before, employment opportunities and the presence of family and friends pull immigrants to New York; lack of opportunity and political repression provide the push to leave their homelands. Special circumstances play a role in the decision to leave: Dictator Trujillo's death allowed Dominicans to go and the oppressive rule of the tyrant who governed the other half of the island of Hispianola, Duvalier, encouraged Haitians to move out. An important example of the effect of political change was the exodus of Soviet Jews from the former Soviet Union and its satellites.[69]

About half of the foreign-born population of New York in 1980 had arrived after 1965, when the Hart-Celler Act, as we have seen, eliminated the quota system and established family reunion and needed skills as the basis for admission. About a million of the new arrivals had the proper documents, but if illegal immigrants (always an estimate) are counted, the total who came and settled in New York at that point becomes even larger, 1.5 million. In 1995, demographers estimated that "easily 30% of the city is foreign born," a proportion that would be even higher if illegals were included. Furthermore, "children of foreign born women account for nearly half of the 130,000 births a year."[70]

Illegal immigration has been more troublesome for states such as California and Texas, and the passage of the Immigration Control Act in 1986, which combined the imposition of sanctions on employers of illegal aliens and a grant of resident status to illegals who applied for amnesty by a given date, has not solved the problem. Other changes in the immigration laws during the period covered in this chapter—notably liberalized refugee legislation—have had a greater impact on New York. Together with the familiar push and pull factors, the various legislative alterations have created still another version of the cosmopolitan city that New York has always been.[71]

There are many practical results stemming from the current immigrant wave. The newcomers pay income, sales, property, and gasoline taxes; contribute to the Social Security Fund; keep small neighborhood stores alive; and provide needed skills. Furthermore, their arrival has stemmed New York's population losses and changed the city in many ways. The original Chinatown, for example, has expanded to include what was Little Italy and, in company with other Asians, the Chinese have changed the population of many areas of Manhattan and even more, in Queens. A downward glance from the number 7 elevated subway train when it stops at the Main Street station in Flushing reveals a conglomeration of shops, restaurants, funeral parlors, and people that truly justify the nickname "Little Asia." The proliferation has aroused considerable interest from visitors and natives alike and, in response, a Visitors Guide is being prepared to describe the ethnic enclaves that have been created along the elevated tracks that stretch from Long Island City to Flushing.[72]

Although the ethnicity of the residents is different, Crown Heights and East Flatbush in Brooklyn present a similar picture. Their streets are filled with "West Indian barber shops, beauty parlors, restaurants, record stores, groceries and bakeries . . . and the sounds of Haitian, Creole and West Indian accents are heard everywhere." Other parts of the city have been equally transformed: Brighton Beach has been dubbed Little Odessa, Hondurans have populated Morrisania in the Bronx, and Dominicans outnumber Puerto Ricans in upper Manhattan. Immigrants have also had an important effect on the areas in which they work but do not live. Korean food markets can be found in almost every neighborhood, and a variety of ethnic restaurants have permitted those New Yorkers who want to go beyond MacDonalds and pizzas to do so.

Most of the ethnic changes have gone smoothly. A Methodist church in Jackson Heights, Queens, for example, has adapted to change by offering services in Korean, Chinese, and Spanish as well as English. Many Roman Catholic churches have made similar accomodations. In some areas of the city, the Catholic Church has been strengthened by the arrival of immigrants from the Caribbean, as well as from South and Central America. Although *new* is hardly the proper word for an ethnic group that has been settling in New York since colonial times, the number of Irish who have made New York their home, illegally during a wave of immigration in the middle to late 1980s and legally after the passage in 1990 of the Family Unity and Employment Immigration Act (Morrison Act) has rejuvenated entire parishes, such as Woodlawn in the Bronx and Woodside in Queens. The Irish newcomers are largely young men and women, eager for work and optimistic about their chances because, unlike so many of the other new arrivals, they are literate in English.[73]

More than neighborhoods have been changed by the post-1965 immigrant wave. For one thing, the newcomers do work that other residents of the city have bypassed. An article published in the *New York Times* in September 1995 gave some idea of the variety: Pictures of an Ethiopian masseuse, a manicurist from Tajikstan, a nanny from St. Vincent in the British West Indies, a doorman from Poland, a newspaper vendor from

Pakistan, and a maid from Brazil combined to present a kaleidoscope of the work being done by immigrants in New York today.[74]

The process has not been without its problems. Indians, for example, have been the targets of racism, manifested by "muggings, purse snatchings, name calling, burglaries and vandalism" and many Koreans, in 1995, are selling out and going back to their home country because they believe that there is a "glass ceiling" in New York which limits their ambitions. Russian Jews in Brighton Beach have experienced hostility from the Jews who settled there earlier, and their high-achieving children have suffered from the demands made on them by teachers who accept the stereotype that all Jews are brilliant students. Other students have been handicapped by a lack of records, which prevents school administrators from placing them in a proper grade.[75]

Of the greatest importance has been the resentment of native workers, who argue that their jobs have been lost to the newcomers who are not unionized and will work for low wages. In 1995, disclosures of garment-making sweatshops in Chinatown and elsewhere, staffed by poor women who have been imported by agents to whom they have to give some of their limited wages to repay the cost of passage, have reinforced the prevailing anger against immigrant workers. There is, however, an important point to be made in favor of the new workers: Their willingness to work cheaply has permitted at least a part of the garment industry to remain in New York.[76]

In spite of the many problems involved in emigration and resettlement, thousands of newcomers continue to see New York as a "Promised City." In 1994, thirty-nine different foreign-language newspapers were being published in the city, three for Spanish speakers, three for Haitians, two for Irish, six for Chinese, and twenty-five for Russians. Clearly, the fiscal crises, economic problems, deteriorated housing, and troubled schools that marked New York in the 1970s and 1980s did not deter people looking for a better life from coming to the city.[77]

This has also been true in the 1990s. In 1990, Congress, aware that Chinese, Korean, Caribbean, and Mexican immigrants were filling most of the available immigration slots, established a lottery system designed to create greater diversity. This proved very useful for Irish and Polish newcomers, who have replenished historically Irish communities such as Sunnyside in Queens and an old Polish neighborhood, Greenpoint, in Brooklyn. New York's attractiveness to all ethnic groups is illustrated when the annual lottery is announced and hordes of people living in the city without the green card that denotes legal residency descend on the Immigration Service headquarters to wait for hours on long lines. For most the wait is fruitless; only 7 percent of New York's immigrants gain legal entry through the lottery.

Another group of immigrants, Turks, not previously attracted to New

York, have added to the ethnic mosaic in Sunnyside. The community was 30,000 strong in 1996 and still growing as were the foodstores selling Turkish delights. Most Turks have found work through the "buddy system" which was historically used by newcomers. Their children now constitute twenty percent of the population at P.S. 150, the neighborhood elementary school.[78]

Immigration became a "hot" subject during the Presidential year 1996. A new welfare law "intended to save 55 billion dollars over the next six years, in part by cutting the benefits for legal immigrants," was enacted by the Republican majority in Congress and signed by President Clinton. Both parties were responding to what seemed to be strong anti-immigrant sentiment in the nation at large. As a result, immigrants have hastened to acquire citizenship. A New York Times headline on September 13, 1996 said "Immigrant Anxiety Spurs a Naturalization Surge" as a result of which 1.1 million immigrants would become citizens by September 30, 1996.[79]

At one point during the debate that preceded the passage of the new act, Priscilla Labowitz, an immigration lawyer, presented some little known facts about the subject in an article which appeared on the "Op Ed" page of the New York Times. Her major sources were Census Bureau and Immigration and Naturalization Service statistics which revealed that in spite of considerable post–World War II immigration from Asia and Latin America, Seventy-four percent of the American population is white and that legal immigration had decreased between 1993 and 1995.[80]

Sociologist Roger Waldinger presented a different aspect of the immigration controversy in a superb book, Still the Promised City? New Immigrants and African Americans in Post–Industrial New York which appeared in the autumn of 1996. Waldinger's thesis is that the failure of native born blacks to achieve upward mobility in New York was not due to the departure of manufacturing plants from the city which eliminated many low skilled jobs. On the contrary, he argued, using the garment industry as an example, blacks rarely held those jobs because both the unions and racist white workers tried to keep them out. He also says that in the sixties, when more opportunities were available, native born blacks shunned low-level jobs, leaving them to immigrants from Central America and the Caribbean. His conclusion is ambivalent: restriction might result in more jobs for American born blacks but, on the other hand, they might not be willing or prepared to take them.[81]

The various changes described in this chapter, including the entry of thousands of people previously not seen in the city, produced considerable disquiet among those who study New York, to say nothing of the apprehensions that concerned government officials and worried ordinary people. As a result, a number of surveys and studies of the city's condition were conducted in the 1970s and 1980s. The results varied; some of the data gave reason for optimism, others for pessimism. One of the first articles, written by Roger Starr of the *New York Times* in 1971, was extremely pessimistic. Starr saw the loss of blue-collar jobs as a virtually insurmountable problem. The diminuition of port activities between 1930 and 1965, for example, had caused the number of waterfront jobs to drop by half, and a further drop had occurred on ferries, tugboats, and barges between 1965 and 1971. Starr saw no reason to expect that the waterfront situation would improve; he also believed that the decline of manufacturing jobs would continue and that there would be fewer corporate headquarter offices in New York.[82]

These facts would be troublesome under any circumstances, but because he was writing in the difficult 1970s Starr saw the economic decline as even more serious when it was coupled with the arrival of thousands of poor and uneducated blacks, Puerto Ricans, and people from Third World nations. He used an interesting device to illustrate some of the resulting problems—an increase in the number of false fire alarms, from 92,000 in 1960 to 264,000 in 1970—and attributed this to the social disorganization that had resulted from the changed population. His other indices—a tripling of the number of people receiving public assistance in the same ten-year period and an increase of 84,000 in female-headed households—were more significant. Starr, as well as other observers, looked to Washington for the remedy, reasoning that federal policies had led to the arrival of poor migrants and immigrants in New York.[83]

Six years later, the Temporary Commission on City Finances, with great caution, tried to lift some of the gloom projected in the pessemists' forecast. Population and the number of jobs would continue to decrease, the report said, but at a much slower rate because the costs of doing business in New York City, such as labor, rent, and energy, were no longer much higher than in other American manufacturing cities.[84]

This modest optimism, however, did not overcome the pessimism of a *New York Times* article written by A. H. Raskin, which focused on the "four decades of expansion in the range, depth and cost of municipal services: welfare, education, mass transit, criminal justice and hospitals, all of which were mostly paid for by city tax money unlike, in other parts of the nation, by state or county governments." These heavy burdens, Raskin said, were the results of 1960s liberalism and the increase in poor New Yorkers. Like Starr, Raskin could see no solution other than increased federal support.[85]

Other voices, however, could also be heard. The January 1977 issue of *New York Perspective*, published by the School of Business of Baruch College, reported the results of a conference on New York's economic profile, held at the college during the previous October, which presented the views of academic economists, government officials, and business leaders on the future of the city and came up with a much more optimistic scenario. The Stock Exchange would remain in the city and grow along with the securities industry; and the Port of New York, if it could be freed from state and federal restrictions and negotiate less costly contracts with the Longshoremen's Union, would continue to be "number one" in general cargo tonnage, value of cargo handled, freighters accomodated, and customs collected.[86]

Only one of the participants at the conference, John Keith, the president of the Regional Plan Association, struck a sour note when he pointed out that "New York had lost half a million jobs, equally divided between manufacturing and office service work," since 1975 and that these jobs were probably lost forever. The City Planning Commission was only slightly more cheerful, expecting some increase in service and financial jobs but in its 1981 report, the Commission also forecasted higher costs for the city's increasing elderly and foreign-born population as well as essential infrastructure improvements.[87]

In the 1980s, the voices of doom were not entirely stilled but they were diminished because, as the decade progressed, some improvements were apparent. A chart comparing various aspects of New York City life in 1977 and 1988 showed, for example, that 3.7 million feet of office space had been built; and that a grocery store on Columbus Avenue on the West Side of Manhattan, which had rented for $800 dollars a year in 1977, was now a boutique whose owner paid $5,000 for the privilege of operating a business in what was becoming a trendy location, attractive to the young middle-class men and women who were moving into the neighborhood.[88]

There was more good news: Graffiti had virtually disappeared from the New York City subway cars and, perhaps as a result, ridership had increased. The results of the civil rights activities of the 1960s and 1970s were apparent in the increased number of blacks, Hispanics, and women on the police force. Best of all, median household income, after taxes, had moved up from $15,000 a year in 1979 to $25,000 eight years later. Unfortunately, the same chart indicated that, at least in the cold months, the number of people forced to live in municipal shelters had also increased, from 2,120 in 1979 to 10,318 in 1988.[89]

All things considered, the optimists had and continue to have more reason for their position. New York has remained the cultural capital of the United States, "the place where artists, actors, musicians, dancers and writers come together to make American culture."[90] In the 1980s, the "lively arts" were revived and are going strong in the 1990s, as the Arts and Leisure pages of the *New York Times* make clear.

The growth of off-Broadway theaters, lines for half-price tickets at Duffy Square and the World Trade Center, crowds in the theater district,

famous musicians who come to Lincoln Center and Carnegie Hall, and
the marvelous exhibits at the city's museums are proof positive that "the
role of the city, now broadcasting on a world wide communications network, assures the supremacy of New York taste, image [and] assumptions." Today, New York can fairly be called the "Center of the Art
World," with twenty museums, large and small, in Manhattan alone and
the Brooklyn Museum across the river for supplementary knowledge if
the others do not suffice.[91]

The aforementioned amenities, delightful as they are, do not exhaust
the reasons for optimism about New York's future. Kennedy Airport is
the busiest in the nation, capitalists from all over the world invest their
money in New York, and the real estate markets in many parts of the
city (such as Brooklyn Heights and the upper East Side) remain strong,
as is also true for older areas, such as Tribeca and Chelsea. New manufacturing has developed in Long Island City and Chinatown, thanks to
the new hands who have come across the oceans to operate the machines.[92]

Nonetheless, it is not possible to say that all is well in the Empire
City. The failure of racial integration in housing and schools was exem-
plified by a *New York Times* report entitled "Battle of Belle Harbor,"
which appeared on November 12, 1995. Parents who lived in private
homes in the white portion of the Rockaway Peninsula in Queens were
battling to expand their neighborhood public school, which operated
from kindergarten through sixth grade, by two more grades in order to
avoid sending their children to the junior high school designated for
them, which is located in the black area of Far Rockaway and serves
children who live in the low-rent city-owned projects nearby.[93]

Another matter, this time related to transportation, illustrates two
troublesome aspects—racial tension and fiscal shortages—that continue
to plague the city. The Metropolitan Transportation Authority (MTA),
which operates the suburban rail systems as well as the subway and
bus lines, announced an increase in the fare on all its systems, but the
percentage asked from suburban commuters was lower than that required from city riders. This led to a suit by civil rights activists, who
claimed racial discrimination because suburban riders are mostly white
and city passengers are heavily black and Hispanic.[94]

The case is yet to be heard but it is on the docket of the federal courts
because any agency that is funded by the federal government (true in
part for the MTA) is barred from discriminating against minority
groups. Another, more lethal racial event occurred just as this manu-
script was being completed. Reawakening earlier grievances, a Jewish
businessman on 125th Street, Harlem's busiest shopping "boulevard,"
tried to expand his store by absorbing an adjacent black-owned record
shop. This led to protests, increased antisemitism, arson, and seven

deaths. Racial conflict aside, the continuing problem of the homeless, seemingly intractable traffic tie-ups, and a tired infrastructure, to name just a few of the difficulties, continue and, if the Republican "revolution" in Washington succeeds, may grow worse.[95]

At the same time, however, people continue to come to New York and older residents stay because of the good things it offers. When New Yorkers are asked why they are willing to pay high taxes and cope with crowding and high rents, the answers include enjoyment of the city's physical beauty, its parks, beaches, stores with the latest fashions, cultural opportunities, as well as low-cost public higher education, good medical care, restaurants for every pocket and taste, chances to meet interesting people, and, most of all, job opportunities. As has been true for almost 400 years, people come to New York and find there a milieu in which the impossible can be attempted.[96]

In several respects, New York in 1995 is not one city. East Harlem, Washington Heights, and the lower East Side, for example, differ in many ways from other areas of Manhattan. Some of the differences are income, education, ethnicity, and race, making the story of the Empire City a "Tale of [more than] Two Cities."[97] The future of the different parts is clouded and one hesitates to predict what the future holds, but in 1996 there is reason to hope. The movement to the suburbs is likely to decline because communities in Nassau, Suffolk, and Westchester counties have already begun to encounter racial conflict and fiscal problems similar to those that have plagued the city. At the same time, it is possible that the quality of life in New York City, such as fewer crimes, cleaner streets, better traffic management, and improved schools, will make the city more attractive to middle-class families. Most important, healthy existing industries, such as tourism, computers, finance, communication, advertising, and publishing, are likely to remain and grow. So will the number of newcomers, who are now more likely to bring their brain power rather than the brawn that built the Empire City in earlier times.

NOTES

1. Bayard Still, "Bicentennial New York, 1976," in Milton Klein, ed., *New York: The Centennial Years, 1676–1976* (Port Washington, N.Y.: Kennikat Press, 1976), 125–127.

2. George Lankevich with Howard Furer, *A Brief History of New York City* (Port Washington, N.Y.: Associated Universities Press, 1984), 301.

3. Still, "Bicentennial," 154.

4. Ibid.

5. Martin Shefter, *The Fiscal Crisis and Its Budgetary Consequences* (New York: Basic Books, 1985), 128; Michael Katz, *Improving Poor People* (Princeton, N.J.: Princeton University Press, 1995), 73–74.

6. Lankevich, *Brief History*, 299.

7. Shefter, *Fiscal Crisis*, 133; Lankevich, *Brief History*, 295–296.

8. Katz, *Poor People*, 74.

9. Shefter, *Fiscal Crisis*, 135; Lankevich, *Brief History*, 296.

10. Shefter, *Fiscal Crisis*, 147.

11. Richard Wade, "The End of the Self-Sufficient City: New York's Fiscal Crisis in History," *City University of New York Magazine*, 1985, 2.

12. Maurice Ballabon, "New York City—Economic Fulcrum," *New York City Perspective*, vol. 1 (December 1973), 2.

13. *New York Times*, April 5, 1977, 1; Herbert Bienstock, "New York City's Labor Market: Past Trends, Current Conditions, Future Prospects," *City Almanac*, vol. 12 (December 1977), 5, 9.

14. Henry Eilbert, "New York City: Its Marketing Potential," *New York City Perspective*, vol. 2 (January 1975), 4; Chase Manhattan Bank, "Distribution of Family Income, 1959–1969 (in 1969 dollars)"; David Rachman, "Problems Facing New York City Retailing," *New York City Perspective* (July 1974), 2–3.

15. Karen Gerard, "New York City's Economy: A Decade of Change," *New York Affairs*, 1983, 5.

16. Roger Waldinger, "Immigration and Industrial Change in the New York Apparel Industry," in Marta Tienda and George Borjas, eds., *Hispanics in the United States Economy* (New York: Academic Press, 1985), 9.

17. Waldinger, "Immigration and Industrial Change," 10.

18. *New York Times*, May 11, 1977, 1.

19. Ibid.

20. *New York Times*, December 11, 1975, 24.

21. Gerard, "New York Economy," 3; Lankevich, *Brief History*, 306.

22. Lankevich, *Brief History*, 321.

23. Gerard, "New York Economy," 8; Lankevich, *Brief History*, 303.

24. Lankevich, *Brief History*, 303.

25. New York State Department of Labor, "Non-Agricultural Employment in New York City, 1950–1980," Table 1.

26. *New York Times*, chart, "Tracing the Strings on New York's Purse" (January 13, 1980), D6.

27. Bienstock, "Labor Market," 15–16.

28. Gerard, "New York Economy," 6.

29. *New York Times*, April 3, 1979, 27; Waldinger, "Immigration and Industrial Change," 30.

30. *New York Times*, September 4, 1995, 1, 22.

31. Gerard, "New York Economy," 8.

32. David M. Reimers and Frederic M. Binder, *All the Nations Under Heaven* (New York: Columbia University Press, 1995), 254.

33. Still, "Bicentennial New York," 132.

34. "Harlem," *Encyclopedia of New York City*, Kenneth Jackson, ed. (New Haven, Conn.: Yale University Press, 1935), 523.

35. *Encyclopedia of New York City*, 115; Reimers and Binder, *Nations*, 206.

36. Reimers and Binder, *Nations*, 229; Emanuel Tobier, *Changing Faces* (New York: Community Service Society, 1984), 38; Philip Kasnitz, *Caribbean New York* (Ithaca, N.Y.: Cornell University Press 1992), 105–106.

37. Reimers and Binder, *Nations*, 229; Kasinitz, *Caribbean*, 105–106.

38. *New York Times,* October 25, 1995, B1, 10.

39. Reimers and Binder, *Nations,* 229.

40. *New York Times Magazine,* January 2, 1992, 11–31.

41. *New York Times,* October 22, 1995, B1, B10.

42. Reimers and Binder, *Nations,* 235, 249.

43. *New York Times,* "The City Council and How It Works," November 26, 1995, C1; Reimers and Binder, *Nations,* 253.

44. Reimers and Binder, *Nations,* 251.

45. "Puerto Ricans," *Encyclopedia of New York City,* 963.

46. Kal Wagenheim, *Puerto Rico: A Profile* (New York: Praeger Publishers, 1970), 197.

47. Clara Rodriguez, *Puerto Ricans: Born in the USA* (Boston: Unwin, Hyman, 1989), 120–121.

48. Reimers and Binder, *Nations,* 251.

49. "Aspira," *Encyclopedia of New York City;* author's conversation with Rudolph Martinez, Assistant Professor in the Academic Skills Department, Baruch College, City University of New York, 1978.

50. Selma Berrol, *Getting Down to Business* (Westport, Conn.: Greenwood Press, 1989), 105–106.

51. Ibid.

52. Martin Mayer, "Higher Education for All?" *Commentary* (February 1973), 38.

53. Ibid., 39.

54. Selma Berrol, "Education and Economic Mobility: The Jewish Experience in New York City, 1880–1920," *American Jewish Historical Quarterly* (January 1976), *passim.*

55. Harold Wechsler, *The Qualified Student: A History of Selective College Admissions in America* (New York: John Wiley, 1977), 275.

56. Selma Berrol, "City University of New York," *Encyclopedia of New York City;* Wechsler, *Qualified Student,* 276.

57. Mayer, "Higher Education?" 39.

58. Ibid., 40.

59. David Lavin, *Rights vs. Privileges: The Open Admissions Experiment at the City University of New York* (New York: Free Press, 1981), 11, 13.

60. Ibid., 15.

61. The author was a Dean at Baruch College from 1970 to 1978 and recalls the "awkward arrangement" very well.

62. Binder and Reimers, *Nations,* 200.

63. *New York Times,* March 23, 1978, B12.

64. Lavin, *Rights vs. Privileges,* 28.

65. Author's conversation with Associate Dean Sidney Lirtzman, Baruch College, December 10, 1995.

66. *New York Times,* June 25, 1995, B1.

67. *New York Times,* November 7, 1995, B1, 3.

68. Ellen Percy Kraly, "United States Immigration Policy and the Immigrant Population of New York City," in Nancy Foner, ed., *New Immigrants in New York City* (New York: Columbia University Press, 1987), 71.

69. Foner, *New Immigrants,* 4.

70. Ibid., 17; *New York Times*, September 24, 1995, 13.

71. Kraly, "Immigration Policy," 46, 48.

72. Foner, *New Immigrants*, 18.

73. *New York Times*, October 24, 1995, 4.

74. *New York Times*, September 2, 1995, 19.

75. Foner, *New Immigrants*, 27; *New York Times*, August 22, 1995, 31, 49; *New York Times*, August 6, 1995, 13; *New York Times*, September 2, 1995, 7.

76. Foner, *New Immigrants*, 24.

77. B. Kim Taylor, "Stats of the City," *Our Town* (January 23, 1995), 7.

78. *New York Times*, January 30, 1996, B2; Ibid., June 1, 1996, B1, 4.

79. *New York Times*, September 13, 1996, B1.

80. Priscilla Labowitz, "Immigration, Just the Facts," *New York Times*, March 25, 1996, 32.

81. Roger Waldinger, *Still the Promised City? New Immigrants and African American in Post–Industrial New York* (Cambridge, Mass.: Harvard University Press, 140, 166.

82. *New York Times Magazine*, November 11, 1971, 62–63.

83. Ibid., 64.

84. *New York Times*, May 15, 1977, 12.

85. *New York Times*, May 18, 1975, 6.

86. Forums I, II, III, IV, *New York Perspective* (January 1977), 2, 4.

87. *New York Times*, April 20, 1981, 13.

88. *New York Times*, January 14, 1974, 16.

89. Ibid.

90. Still, "Bicentennial New York," 155.

91. Eric Homberger, *Historical Atlas of New York* (New York: Henry Holt & Company, 1994), 147, 152.

92. *New York Times*, September 4, 1995, 1, 22.

93. *New York Times*, November 12, 1995, 1, 12.

94. *New York Times*, November 2, 1995, 27.

95. *New York Times*, December 8, 1995, 1; *New York Times*, December 18, 1995, B3.

96. Homberger, *Historical Atlas*, 150–151.

97. Ibid., 147.

Bibliographical Essay

As noted in the preface, most books on New York deal with a specific aspect of the city's history, but there are some that range widely enough to be considered general works. Two of them are reference books: Eric Homberger's *Historical Atlas of New York City* (1994) describes the geographical history of the city from Dutch days onward, and the *Encyclopedia of the City of New York* (1995), edited by Kenneth Jackson, provides data in small doses on an enormous variety of topics.

Books that cover urban history as a whole but also provide information on New York City include texts such as Charles Glaab and A. Theodore Brown's *History of Urban America* (1967) and Sam Bass Warner's *Urban Wilderness* (1972) or collections of essays written by different historians, such as Wilson Smith's *Cities of Our Past and Present* (1964) and another edited by two distinguished historians, Allan Nevins and John Krout, *New York: The Greater City* (1948). There is only one monograph that includes all of the most important aspects of New York City history: George Lankovich and Howard Furer's *A Brief History of New York City* (1984).

Bayard Still's *Mirror for Gotham* (1956) covers many years, but his information is limited to what travelers to the city said about it; this is interesting but must be used in conjunction with other sources. A somewhat similar but more reliable work is Milton Klein's *Centennial Years* (1976), which tells readers what happened in New York in 1676, 1776, 1876, and 1976. Ira Rosenwaike's *Population History of New York* (1972) is extremely useful because he has collected and organized a variety of essential statistics.

Several books which concentrate on specific developments in New York history, usually limited to a particular time period, are also very useful. Nelson Blake's *Water for the City* (1956), which, as the title indicates, discusses the building of a much-needed aqueduct system for the city, and Anthony Jackson's *A Place Called Home* (1976), which is devoted to the housing history of nineteenth-century New York, are examples. Two others are David McCulloch's *The Great Bridge* (1972), a marvelous description of the building of the Brooklyn Bridge and Eugene Moehring's *Public Works and Patterns of Urban Real Estate Growth in Manhattan, 1835–1894* (1981), both of which contain considerable information related to the growth of the city. Twentieth-century physical change was the work of Robert Moses, discussed in valuable detail by Robert Caro in *Robert Moses and the Fall of New York* (1974). Both Robert Daley's *The World beneath the City* (1959) and Peter Derrick's long essay "Rapid Transit in New York: Its Development and Impact on the City," which appeared in *New York Affairs* in May 1986, discuss the building of an essential component of New York City life: the subways.

The physical city, at all periods, was closely tied to the economic sector. In this regard, Robert Albion's classic *Rise of the Port of New York, 1845–1860* (1939), when combined with Edward Spann's *A New Metropolis: New York, 1840–1857* (1981); Allan Pred's *Spatial Dynamics of United States Industrial Growth* (1981), which gives New York its due; and Henry Lanier's *A Century of Banking* (1922) provide comprehensive information on the economic life of the nineteenth-century city, as does Thomas Cochran's essay "The City's Business," which is included in the Nevins and Krout collection cited previously.

New York City history, in general, is a cheerful story, but there are also dark sides. Jacob Riis wrote several well-known books about poverty in the late nineteenth century, such as *The Battle with the Slums* (1902) and *The Children of the Poor* (1892). Raymond Mohl did the same for the earlier part of that century in his *Poverty in New York, 1783–1825* (1971). Jeremy Felt's book on child labor, *Hostages of Fortune* (1965), discusses one aspect of the poverty Mohl and Riis describe; and Charles Rosenberg's *The Cholera Years* (1962) discusses the epidemics that plagued the city before purified water was available and shows how the deadly disease afflicted the poor, who were unable to flee the city.

Another result of poverty was violence. Joel Tyler Headley's *Great Riots of New York, 1712–1873* (1970) describes them very well, as does Paul Weinbaum's *Mobs and Demogogues* (1979). Part of the response to the riots was the creation of a uniformed police department, discussed by James Richardson in his book *The New York Police* (1970). This step was closely connected to the political life of the city, which is described in several works. Of particular interest is David Hammack's *Power and So-*

ciety: Greater New York at the Turn of the Century (1982), which concentrates on the joining of the four nearby previously separated counties to Manhattan. William Henderson's *Tammany Hall and the New Immigrants* (1976) discusses the workings of that famous political machine in the early twentieth century, and Charles Garrett discusses the end of its power in *The LaGuardia Years: Machine and Reform Politics in New York City* (1976). Thomas Kessner's *Fiorello LaGuardia and the Making of Modern New York* (1989) is also very useful, especially for the city's history during the great Depression and World War II.

Two books (both coauthored)—Daniel Moynihan and Nathan Glazer's *Beyond the Melting Pot* (1970) and David Reimer and Fred Binder's *All the Nations under Heaven* (1995)—link the city's history to the lives of the immigrants and migrants who settled there. Both provide data for the thesis of this book—the variety of the people who have settled in New York and improved their lives and, in the process, improved the city. Several books on the history of American immigration as a whole, such as Carl Wittke's *We Who Built America* (1939), Roger Daniels's *Coming to America* (1990), and Philip Taylor's *Distant Magnet* (1971) contain information specific to New York, the nation's premier immigrant-receiving city.

Hundreds of specialized books have been written on immigration and ethnicity in New York, the most important of which were Thomas Janvier's *Dutch Founding of New York* (1903), Hyman Grinstein's *Rise of the Jewish Community of New York* (1945) (both important for the early chapters of this book), Robert Ernst's *Immigrant Life in New York, 1825–1863* (1949), and Kirby Miller's *Emigrants and Exiles* (1985). The latter is useful for the mid-nineteenth-century arrivals of Irish and Germans, as was Moses Rischin's *Promised City* (1962), Deborah Dash Moore's *At Home in America* (1979), and Thomas Kessner's *The Golden Door* (1977) for the eastern European Jews who came from 1880 to 1924. Robert Orsi's *The Madonna of 115th Street* (1985), Richard Gambino's *Blood of My Blood* (1974), and Jerre Mangiano and Ben Morreale's *La Storia* (1980) tell the story of the other group that arrived in large numbers at that time: the Italians. As a rule, the new arrivals were too busy getting a foothold in New York to quarrel with those who had preceded them, but ethnic hostility was certainly present, as Ronald Bayor's *Neighbors in Conflict* (1988), which discusses Irish-Jewish relations in upper Manhattan, makes clear.

Essential to the story of the people of New York are the black men and women who were always part of the city but came in increasing numbers from 1900 on. Their story is well told in several works: Gilbert Osofsky's *Harlem: The Making of a Ghetto* (1968), James Weldon Johnson's *Black Manhattan* (1969), and Edward Levinson's *Black Politics in New York*

(1974). Post-World War II arrivals are the subject of Nancy Foner's *New Immigrants in New York* (1987), as well as Virginia Sanchez Korral's *From Colonia to Community: History of the Puerto Ricans in New York* (1983) and Elena Padillo's *Up from Puerto Rico* (1958). The continuing migration of Spanish-speaking people to New York is discussed in Philip Kasnitz's *Caribbean New York* (1992) and in Emanuel Tobier's *Changing Faces* (1984).

The newest immigration from Asia is given space in Reimer and Binder's *All the Nations under Heaven,* cited previously, but a full-scale study has yet to be written. For this reason, the author of any book dealing with the changing population of the city must rely heavily on the *New York Times* and other periodicals, such as the *Journal of Ethnic History, Journal of American History, New York History, American Jewish History,* and lesser known specialized journals, such as *New York Affairs* and *New York Perspective. Reviews in American History* is also valuable.

Sources for special topics, such as the educational history of the city, include Diane Ravitch's *Great School Wars* (1974) and my own *Immigrants at School* (1967) as well as the assorted papers and articles listed in the notes to Chapter 6. The notes are also useful for less important works on all the topics discussed in the preceding pages and for primary sources, such as publications of the United States Labor Department and the Bureau of the Census.

Index

Aid to Families with Dependent Children (AFDC), 142, 150
Amalagamated Houses, 110
American Labor Party (ALP), 112
Anti-poverty organizations, 61
Articles of Capitulation, 9
Asian immigrants, 132
Association for the Improvement of the Condition of the Poor (AICP), 57
Astor, Jacob, 27, 52

Banker's Agreement, 111
Banks, 27, 51
Battle of Golden Hill, 21
Beame, Abraham, 150–151
Before the Melting Pot, 3
Bilingual education, 160, 165
Black Ball Line, 30
The Black Family in Slavery and Freedom, 85
Blacks: during World War II, 121–122; in early New York, 24, 25, 26; effect of immigration on, 119; hostility to, 67, 68, 158, 170; improved status, 140, 156; in New Amsterdam, 1, 6, 7; in nineteenth-century New York, 49, 50; riot in 1935, 121; in the twenties in Harlem, 120–121; West Indians, 139
Board of Aldermen, 63
Board of Assistant Aldermen, 63
Board of Brokers, 31
Board of Commissioners of Emigration, 44
British immigrants, 41
Brooklyn, 79
Brooklyn-Battery Tunnel, 129
Brooklyn Bridge, 80–81
Brooklyn-Manhattan Transit (BMT), 108
Butler, Nicholas Murray, 81

Castle Garden, 44–45
Centralized school system, 81
Central Park, 66–67
Children's Aid Society, 61
Chinatown, 86, 87
Chinese, 48–49, 87, 114
City College of New York, 63
City Planning Commission, 171
City University of New York (CUNY), 161–163

Clinton, DeWitt, 31
College Discovery Program (CDP), 162
College Preparatory Initiative (CPI), 165
Croton Water System, 58
Crystal Palace, 52
Currency Act, 20

Dauphine, 1
Da Verrazano, Giovanni, 1
Doggett's New York Business Directory, 51–52
Dongan Charter, 12
Draft riots, 66–68
Duke of York, 9, 24
Dutch West India Company: and Henry Hudson, 1; and immigrants, 4; and Indians, 3; and New Amsterdam, 2; and religion, 5

Economic distress in the sixties and seventies, 152–153
Economic recovery in the eighties and nineties, 54–155
Emergency Financial Control Board (EFCB), 151
Empire State Building, 108
Epidemics, 13, 28, 59
Empress of China, 26
Erie Canal, 31
Ethnic friction: blacks and Jews, 139, 140, 158–159; Irish and Jews, 118–119
Ethnic neighborhoods in nineties, 167

Fiscal crisis of seventies: effects of, 151; reasons for, 150
Five Points, 57
Free School Society, 62
French, 28
French and Indian War, 19

George Washington Bridge, 106
Germans, Hessians, 28; Kleindeutschland, 40, 57; occupations in eighteenth-century New York, 16; occupations in nineteenth-century New York, 60; reasons for emigration, 45–46
Goodfriend, Joyce, 3
Gracie, Archibald, 52
Greater New York, 81–83
The Great School Wars, 116
Greeley, Horace, 60
Guiena, 9

Hamilton, Alexander, 29
Harlem, 86
Harlem, the Making of a Ghetto, 120–121
Hart-Celler Act, 132, 166
Havemeyer, William, 27
Holland Tunnel, 106
Housing: abandonment, 146; apartment houses, 109–110; city-built projects, 110; conflict, 158; skyscrapers, 108–109; slums, 56–58; sponsored housing, 110
Howe, General William, 22
Hudson, Henry, 1
Hughes, Bishop John, 62
Huguenots, 10, 16

Idlewild International Airport, 129
Impelliteri, Vincent, 130
Interboro Rapid Transit (IRT), 108
Irish: in eighteenth-century New York, 16, 28; emigration from Ireland, 42–44; and poverty of, 32, 60; victims of bigotry, 66
Italians: depression years, 117–118; emigration background, 90; Little Italy, 88–89; occupations, 16, 90–91; and poverty, 91

Jay, John, 29, 45
Jews: background to emigration, 46–47, 93–94; Hasidim, 131; Lower East Side conditions, 95; movement from Lower East Side, 115; in New Amsterdam, 1–8, 15; in New York, 47–48; school experience, 92; teachers, 116–117

Kips Bay Battle, 22
Kleindeutschland, 40, 57, 58, 94
"Know Nothings" (American Republican Party), 64
Koch, Edward I., 154
Koreans, 168

"Ladies Mile," 75
LaGuardia, Fiorello, 111, 112, 113, 114
LaGuardia Airport, 106
The LaGuardia Years, 108
Leisler, Jacob, 11
Lenox, Robert, 52
Lark, 44
Lincoln Center, 126
Lincoln Tunnel, 126
Lindsay, John, 141
Literacy Act, 103
London, 21
Low, Seth, 97

McCarren-Walter Act, 127
McCoy, Rhody, 144
Mills, C. Wright, 136
Molasses Act, 20
Moses, Robert, 107–108
Municipal Assistance Corporation (MAC), 151

Nancy, 21
National Origins Act, 104
Naturalization, 168–169
Navigation Acts, 9, 20
Newcomer School, 165
A New Metropolis: New York City, 1840–1857, 50
Nieuw Nederlandt, 1–2
Normandie, 109

Ocean Hill–Brownsville controversy, 143
O'Dwyer, William, 128
Open admissions, 145, 163

Parkchester, 110
Poles in New Amsterdam, 4
Police, 64

Port of New York Authority, 106
Post–World War II population shifts, 131
Public Education Association, 81
Public School Society, 62
Public Works Administration (PNA), 113
Puerto Ricans: continuing problems, 160–161; effects of the Depression, 134; increase after Word War II, 128; move into East Harlem, 132; reasons for migration to New York, 133–134, 135; school difficulties, 136–138

Quartering Act, 20
Queen Mary, 109
Queens Midtown Tunnel, 106

Raskin, A. H., 170
Religions, 15
Remediation needs at city colleges, 164–165
Rockefeller Center, 108
Rohayton, Felix, 151

School decentralization, 143–144
School integration, 143
The Seaport City, 5
Search for Elevation, Education and Knowledge (SEEK), 162
Ships: *Dauphine,* 1; *Empress of China,* 26; *Guiena,* 9; *Lark,* 44; *London,* 21; *Nancy,* 21; *Nieuw Nederlandt,* 1–2; *Normandie,* 109; *Queen Mary,* 109
"Singel," 4, 5, 6
Society for the Prevention of Pauperism (SPP), 61
Sons of Liberty, 21
Stamp Act, 19–20
Starr, Roger, 170
Stewart, A. T., 55
Stuyvesant, Peter, 3, 5–6, 9
Stuyvesant Town, 110
Subways, 108
Sugar Act, 19
Sullivan, "Big Tim," 97

Tammany Society (Hall), 65, 97
Tea Act, 20
Temporary Commission on City Finances, 170
Tenement House Law, 58
Terrible Honesty: Mongrel Manhattan in the Twenties, 121
Townshend Acts, 21
Trade, 8, 9, 10, 26, 50–51
Transportation, 54, 77, 79
Transport Workers Union, 129
Triangle Shirtwaist Fire, 96
Turks, 168
Tweed, William Marcy, 64–65

United Federation of Teachers, 144
United Nations, 122

Verrazano Bridge, 126
Visiting Nurse Association, 89

Wagner, Robert, 140–141
Waldinger, Robert, 169
Walker, "Jimmy," 110–111
Walloons, 2
War of 1812, 30
Welfare, 141–142
West Indian immigrants, 85, 156
Wood, Fernando, 64

About the Author

SELMA BERROL is Professor Emerita at Baruch College. A lifelong New Yorker, she is the author of five books, all of which deal with the immigrants, schools, and history of New York City.

ISBN 0-275-95795-0

90000>

EAN

9 780275 957957

HARDCOVER BAR CODE